REHABILITATION AND ACQUIRED DEAFNESS

REHABILITATION AND ACQUIRED DEAFNESS

Edited by William J. Watts

CROOM HELM
London & Canberra

© 1983 William J. Watts
Croom Helm Ltd, Provident House, Burrell Row,
Beckenham, Kent BR3 1AT

British Library Cataloguing in Publication Data

Rehabilitation and acquired deafness.
1 Hearing impaired — Rehabilitation
I. Watts, William J.
362.4'28   RF297

ISBN 0-7099-2746-0

Printed and bound in Great Britain
by Billing & Sons Limited, Worcester.

CONTENTS

Foreword *Jack Ashley*, MP		vii
Preface *R.J. South*		ix
1.	Perspectives in Aural Rehabilitation *William J. Watts*	11
2.	Human Development and Communication *William J. Watts*	26
3.	Experiences of Acquired Deafness *Kenneth S. Pegg*	50
4.	Denmark as a Contemporary European Model of Aural Rehabilitation *Andreas Markides*	55
5.	The Role of the Otologist *John Groves*	87
6.	The Treatment and Prevention of Deafness in Adults *John C. Ballantyne*	93
7.	Audiological Procedures in Differential Diagnosis *John J. Knight and Peggy Chalmers*	108
8.	The Audiological Physician *Larry Fisch*	134
9.	The Design and Use of Hearing Aids *Michael C. Martin*	146
10.	Ear Impressions and Hearing Aid Earmoulds *Roger Wills*	174
11.	Environmental Aids *John D. Pym*	189
12.	Speechreading in Practice *Winifred S. Brinson*	205
13.	The Basis of Practical Auditory Training *Gaynor M. Freestone*	219
14.	Speech Conservation *Ann Parker*	234
15.	Hearing Therapy *Christine Richardson*	251
Contributors		257
Index		258

FOREWORD

The onset of deafness, sudden or slow, can be a disaster for the individual. Sudden deafness is traumatic whereas its slow development is insidious. But ultimately the effects are the same. There is a loss of confidence, growth of misunderstanding, social isolation and, in extreme cases, demoralisation.

Some people are able to cope with deafness better than others. Yet all of them can benefit from skilled advice. No one with any other severe disability would dream of neglecting the professional assistance available, but many deaf people struggle on alone.

The reasons are that too many deaf people refuse to admit that they are deaf; it is, somehow, a disability which people seek to disguise; and most of those afflicted are unaware of the existence of, and advances in, rehabilitation.

This book will be an invaluable aid in enlightening deaf people. It will also help and stimulate those who are active in the field. Its wide-ranging scope covers many of the multitudinous aspects of acquired deafness and embraces both the philosophy and practical aspects of rehabilitation. It fills an important gap in the literature of deafness and will help to chart a better future for deaf people.

Jack Ashley, MP
House of Commons
Westminster
London

PREFACE

Hearing impairment is a subtly cruel handicap, allowing many opportunities for misunderstanding and frustration in everyday social intercourse. At the City Lit Centre for the Deaf we believe that the caring professions should co-operate far more effectively to develop aural rehabilitation for those who have acquired a hearing loss in the middle or later years of life. The potential benefits are enormous, not only in terms of personal relationships but also in maintaining the use of otherwise reducing forces in the nation's productivity. The failure to arrest the decline in the quality of the lives of the great majority of the victims must largely be placed at the door of excessive professional specialism because, as with so many aspects of human life, successful rehabilitation will only come through interdisciplinary teamwork.

At the City Lit Centre for the Deaf, considerable teamwork with other agencies and hospitals was developed over many years under the able leadership of Kenneth Pegg. A wide range of learning services for all adults with impaired hearing has involved partnership with special schools and partially-hearing units, 'hearing' colleges and the Careers Service, and has included such elements as auditory training, lip reading and job counselling for the deaf. With its unique experience in this comprehensive service the Centre was asked by the Department of Health and Social Security to establish a full-time interdisciplinary course for a newly recognised caring profession, Hearing Therapy. In 1978 the first course was offered to a group of students selected from the National Health Service, each to be trained to work single-handed as a member of a multidisciplinary hospital team including clinical, technical and social-work staff.

The editor of this book, Dr. William Watts, was responsible as tutor organiser for the weaving together of the various specialisms within the course, including speechreading, auditory training, the psychology of deafness, development and ageing, introductions to counselling skills, to the medical and surgical treatment of deafness and to hearing aids. This book presents the fruits of his experience: the different subjects of study, practical and theoretical, are vividly reflected in the titles of the contributions by eminent specialists.

The rich variety to be found in the topics indicates the many areas of concern for Hearing Therapy. Underlying all these perspectives, however, is the common aim to maximise the rehabilitation of adults with acquired hearing loss. When these perspectives meet in genuine interdisciplinary teamwork, the Hearing Therapists of the future will without doubt be seen as important partners in a major advance in the life-enhancement and self-understanding of many adults at present socially crippled.

R.J. South
Principal
City Lit
London

1 PERSPECTIVES IN AURAL REHABILITATION

William J. Watts

Aural rehabilitation for people suffering from acquired deafness, who are often referred to as the hard of hearing, involves a variety of techniques. When medical or surgical intervention has nothing to offer, the main rehabilitation techniques are concerned with hearing strategies, learning to listen and to use a hearing aid effectively under difficult conditions, and with communication skills, especially those of speech-reading and auditory training. Psychologically, aural rehabilitation involves adjustment to the handicap and new ways of dealing with one-self in self-actualisation; it also involves new and differing interactions with other people.

This book introduces some of those professionally engaged in this work and the techniques they use both before and after aural rehabilitation programmes have begun. These techniques involve a number of different kinds of professional people and each of our contributors plays an important part in the overall rehabilitation process. We have aimed the text at a broad range of readers, but specifically at student hearing therapists, graduate students and others professionally involved with hearing impairment. It should also be of interest to physicians, psychologists, sociologists, teachers, speech therapists, nurses and all who may have become interested in the adult hard of hearing.

This chapter describes the general concept of aural rehabilitation and seeks to consider briefly the contemporary perspective in which such programmes are carried out. We are thus immediately involved with the welfare of people who suffer from acquired deafness and with positive ways of helping them. Simply stated, aural rehabilitation can be defined as covering those techniques designed to help the hearing-impaired person to adjust to his handicap, or to lessen or reduce that handicap.

The important characteristics of hearing loss as they relate to aural rehabilitation are bound up with the degree of loss, the time of onset, the type of loss and the auditory discrimination possible. People with acquired deafness, who form the central theme of this book, are those who lose their hearing in their late teens, in adult life and thereafter into old age. They have normal speech and language, but they have difficulty in verbal communication and other social, emotional and vocational problems may well occur. Those who acquire hearing loss as adults will then have varying degrees of difficulty in receiving speech and environmental stimuli which allow us as human beings to communicate and interact with other people.

To some extent auditory discrimination and the degree of loss as measured are independent. In this way, for instance, some minimal auditory discrimination may still be present even if speech reception is limited, since hearing may be used for signal-warning purposes or simply to maintain contact psychologically with the auditory environment of the world around. In a different way the person of advanced years with a small degree of hearing loss may have very poor speech discrimination. This phonemic regression is quite common in the hearing loss of old age, where speech discrimination often bears no relation to the measurable hearing loss, and which may well point to some degree of central degeneration.

The Adult With Acquired Hearing Loss

No doubt we would all readily recognise that the problem of the adult who has become deaf slowly but progressively over the years, or who becomes deaf suddenly, is one of communication. However, the problems of the adult with acquired hearing loss are much more complex than is at first realised. Having passed from a stage where people seem no longer to speak as clearly as they once did, through a stage of increasing social isolation as he is forced to accept that there is something very wrong with his hearing, and then to a stage of seeking medical help only to find there is no treatment appropriate to his case, it is small wonder that this cumulatively brings about a sense of disappointment and despair. He may find the first ray of hope after a very long time in the fact that he is told he can be helped by a hearing aid, but even this may lead to disappointment. Many adults with a socially significant hearing loss which cannot be helped medically can still obtain help from hearing aids. In many countries the issue of a hearing aid with little follow-up support is the only remedy offered. The instrument which the hard-of-hearing person thought would restore his hearing, whilst it makes sounds much louder, does not necessarily make the sounds of speech clearer, and he is quite unprepared for this. Small wonder indeed that he experiences yet more frustration and ceases to use the instrument he thought would restore his hearing. Only the fortunate find one of the few centres for the deaf where they will be shown how to use a hearing aid and told what it will do and what it will not do, and where it will work most effectively and where it will not. Only the fortunate will be introduced to the skills of speechreading and auditory training which will measurably help them with communication and social adjustment. Surely these facilities and techniques should form the basis of communication rehabilitation for all adults with acquired hearing loss and should be readily available to those who require them.

Aural rehabilitation methods should always take in amplification procedures such as hearing aid evaluation, adjustment and orientation. Particularly in hearing aid orientation people need to learn about the purpose, function and maintenance of these aids. The user new to the aid often needs simple and direct instruction about the instrument and his hearing loss. Adult aural rehabilitative services which include the teaching of the skills of speechreading and auditory training are needed for some people with acquired deafness, whether long-standing or brought about through progressive or traumatic hearing disorders.

Rehabilitative communication for those with acquired hearing loss would seem to centre round the effective use of hearing aids, the development of hearing strategies, speechreading and auditory training, counselling and psychosocial remediation. Aural rehabilitation includes all procedures which seek to improve communication, but it is much more than this because it is concerned with the whole person and his adjustment to life.

Communication Rehabilitation

The major impact of hearing loss, as we have seen, is in the area of communication. People with acquired deafness may well have difficulties at home and at work. In the past this problem of communication has been helped by the provision of speechreading and auditory training. In recent years there has been a turning away from these more classic methods of rehabilitation and much more reliance now seems to be placed on better hearing aids and their orientation. Such movement away from these basic skills may well be open to question. We take the line that the older skills are still essential for some sufferers with acquired deafness and become that much more effective with the use of better hearing aids.

In the USA there are reports of difficulties in acceptance of aural rehabilitation. Diagnosis forms the major element of audiology and rehabilitation has been given a much lower status. To some extent aural rehabilitation has remained very much in the background and little practicum in speechreading and auditory training has been required (Ventry 1965). There are reports that in some universities with renowned programmes in audiology junior staff and graduate students have been employed in the teaching of aural rehabilitation courses (Rosen 1967). The Academy of Rehabilitative Audiology in 1966 was organised to help audiologists with rehabilitative interests to direct their efforts towards changing these trends (Oyer and Frankmann 1975). One reason for the neglect of rehabilitation in the USA has been the hearing aid situation. There were aggressive sales practices by hearing aid dealers and the policy of the American Speech and Hearing Association (ASHA) until very recently prevented the audiologist from dispensing hearing aids. Although hearing aids were readily available under the National Health Service in Great Britain the position of aural rehabilitation had not been extended beyond its original concept, with the audiological technician providing these aids. In practice the audiological technician did not have the time for aural rehabilitation nor had he been trained in the necessary skills.

The Status of Speechreading and Auditory Training

In the early 1900s speechreading for those suffering from acquired deafness was started in many places throughout the world. Irene Ewing pioneered much of the work in speechreading and the use of hearing aids in Britain (Ewing 1946). In the USA at about the same period considerable public recognition was gained through speechreading courses and the methods used. After World War II the needs for servicemen were met by special classes in Britain and by special rehabilitation centres in the USA. In these situations a considerable amount of speechreading and auditory training was provided in addition to hearing aid orientation.

It is sometimes said that the reason for the relatively poor status of aural rehabilitation until quite recently is that too much emphasis has been placed on speechreading and auditory training. According to this view, the usefulness and validity of these two procedures have never been entirely clear. Those who hold this view consider that amplification should be used as the major rehabilitative tool. They feel that because of habit and tradition, speechreading and auditory training still receive an inordinate amount of attention. The aural rehabilitation provided at the City Lit Centre for the Deaf, London, reflects a somewhat different view. For us, speechreading and auditory training are central and integral parts of aural rehabilitation. Making use of effective amplification, providing personal adjustment and educational counselling and a truly holistic approach to patient-centred needs are also, however, to us very important aspects of aural rehabilitation.

A 1973 survey of hearing clinics in the USA indicated that only 40 per cent of the respondents could provide aural rehabilitation for older hearing aid users and only about 20 per cent specifically mentioned speechreading and auditory training (Schow and Norbonne 1980). In short, speechreading was given lip service, but was probably available in only about two of every ten clinical settings. It was claimed that the scarcity of speechreading instruction indicated that many professionals question the utility of speechreading therapy. This is a doubtful argument especially in view of the position taken by Rosen (1967) who stressed the lack of academic training provided for the typical audiologist. Often such a person was found to mention lipreading, auditory training or training in the use of a hearing aid, but probably would not offer these services himself. Furthermore the advice was likely to be offered half-heartedly, as if the audiologist was not really aware or convinced of its value. It could well be that the lowly position attributed to aural rehabilitation meant that the skills of speechreading and auditory training had never been successfully taught or used in many places. Some individuals have been particularly critical of the more traditional methods of speechreading and auditory training used in aural rehabilitation (Alpiner 1971; Hardick 1977; Best 1978). They take no account of the fact that very few centres have provided such facilities and where they did the provision may have been less than adequate (Rosen 1967).

This decrease in the emphasis placed on the more traditional methods used in aural rehabilitation has led to the development of a number of none the less interesting alternative approaches. Thus we have 'progressive rehabilitative audiology' by Alpiner (1971) which focuses on counselling and improving communication ability rather than making use of speechreading and auditory training programmes. Fleming (1972) presented as an alternative a 'communication therapy program'. Tannahill (1973) described a group hearing aid adjustment programme designed to help persons understand their hearing losses and hearing aids, with better information presented through instruction, group discussions and individual counselling. Hardick (1977) described a similar programme in which the major focus was on hearing aid fitting and orientation. The common factor of these new approaches is the claim that hearing aid adjustment, orientation and general communication help are central issues and that speechreading and auditory training are occasionally ancillary procedures. Goldstein and Stephens (1980) produced 'an audiological rehabilitation management model' which takes into account such processes as attitude, instrumental, strategy and ancillary processes together with communication training. Their approach was presented as a positive move from the position that hearing aid evaluation has so often taken in the past where it has been treated as the beginning and the end of the rehabilitation process. The model has also recently been extended in its application (Stephens 1982).

While not fully accepting the de-emphasis on the traditional communication methods of speechreading and auditory training which has taken place in the USA in the past decade, we can at least learn from the very positive emphasis placed on the effective use of amplification and communication rehabilitation in general. A combination of past methods and present procedures seems to be a much more realistic approach to aural rehabilitation. For this reason brief details are given here of a research investigation carried out in validation of speechreading and auditory training techniques which have served us so well in recent decades (Watts and Pegg 1977).

In Validation of Speechreading and Auditory Training

This investigation was carried out in an attempt not only to increase knowledge and understanding of the problems faced by adults with acquired hearing loss, but also to evaluate the effectiveness of the speechreading and auditory training techniques provided to help with rehabilitation.

The background to the investigation took into account that for many years the teaching of speechreading has been advocated for adults with acquired hearing loss. However, only in more recent times does it seem to have been realised that a rehabilitation programme is in many cases more effective if it includes both speechreading and auditory training. We feel strongly that such a programme should be available for every adult who requires help, and this should be provided as soon as possible after a hearing impairment has been ascertained. There appears to be little evidence in Britain to indicate the benefits or otherwise of those courses that do exist to help adults with acquired hearing loss.

Our investigation was carried out at the City Lit Centre for the Deaf, London, and was designed to evaluate the effectiveness of speechreading as a single mode of instruction and also the effectiveness of speechreading and auditory training as a combined mode of instruction.

Students attending the Centre for the Deaf travel from all parts of London and the neighbouring Home Counties for either day or evening classes. They differ in one essential respect from the usual adult hospital patient with acquired hearing loss in that they have taken the initial step towards satisfactory rehabilitation by enrolling for a course of instruction. For the purpose of this investigation two randomly selected groups of students were formed. The first group received speechreading instruction and the second group speechreading and auditory training combined. While students normally attend for a full academic year, for our purposes the period of continuous controlled instruction was six months or two academic terms per year in a two-year investigation.

During the first year 4 students completed the course of speechreading and 5 students failed to complete the course. At the same time 6 students completed the course of speechreading and auditory training and no students failed to complete the course. Instruction was provided for a large number of students during the second year; 20 students completed a course of speechreading and no students failed to complete the course. At the same time 19 students completed the course of speechreading and auditory training and 1 student failed to complete the course. We had therefore in total over the two-year period two groups defined by the method of instruction: Group 1, Lipreading (24 students) and Group 2, Lipreading and Auditory Training (25 students) for the purposes of the investigation.

Case notes were kept for each student and these included the results of the testing procedures used, and general information regarding the effect of acquired deafness upon family, social life and employment. The students who took part had not previously received formal instruction in speechreading or auditory training. Ideally the whole of the testing, speechreading and auditory training should have taken place during day classes but it was not possible to arrange this. Some students, for example housewives and retired persons, found day classes convenient, while others could only attend in the evenings after completing a full day's work. We had no way of assessing the fatigue factor of this latter group and their progress might have been greater in different circumstances.

It was found that some 43 per cent of those taking part were using

National Health Service Medresco hearing aids, whilst the remainder used commercial hearing aids of various kinds. Several students were prepared to accept a commercial hearing aid with inferior performance for the sake of convenience and cosmetic value. There was confusion amongst the students regarding the cause of their deafness. It was found that while some 36 per cent had a reasonable understanding of their problem, the remainder either did not know or had misunderstood what they had been told at the time when their deafness had been ascertained.

Instruction in Speechreading and Auditory Training

Students designated to both groups received continuous controlled instruction. A record was kept of those selected to attend for speechreading only. This record listed the number of attendances, total hours of instruction, special difficulties experienced and type of instruction received. A similar record was kept of those selected to attend for speechreading and auditory training. Before auditory training began certain preliminary checks on the hearing aid were made. These covered maximum intelligibility of the hearing aid, correct adjustment and suitability. From the results of the criterion tests used, an auditory training programme was devised to meet the needs of each individual student. Each programme was necessarily based upon the requirements of each particular student and ranged from discrimination of gross sounds through to the fine speech discriminations connected with the effective use of a telephone. Students who completed the course of instruction, irrespective of the experimental group to which they belonged, received not less than 20 hours of speechreading instruction in a group situation. Those in the speechreading and auditory training group received, in addition, not less than 6 hours of individual auditory training over the same period.

Hypotheses

There were two hypotheses for which support was sought. The first was concerned with the single sensory mode of instruction, the second with the bisensory mode of instruction; (1) That a single mode of instruction using speechreading improves the communication ability of the adult with acquired hearing loss, and (2) That a combined mode of instruction using speechreading and auditory training will show even greater improvement than the single mode.

Criterion Tests Used

(1) Pure tone tests of minimal threshold (a) air conduction (b) bone conduction
(2) Speech trainer speech test of hearing using phonetically balanced monosyllabic word lists
(3) Free field speech tests using phonetically balanced monosyllabic word tests at 3ft, 6ft and 9ft (a) unaided hearing (b) aided hearing (c) unaided hearing plus lipreading (d) aided hearing plus lipreading
(4) Social Hearing Index (initial assessment) (Ewertsen and Birk-Neilsen 1973; Birk-Nielsen and Ewertsen 1974)

Results

The first simple analysis carried out consisted of taking the before and after training scores, which for lack of space are not included here, and computing means for each of the two groups according to the mode of instruction under the five conditions of test application. For this purpose the speech trainer measures were summed for both ears as were the measures over the varying free field distances. A summary of these group mean differences is provided in Table 1.1.

Table 1.1: Phonetically Balanced Monosyllabic Word Testing Initial Analysis Group. Mean Differences Using Before and After Training Scores

Application	Group 1 Speechreading	Group 2 Speechreading and Auditory Training
1. Amplivox Speech Trainer	00.42 loss	19.20 gain
2. Free Field Unaided Hearing	01.58 loss	16.80 gain
3. Free Field Aided Hearing	02.50 gain	28.40 gain
4. Free Field Unaided Hearing and Speechreading	39.59 gain	29.60 gain
5. Free Field Aided Hearing and Speechreading	28.34 gain	36.00 gain

The initial analysis provided little more than insight into some basic trends. It can be seen that Group 2 was superior on every measure except for free field unaided hearing and speechreading. Although Group 2 did in fact show considerable improvement with free field unaided hearing and speechreading, it was not of the same magnitude as that of Group 1. Analysis made in this way has some considerable limitations in that it is only possible to make comparison between groups on one specific test application and does not allow for a cross-test application. For example the 39.59 gain shown by Group 1 under Application 4 cannot be compared with the 36.00 gain shown by Group 2 under Application 5. This is because in this instance the before and after scores of Group 1 were (3430-4380) and those of Group 2 (4890-5790), clearly showing that the finishing point of Group 1 was still lower than the starting point of Group 2. Also this initial analysis does not show that difference between groups cannot be explained in actual physical improvement to hearing. Therefore we must seek other means of analysing the data.

Faced with the task of analysing and seeking to understand human behaviour, we need models which will test hypotheses involving a greater quantity and complexity of behavioural variables. For readers who may not be familiar with statistical techniques the following explanation is provided.

In general, multivariate procedures may be considered in two ways. First they are a means of analysing behavioural phenomena, based upon the realisation that hardly any form of human behaviour has only a single facet. Behind any measurable trait are components that covary only partially so that description of any behaviour needs some degree of finer analysis. In addition the principle of multiple cause has to be taken into account. The second conceptualisation of multivariate analysis concerns the fitting of a set of algebraic models to situations with multiple random variables, usually criterion or outcome variables which are measures of the same sample (Finn 1974). The class of experimental designs known as repeated measures designs of course denotes a multivariate situation. The present investigation concerning adults with acquired hearing loss undergoing instruction is very much on these lines. For this reason use has been made of multivariate analysis procedures. For this investigation we have used a univariate and multivariate analysis of variance, covariance and regression based on the work developed at the University of North Carolina. This has been converted for ICL 1900 and we have added some versions and facilities. As before the method of instruction or skill being taught governed the formation of the groups, and the multivariate procedures were designed to provide a much greater degree of in-depth analysis than the initial analysis already described.

After transformations 18 variables were used in the multivariate analysis and there were two levels of instruction: Group 1 (Speechreading) and Group 2 (Speechreading and Auditory Training). The variables were used to denote measures of change, so that a positive score from before and after measures was an indication of improvement following instruction. All the variables except those for the pure tone measurement were treated in this way. Scatter diagrams of all pairs (before and after variables) showed that the data were sufficiently close to normal distribution. The standard deviations for each subgroup of variables were found to be similar. It was found that Group 2 (Speechreading and Auditory Training) were superior on every measure except unaided speechreading (see the last column of rows 13, 14 and 15 in Table 1.2). Table 1.2 provides a summary of the information already referred to and includes a description of the variables in their subgroup standard deviations and the least square estimates of effects.

Table 1.2: Multivariate Analysis Summary

Description of Variable	Standard Deviation	Least Square Estimates of Effects	
		Mean	G2-G1
Pure Tone Measurement			
1. Left Ear Before db.	19.9020	70.98917	7.06167
2. Left Ear After db.	19.4837	72.44167	6.71667
3. Right Ear Before db.	19.9184	71.03583	6.48833
4. Right Ear After db.	20.0699	70.91417	4.41167
Amplivox Speech Trainer			
5. Speech Audiometry Left	8.5850	4.40000	8.80000
6. Speech Audiometry Right	7.9785	4.99167	10.81667
Free Field			
7. Unaided Hearing at 3ft.	7.6622	1.38333	4.43333
8. Unaided Hearing at 6ft.	5.5493	0.18333	2.03333
9. Unaided Hearing at 9ft.	7.2042	1.61667	1.56667
10. Aided Hearing at 3ft.	9.5604	5.20833	9.58333
11. Aided Hearing at 6ft.	11.6692	5.00000	10.00000
12. Aided Hearing at 9ft.	11.1048	5.04167	5.91667
13. Unaided + Speechreading at 3ft.	11.5579	8.42500	−5.65000
14. Unaided + Speechreading at 6ft.	12.9790	11.23333	−0.86667
15. Unaided + Speechreading at 9ft.	14.2376	14.51667	−2.63333
16. Aided + Speechreading at 3ft.	9.9865	5.68333	3.03333
17. Aided + Speechreading at 6ft.	8.9203	12.64167	1.11667
18. Aided + Speechreading at 9ft.	11.3098	13.84167	3.51667

When the 4 pure tone covariates were eliminated and the least square estimates adjusted for covariates effect the whole of the previous pattern remained. Group 2 remained superior to Group 1 except with unaided speechreading. Since differences between groups might be attributed to difference in hearing change rather than training, it was necessary to attempt to explain all group differences in terms of pure tone measurements. If a significant difference then remained it could not be due to hearing differences. The error correlation matrix showed that the correlation between occasions for the measures of pure tone were left ear 0.986929 and for the right ear 0.992280. The hypothesis of no association between dependent and independent variables gave an F-ratio of 0.9095 with 48 and 125.3 degrees of freedom. That a ratio as large as this could arise by chance with a probability of 64 per cent from samples drawn from a population in which there was no association, would suggest that the pure tone measures have no significant relationship with the other measures of performance.

In this multivariate model the first null hypothesis that there was no effect due to training was not supported. The significant differences in this way which remain are not due to hearing differences and can therefore be safely attributed to instruction or skill training. The second null hypothesis that Group 2 did not differ from Group 1 was also not supported. It is of course not possible to provide the very considerable computer data of the present multivariate analysis but interested readers can find this in full in our previous work (Watts 1976; Pegg 1977).

Conclusions

It seems that for many adults with acquired hearing loss the visual clues of speechreading may not provide enough information for efficient communication. Similar restrictions apply to auditory training where in many cases no amount of training leads to a satisfactory level of speech discrimination. While both of these conditions may be generally recognised, to a large extent the implications for rehabilitation training are not put into practice. When we combine the two sensory channels provided by speechreading and auditory training each channel makes some unique contribution to speech intelligibility not provided by either as a single sensory mode. This investigation has pointed to the fact that a most effective form of aural rehabilitation is one in which wherever possible visual and auditory channels are combined in order to reduce sensory confusions. Although both research hypotheses received support the most effective form of instructional rehabilitation was found in the second hypothesis where the combined mode of instruction in speechreading and auditory training produced significantly more effective communication ability.

Many investigators have sought to explain various aspects of speechreading and auditory training. We would be the first to agree that these skills appear to be wide-ranging or global and thus difficult to quantify. In our research study we have described in detail an objective evaluation which has suggested that the processes of speechreading and auditory training do play a very important part in aural rehabilitation. The data we have provided represent a definitive evaluation of the remediative effect of speechreading and auditory training and their combination. We have been confirmed in our feelings that these processes should be used as and when they are required. There is surely much to be gained in the use of those elements we have already found to bring effective results. In the words of Ethel Mussen, 'as you consider these rehabilitative responsibilities of audiology incorporate into your clinical style those elements others have already found to be effective.' (Mussen, in foreword to Schow and Norbonne 1980). The field of aural rehabilitation is enlarging rapidly and in some of the more recent publications we find reflected the idea of rehabilitation becoming a major aspect of audiology with definite structure and wide-ranging information (Schow and Norbonne 1980; Bode, Tweedie and Hull 1982). For those engaged in aural rehabilitation there can be no such thing as a static body of knowledge, but rather the effective use of many processes some of which may be marked by change and emphasis.

Contemporary Aural Rehabilitation

We will now take a quick look at the present provision for adults who suffer from acquired deafness. In Western Europe the audiological and rehabilitation services are exemplified by the work in Denmark. Provision in Denmark (described in detail in Chapter 4) is well-organised, comprehensive and highly professional with the medical, technical and pedagogical components of the service developed as separate professional entities with a high degree of co-operation. Similar services have been established in Sweden. Although not as advanced as the services in Denmark they have a sound organisational basis and their development has been continuous and well planned. In North America a considerable amount of highly successful work has been carried out with the hard of hearing. Systematic information, especially regarding the USA, is particularly difficult to obtain and the general impression is of centres of excellence and also areas of inadequate provision, varying from state to state (Pegg and Martin 1978). In the Far East there has been a move in Japan to establish aural rehabilitation with an educational base (Makamishi 1981).

Until very recently aural rehabilitation services provided in Britain for adults with acquired deafness were extremely limited and represented the endeavours of only a few pioneers and voluntary bodies. Today the already well-established audiological services within the National Health Service have been further strengthened by the provision of Hearing Therapists (DHSS Health Service Circular, 1978).

References

Alpiner, J.G. (1971) 'Planning a strategy of aural rehabilitation for the adult', *Hear Speech News, 39*, 21-6
Best, L.G. (1978) 'Research aspects of rehabilitative audiology' in Alpiner, J.G. (ed), *Handbook of Adult Rehabilitative Audiology*, Williams and Wilkins, Baltimore, pp. 250-60
Birk-Neilsen, H. and Ewertsen, H.W. (1974) 'Effect of hearing aid treatment: Social Hearing Handicap Index before and after treatment of new patients', *Scand Audiol, 3*, 35-8
Bode, D.L., Tweedie D. and Hull, R.H. (1982) 'Improving communication through aural rehabilitation' in Hull, R.H. (ed.), *Rehabilitative Audiology*, Grune and Stratton, New York
Department of Health and Social Security (1978) Circular on Health Service Development, Appointment of Hearing Therapists, DHSS, London
Ewertsen, H.W. and Birk-Neilsen, H. (1973) 'Social hearing handicap index: Social Handicap in relation to hearing impairment', *Audiol, 12*, 180-7
Ewing, I.R. (1946) *Lipreading and Hearing Aids*, Manchester University Press, Manchester. second impression
Finn, J.D. (1974) *A General Model for Multivariate Analysis*, Holt, Rinehart and Winston, New York
Fleming, M. (1972) 'A total approach to communication therapy', *J Acad Rehab Audiol, 5*, 28-31
Goldstein, D.P. and Stephens, S.D.G. (1980) *Audiological Rehabilitation, Management Model 1, Technical Memorandum 3*, Royal National Throat, Nose and Ear Hospital Auditory Rehabilitation Centre, London
Hardick, E.J. (1977) 'Aural Rehabilitation Programs for the Aged can be successful', *J Acad Rehab Audiol, 10*, 51-66
Makamishi, Y. (1981) Personal communication with Professor Y. Makamishi of the University of Tokyo
Oyer, H. and Frankmann, J. (1975) *The Aural Rehabilitative Process*, Holt, Rinehart and Winston, New York
Pegg, K.S. (1977) 'The Rehabilitation of Hearing Impaired Adults', MPhil thesis, University of Sussex
Pegg, K.S. and Martin, M.C. (1978) Report to the Inner London Education Authority and the Royal National Institute for the Deaf on a visit to the USA and Mexico under the auspices of the Hearing Therapy Trust, London
Rosen, J. (1967) 'Distortions in the Training of Audiologists', *Asha, 9*, 171-4
Schow, R.L. and Nerbonne, M.A. (eds) (1980), *Introduction to Aural*

Rehabilitation, University Park Press, Baltimore
Stephens, S.D.G. (1982) *Auditory Rehabilitation: Extending the Model, Technical Memorandum 4*, Royal National Throat, Nose and Ear Hospital Auditory Rehabilitation Centre, London
Tannahill, J.C. (1973) 'Hearing Aids: Trial and Adjustment by new users', *Audecibel*, *22*, 90-7
Ventry, I.M. (ed) (1965) *Audiology and Education of the Deaf*, Joint Committee on Audiology and Education of the Deaf, Washington DC
Watts, W.J. (1976) *Speechreading and Auditory Training in the Rehabilitation of Adults with Acquired Hearing Loss*, Phillips Research Unit, University of Sussex. Research Report made to the Department of Health and Social Security, London
Watts, W.J. and Pegg, K.S. (1977) 'The rehabilitation of adults with acquired hearing loss', *Br J Audiol*, *11*, 103-10

2 HUMAN DEVELOPMENT AND COMMUNICATION

William J. Watts

A Psychological Framework for Aural Rehabilitation

It is hoped that this book will provide a guide to better understanding not only of men and women suffering from acquired deafness but also of the professional people and procedures involved in aural rehabilitation. Having taught on aural rehabilitation courses for a number of years, and on other aspects of psychology and education before that, I am now more than ever convinced that to achieve successful rehabilitation we need to know more about how other human beings think and feel. In particular, we need to improve our knowledge of human development and communication. All the love available to meet human problems will not be enough unless it is based on a foundation of psychological evidence and above all on the intimate understanding of the thoughts, feelings and actions of individuals.

However, the characteristic of life today is size, the metropolis, the supermarket, the mass-producing plant, all of which drain the life blood from smaller concerns and individuals. Handling masses of people seems to lead to mass regimentation. In the midst of the masses the person handicapped with acquired deafness, lacking in communication, can be more alone than ever before.

The problems of acquired deafness are exemplified in what Beethoven had to say about his deafness some 180 years ago:

> If at times I decided just to ignore my infirmity, alas, how cruelly was I then driven back to solitude by the intensified sad experience of my poor hearing. Yet I could not bring myself to say to people: 'Speak up, shout, for I am deaf'... Moreover my misfortune pains me doubly, for inasmuch as it leads to my being misjudged. For there can be no relaxation in human society, no refined conversation, no mutual confidences. I must live quite alone and may creep into society only as often as sheer necessity demands. I must live like an outcast. If I appear in company I am overcome by a burning anxiety, a fear that I am running the risk of letting people know my condition... But how humiliated I have felt if someone standing

beside me heard the sound of a flute in the distance and I heard nothing — such experiences almost made me despair, and I was at the point of putting an end to my life — the only thing that held me back was my art. For indeed it seemed to me to be impossible to leave this world before I had produced all the works that I felt the urge to compose.

Things do not change greatly over the years and the recently written comments made by a housewife suffering from deafness, who was undertaking a rehabilitation programme, are little different:

'You don't look deaf!' This was said to me last week and led me on to a train of thought. What is a deaf person meant to look like, and if we don't fit into the image, does this cause a breakdown in communication? If one wears a small post-aural aid and still has a spring in the step, is it too much to expect normal hearing people to co-operate? Do we have to do all the hard work of making sense of what others say, trying not to inconvenience them? Advertisements for hearing aids tell us: 'Wear such and such a hearing aid and your friends will never know you are hard of hearing.' Why the guilt complex?

Even when your friends know, they aren't much help. An evening spent in their home and you end up feeling like a puppet, nodding and smiling at what you hope are the right moments. If you are dining out it is easier, the range is closer, but if you lipread everything stops while you tackle your meal! If you are not the type to be constantly demanding, 'Speak up, I am deaf', what can you do?

In the past few years, people have said to me, 'You manage very well, you don't inflict your handicap on others' — but I have still suffered in the process. In this enlightened and permissive age, when anything and everything from drugs to sex are frankly discussed, surely public opinion and imagination could be stimulated to help the deaf, whose only shortcomings are not being able to comprehend their native tongue.

This chapter provides a brief synoptic account of human development and communication in order to stimulate interest in further knowledge. It should be looked upon as complementing the work of anyone who seeks to exercise an empathic understanding of other human beings, and especially those involved in aural rehabilitation. Its focus on developmental evidence and upon the intimate thoughts, feelings and activities of individuals provides a microcosmic but nevertheless tantalising broadcloth of knowledge concerning the predominant experiences and processes of human development as people are born, grow up, mature, age and die. Any member of a helping profession such as audiology, of which aural rehabilitation forms a part, should have an intimate personal understanding of people. Although audiology has been described as the profession that provides knowledge and service in the areas of human hearing, and more broadly, human communication and its disorders, it has seldom been emphasised that a knowledge of human beings is also essential. No doubt it was this lack which caused Ethel Mussen when considering aural rehabilitation to emphasise this very point: 'If one read all that is presently available, there still would be no substitute for an individual's grasp of the nature of communication, the social and cultural style of the people involved, and the skill to wed them to a process of growth and change' (Mussen, in foreword to Schow and Nerbonne, 1980). Each of us needs to use the knowledge gained by others through psychological inquiry, but we also have to discover everything anew for ourselves and practise it. Only through practice can we really believe what we feel and know. The awareness of the thoughts and feelings of oneself and others provides a basis for the dispassionate empathy so necessary to aural rehabilitation.

For our purpose aural rehabilitation takes in the services which are needed for the help of the adult with acquired deafness. They may be for individuals with long-standing hearing loss as well as for persons who acquire loss during adulthood through traumatic or progressive hearing disorders brought on by accident, heredity, disease, noise or advancing years. We have deliberately refrained from discussion of children and congenital deafness where the problem centres round language development and educational attainment. People with acquired hearing loss may have communication problems but these are not usually related to language development. People with acquired deafness are the 'you and I' of society who have gone deaf and seek to remain integrated into the total community of the hearing, talking world.

Conception, Birth and the First Months

Before each of us was born we were involved with the predominant life experience which starts with pregnancy. The experience of pregnancy seems to be very much a private matter, a time in which the mother's feelings and fantasies play a central role in the anticipation of a largely unknown future event. Although on the one hand it is so private, it is also from the very beginning a social event of considerable importance for the mother, as she shares the news with others and looks for confirming enjoyment from the father. Personal adaptations, change and modifications in the lifestyle take place as a result of the widespread hormonal changes which anticipate motherhood (Chamberlain 1969). The often illogical personal likes and dislikes and the drives of contrary activity are well known phenomena of pregnancy. However, many of those ideas also remain private with little more than a recognition that imaginative activity or fantasy has a significant effect (Segal 1973). Central control or ego activity seems to be concerned with testing, checking out and refining imaginative activity so that satisfactory adaptive behaviour comes about.

Most women are concerned with how they themselves will function as mothers, and they are often found making comparisons with their own mothers and drawing on the often vague memories of their own childhood. Many women want to pass through pregnancy with the minimum of interference from medical and other professionals. Although this may be so, they nevertheless anxiously want to rely on their help and advice over some things. Usually the most important person for a woman's contentment and happiness during pregnancy is her husband. Not only does he provide the fundamental need of assurance for material and physical security, but he also plays a more than central role in the intimate valuing of each other, so necessary in human relationships, and even more necessary at this time. Although as yet the way one person helps alleviate the anxiety of another is not fully understood, such caring helps greatly during pregnancy. The husband in day-to-day living can act as a receptor, a source of continuing strength to help with his wife's often anxiety-ridden fantasies and fears.

The later stages of pregnancy are marked by the stimulating movement of the unborn child and by changes in the mobility of the mother. At this time a peculiar withdrawal takes place into ideas centred round self and child, epitomised by quietness and relaxed preoccupation. It is a time of fundamental life change or life crisis (Caplan 1964). There is increased dependency on others for physical and emotional well-being. This security, together with the web of related private worlds of the mother, go to form the necessary psychological environment which will encompass the newborn child.

So the child is born. Nothing can describe this experience of human joy. With this release of happiness comes immediate responsibility, for the child at birth is incapable of surviving alone. From the very beginning he starts to attune to those who organise his life, his parents in particular, and they in turn attune to him as they provide the material support and stimulation necessary for his survival. At birth a fundamental change takes place in the baby's psychological organisation and physiological functions such as breathing, sucking, crying and bodily excretion, none of which had been exercised fully before, start their reflex patterns of sensory organisation. At this stage the baby's control system and his capacity to discriminate and react in a selective manner are essentially rudimentary and undifferentiated. With a smooth pattern of modest stimulation when awake, and minimal stimulation when asleep, the baby rapidly builds a system of relaxed harmony with his mother. She relieves his distress by stopping or modifying the disturbing experience, and comforts him by holding, caressing and cuddling, all of which involve movement and stimulation of a gently erotic nature. Sometimes it is thought that in the first few months the baby is capable of very little except sleep, a few rudimentary reflexes and the ability to feed. However, in the early months the eyes are beginning to focus, spatial discrimination has its beginnings in the grasping movements being made, defensive head movements are taking place and there is evidence of odour discrimination. The startle response to loud noises is well known but much finer discriminations are taking place, with the baby's body and mouth responding in minute but quite specific ways to different patterns of sound in the first early months (Lewin 1975). There is mimicry of the mother's spoken mouth movements and response to her smile. The quickly developing competence in sensory discrimination and motor activity which is present very early in the child's life suggests an innate basis for these activities. There may well be embryonic meaning and perception, and there is certainly a peculiar awareness, meaningful from the beginning, which continues to develop through experience (Lewis 1963).

As a result of their togetherness or accord, mother and child establish a form of communication marked by conversations which involve the caress of sound rather than words. These early visual-muscular and auditory signals, together with feeling experiences, go to form the roots and mechanism of human communication. Under the control of the developing intelligence the child will take on the symbolic activities of early childhood, and in particular the symbolisation of language.

Speech and the Early Years

The early prelinguistic communication between mother and child is concerned with the infant's immediate needs and feelings, and the mother soon becomes adept at interpreting and responding, using convenient verbal or mimed symbolism. We are still far from certain as to how the young child combines perception, symbolism and motor activity so as to produce speech. Although we may not be able fully to explain the processes we cannot fail to see that the impulse to communicate in speech and gesture is there from the beginning.

The raw materials out of which the child builds his speech are the speech sounds or phonemes produced in early infancy. There is a strong case for considering that these early vocalisations have an innate basis because children of all races and nationalities seem to have a similar repertoire of prelinguistic utterances.

Not all the phonemes used by adults are present at the beginning, but they are to some extent present within the first few months. These initial sounds, and combinations of them, spring from the emotionally based conditions of harmony between mother and child. The very young child learns to listen at close proximity, at a high level of loudness, in secure and satisfying conditions repeated day after day, where the same simple words and phrases are basic to his life. A satisfying emotional relationship provides the atmosphere for distinguishing the tones of his mother's voice and the expressions on her face and later the movement of her lips. These intimate activities play an essential part in the child's understanding and acquisition of spoken language. This intensive stimulation in the child's mother tongue helps to encode the patterns of speech more clearly in his mind.

Although the sounds of speech are continuously reinforced by the mother, they do not acquire real linguistic significance for the child until they become representative of objects, situations and activities, and he begins to use them to communicate his thinking. The initial sounds are used over and over again before they are ready to be used in meaningful ways. Thus the repetitive sequence of babbling or lalling begins somewhere round the age of five months. The discovery of these skilled movements provides sufficient reinforcement for its own practice, and has the important function of providing the child with practice in the processes that are later to be used in speech. There is evidence to suggest that deaf babies lacking in auditory ability and consequent reinforcement do not babble in the fullest sense (Murphy 1964).

Although babies normally babble at about the fifth month, it is not until they are nearing the end of the first year that they begin to speak (Bruner 1975). The first word is very much a landmark in the development of speech and is of considerable interest to the parents. Communication between mother and child establishes many of the conversations that underlie the use of language and language development is facilitated by these social interactions in that language encodes routine with which the child is familiar.

We can expect many children to be saying at least one word by the end of the first year. The development of spoken language is highly individualised but it is possible to see a broad framework of the more usual ages and stages. The first words are usually rough imitations of something which has been continuously heard. Much attention is lavished upon the child when he produces a passable copy of the vocal patterns set for him. The fact that the child finds the copying of parental vocalisations self-rewarding provides much of the motivation required in the learning of speech.

Maturational factors are of course involved in speech development. The vocalisations made by adults cannot be copied by the child until the auditory mechanism and their central connections are sufficiently developed. Always the young child's speech performance lags behind his perception, or in other words his spoken language encompasses what he appreciated and understood some considerable time before. A child may be able to recognise and imitate a speech sound accurately for a long time before he can call it from his internal memory store and use it spontaneously in speech.

The first word often consists of a vowel and a tune and is usually accompanied by some explanatory gesture to reinforce meaning. At first the child's speech may be comprehensible only to his mother. His consistency in the use of the same primitive word form for any given object or activity allows his mother to interpret and reinforce it. The child's early words are meaningful word sentences or holophemes which may signify some general situation rather than a specific thing, activity or relationship. In this way the expression 'da-da' may mean 'da-da come here', 'da-da do this', 'da-da don't go' or 'da-da I love you'. The child's one word utterances express an intention and include labelling, repeating, answering, requesting, calling, greeting, protesting and practising (Halliday 1975).

The meaning of a word for the child may originate in a particular individual experience as well as from accumulated culture experiences. The use and meaning of many words is acquired as people indicate things represented, by handling things in play, and particularly by associating action with appropriate words. The child learns much of his speech as he is acquiring aspects of his social heritage such as ways of eating, drinking and dressing within the home and in the world outside his home. The meaning of many new words comes through the ever increasing influence of experience and gradually the context of language plays its part. At a later stage through context the child will use language to learn more language.

If we return to the idea of a broad framework in the development of spoken language it is possible to discern the more usual stages (Sheridan 1964). Moving from the first word utterance we find that at 13-14 months the child while continuing to use primitive chatter quite freely to himself and other people begins to speak spontaneously one or two recognisable words related to the here and now. By 15 months he may be using something approaching half a dozen recognisable spoken words and understands many more. At 18 months his indistinct utterances to himself and others have gradually assumed the characteristics of real speech. He may be using up to 20 recognisable words but he still does not understand complex sentences. Activities and strategies are continually enlarged by the thinking child largely through experiences, so that by 21 months he begins putting words together in simple sentences. This ability to formulate an idea and express it in spoken words marks the true beginning of formal language. All forms of symbolic function reflect thought and this is especially true of the sophisticated symbolisation of language (Piaget 1951). By the age of 2, the child is using 50 or more recognisable words. He refers to himself by name and engages in a continuous explanatory monologue as he plays, as though at this stage it is essential for him to clothe his thinking with words. Increasing experience means that his mind teems with ideas so that he is always demanding to be told the name of things and asks innumerable questions about the things around him. He begins to speak about the 'not here' and 'not now' aspects of life. In his make-believe play he can invoke symbols from his inner language store and he is learning how to manipulate them. By the age of 2½ his language handling has increased greatly and he begins to use the pronouns 'I', 'me' and 'you'. Not only does he recognise nursery rhymes but he begins to repeat them and enjoys simple familiar stories read to him from picture books. At 3 years he has a large working vocabulary of anything from 250 words or more and most of what he says is now intelligible. He uses plurals and pronouns and is continually asking 'Why', 'How' and 'When' type questions.

By the age of 4 the child's speech is so advanced that it shows only a few infantile speech sounds. He can give accounts of his recent experiences and other events. He loves stories, but confuses fact and fantasy, and now he is continually searching for the meaning of words which are new to him. It is the astonishing speed with which a child learns to speak and use his own language which has led linguists to argue strongly for the existence of some inherent language acquisition device (Chomsky 1957, 1965; Lewis 1963).

The Developing Intellect

For the child the first months of life are a time when sensori-motor patterns of behaviour are developing. These new integrations come about as a result of interplay between the child's innate reflexes or patterns, and the learning which comes about as a result of experience. It is in this early sensori-motor activity that the basis of the developing intelligence is found. The baby is marked by spontaneous exploration of stimuli and in this way begins to integrate meaningful intellectual structures or schema for himself. He develops an ever-expanding store of sensori-motor patterns or circulatory reactions.

The growing child is constantly constructing his understanding of himself and his world. Right from the start he builds up in his mind a kind of working model of the world around him. This is a model of a world of persisting and moving objects, and recurring happenings set in a framework of space and time and showing regular order. This model-building is carried on in a functional yet unmistakable way even in the first early months of life, before language or explicit thought have developed.

Once the basic model is formed in the child's mind, the rest is mainly a matter of building on, filling in and organising. The structure remains the same even though it is being continually expanded and enriched (Piaget 1950, 1954). It does in fact remain with the child for the rest of his life and continually regulates all his planning and action. This pattern of behaviour or schema is not just a static impression made by past experience, it is an active dynamic process in which there is a cumulative development between past and present.

There are of course numerous theories of intellectual development, but Piaget's contemporary theory is put forward as being probably the most significant. Piaget sees the mental development of children as a process by which they progress through childhood stage by stage to the formal thought of the adult. He is very much concerned with the psychological nature of human knowledge, and considers thought to be internalised action, and uses the expression operation to describe it.

According to Piaget's theory of intellectual development the first stage is the Sensori-Motor Operations Period which extends from birth until the appearance of language approximately during the first 18 months of life. At first the child perceives the world as a series of fleeting pictures and sounds. Gradually he acquires a degree of objectivity outside himself as his innate reflexes become modified by learning experience. By the end of this period he has advanced to the highest degree of intelligence that is possible without symbolic functioning.

Piaget sees a second broad stage of development from the age of 2 until 7 which he calls Pre-operational Thought. At first up to the age of 4 the child appears to re-learn on a conceptual level much of what he had previously learned from earlier sensori-motor experience of perceptions and conceptions. The emergence of real symbolic activity especially the use of language also occurs during this period of development. Then between the ages 4 to 7 we begin to see the emergence of intuitive thought. At this stage the child's thought is less under the influence of mere perceptions than before.

The Stage of Concrete Operations represents a third broad stage extending from about age 7 until 11 or 12 and consists of a period in preparation for, and realisation of, concrete experiences in particular of classes, relations and numbers. The child now becomes able to reason logically concerning these concepts. He shows his understanding of classes as he looks for all things which are the same colour or shape. He begins to understand relations between objects and people, and enters into an appreciation of numbers in the sense that he understands and can manipulate the bonds comprising a number.

The final stage in intellectual development, described as Formal Operations, begins early in adolescence. Before this time the child could classify, count and put into series the various objects and events he perceived. An adolescent at this stage through formal thinking becomes concerned with what is hypothetically possible, as well as with what is real. He is now able to reason scientifically, forming hypotheses and testing them in reality and thought. Previously his thinking had involved a great deal of concrete objects and experiences, but now the adolescent can imagine what is possible. He learns to speculate using logical rules and by the time he is about 15 he is able unconsciously to use aspects of formal logic in solving problems.

Piaget stresses the need not to use these so-called stages of intellectual growth in a rigid way. He is concerned with the working of the child's developing mind as he restructures his thinking. He uses the idea of stage only to describe how the child moves from his present developmental level to a new more advanced stage of thinking. He sees action as the source and medium of intelligence and feels that the reality of concepts must be sought in the action of thinking which can, of course, be embodied in symbolic functioning. Human intelligence is not tied to a particular type of internal image, nor to any particular type of symbols. It seems that the human mind is inventive enough to create the symbols that can best serve intelligence. This is particularly true in the symbolisation of words where, as need arises, new words are generated and added to the living language. Language demonstrates to us the place of the symbol in human intelligence. Language is learned to a great extent through social imitation and the young child enjoys its use because it enables him to further establish and demonstrate his grasp of reality. It seems that the most important function of language, shared with other symbolic activity, is in the service of thinking and that communication to some extent is almost secondary. Thinking becomes a personal elaboration and words appear to be a way of getting thinking going.

The work of Piaget on human intellectual development is put forward not so much as an established theory, but rather as a point of view which is worth following further (Piaget and Inhelder 1969). If it is used as a working model it will give considerable purpose to much of our thinking about, and understanding of, human intellectual development and change.

Thinking and Language in Human Communication

Before we can give any consideration to the relationship of thinking and language in human communication we must first of all provide operational definitions. There are many definitions of thinking and language, but for our discussion we will accept that provided by Furth (1966). He defined thinking as 'any activity which is related to or which demonstrates human intelligence. It includes all such activity, from the first manifestations of intelligence in an infant's behavioural repertoire to the adult intelligence as exemplified in logical operations... thinking as human behaviour is not something neatly separated from other human activities. It is as much a continuing part of our psychological life as the heart beat or the functioning of the nervous system is part of physiological activity.' When discussing an operational definition of language Furth suggests that 'the term language should be taken in the narrow sense of the natural, verbal language of society. It does not include all systems of communication or signals, nor does it encompass formally taught symbols, such as mathematics or symbolic logic. It refers here to the quite specific denotation of the mother tongue, the language of a society which practically all human infants are exposed to and learn by the time they are four years old.'

When we talk of language we must also be clear that for the first five or six years of a child's life we generally mean spoken language. In other words, in the normal child, language is acquired through auditory channels with some slight reinforcement from the other senses. Communication has at least two simultaneous elements. One element is directed to oneself, the other element to the person or persons with whom the communication is made (Murphy 1968). Communication depends for its efficiency on some mutual system of symbolisation. Symbolic systems may well use speech, gesture, drawing, mime and so on. Where such symbolism occurs and becomes a recognised mode of expression, we describe it as language. Human language can be described as a form of symbolisation of thought using words. In depicting language in this way we are able to appreciate the work of Furth and his associates who have shown that deaf children lacking any formal communication structure are still capable of highly sophisticated problem-solving (Furth 1963a, b.). While searching as an empirical psychologist for knowledge concerning thinking and language, Furth found considerable evidence to suggest that the basis for the development of intelligence was not found in language. As a result of his work he concluded that 'both theory and research indicate that intelligence does not build on language, but rather, language builds on intelligence.'

Interest in the relationship between thinking and language has varied in intensity over the years. Even today the efforts made to unravel this problem have not yielded a generally accepted solution. Many of the results of research have only highlighted the complexity of the inter-relationships of thinking and language. Sometimes contemporary psychology seeks to explain the acquisition of concepts in terms of verbal explanations and connections and fails to take into account the fact that deaf children with little or no language develop concepts. The fact that most deaf children are denied to a large extent the ready-made symbol system of the hearing world, not only for communication, but also for thinking, suggests that thinking cannot find its base in verbal behaviour. So the validity of theory which relies on verbal explanations of thinking appears to be unacceptable. It is easy to fall into the pitfall of explaining thinking in terms of verbal behaviour, for as consideration is given to a problem, there is an awareness of the use of internal language. It is all too easy to consider thinking as a kind of internal screen, which seems almost to identify the verbal symbol with the process of thinking. To explain thinking in terms of verbal or other symbols assumes that concepts are real units of thinking, that concept and symbol and particularly words are identical. Symbols are then assumed to work as substitute stimuli. It is, of course, wrong to give a reality to the symbols which they do not possess, and equally wrong to assume that symbolic units carry the actual meaning of concepts.

None of what has been said about thinking and language reduces the importance of these processes, especially the use of language in human communication. We have, however, sought to present a perspective in which language demonstrates to us the place of the symbol in the service of human intelligence. Language increases the power of thinking in range and rapidity. Piaget sees the symbolic function as detaching thinking from action and as being the source of representation.

> Unlike images and other semiotic instruments which are created by the individual as the need arises, language has already been elaborated socially and contains a notation for an entire system of cognitive instruments, relationships, classifications and so on for use in the service of thought. The individual learns this system and then proceeds to enrich it. (Piaget and Inhelder 1969, p. 87)

Every child has to construct his own knowledge of reality. Whereas the words that other people use may help, they are useful only if they can be related to the totality of the child's schema or what he knows. In particular it is necessary to remember that the roots of logic are to be found in actions not in words (Piaget 1951). Language is, of course, full of expressions of logical relationships, levels of classification, cross-classification and general relationships. But teaching children the use of these linguistic forms does not appear to help them develop clear ways of thinking. It cannot be overemphasised that it is by thinking that people get better at thinking (Furth 1973). This view was supported by Sinclair (1967) who, as a result of his work, concluded that language development is dependent on the level of thinking rather than being responsible for the thinking.

The development of logical actions through childhood into adolescence is traced by Piaget who considered that at every stage children carry out intellective activities without necessarily using language that revealed a knowledge of these processes. It must be quite clear that the emphasis of this is that in order to know something or to think about something we do not have to use words. It is still held by many people that even if we do not always need words to think about thoughts which are already in our minds, it was through words that the thoughts were generated. It is true that something a person is told may be connected with what is already known, but if real understanding is there new internal connections are made. However, if a person is unable to grasp what he has been told it is usually because he cannot make the necessary new connections for himself because of lack of internal structure or knowing. To a very great extent internal structures have been built up from very early childhood, and their roots lie in actions and not in words.

We have been briefly concerned with the development of the intellective and symbolic grasp of reality in this section on thinking and language in human communication. Above all it seems that the semiotic or symbolic function reflects thought and this is especially true of the sophisticated symbolisation of language. Piaget more than adequately sums up these aspects we have been considering in what he has to say about early child development. 'In spite of the astonishing diversity of its manifestations, the semiotic function presents a remarkable unity. Whether it is a question of deferred imitation, symbolic play, drawing, mental images and image memories or language, this function allows the representative evocation of objects and events not perceived at that particular moment. This semiotic function makes thought possible by providing it with an unlimited field of application in contrast to the restricted boundaries of sensori-motor action and perception. Reciprocally it evolves under the guidance of thought, or representative intelligence.' (Piaget and Inhelder 1969, p. 91). If acceptance is given to the meaningfulness of the idea that language reflects thought it should cause considerable changes in our schools. With the child seen as a doer or active participator in learning there must be a change in the role of the teacher with a diminution of his role as importer of information. Piaget has clearly shown that the activities and strategies developed by the thinking child are acquired to a large extent through experience. Furth has also confirmed this point of view and introduced us to a perspective in which the ability of the child to think operatively occupies a key role in development.

It is interesting that even a brief look at the relationship of thinking and language in human communication has caused us to question the idea that language provides the critical means of enabling human psychological development and function to take place. It should also cause us to question much of current educational theory and practice.

From Childhood into Adolescence

Throughout childhood intellectual development has been taking place and during adolescence we have seen that formal thinking comes about. Probably the other most important psychological changes which appear in adolescence relate to aspects of personality. These changes take place under the impact of physiological change and social pressures, which make the behaviour of childhood inadequate and call for a great deal of change and readjustment.

Adolescence can be described as the period between childhood and adult life and in its broadest sense refers to the psychological changes consequent upon puberty (Fleming 1951). Adolescence is better thought of as a process rather than a state. There are essential steps to any process and none more so than with adolescence as one of the normal life crises through which human beings pass. Although the start of adolescence is biologically determined, it can be a drawn out process and can be made flexible by both social pressures and individual needs. The terminal point of adolescence can only be approximated, for although sexual maturity can be achieved in some cases quite quickly there is no sharp physical distinction or event between adolescence and adulthood. Each society introduces its own criteria as to the full status of maturity. All this reminds us that the process of adolescence should be seen as having a biological beginning and a sociologically defined ending. The term adolescence, derived from the Latin *adolescere*, means approach to maturity and supports the idea of adolescence being a process. The age of onset of pubescence varies somewhat as to sex, race, climate and general living conditions. Biologically it is marked by the onset of menstruation in girls, which occurs in the white population at about the age of 13. It is often preceded by the appearance of pubic hairs and noticeable bust development. In boys the most significant single event marking the onset of puberty is ejaculation and it appears that the average age when this takes place is a little under 14.

With boys the development of pubic hair usually precedes ejaculation whereas the characteristic voice change of boys usually follows it. These developments are of course in line with the generally accepted idea that girls are ahead of boys in achieving sexual maturity.

Adolescence as a process is marked by a movement away from expecting adult care towards self-responsibility and this entails changes in thought and behaviour towards oneself and other people. In the past psychologists placed undue emphasis upon clearly defined periods of typical adolescent behaviour and very little place was given to the effects of society. They also predicted emotional upheavals and erratic unstable behaviour as being almost inevitable in adolescence. Today contemporary psychology would consider adolescence to be a normal crisis of life, a necessary healthy process, and place less emphasis on so-called typical behaviour. From a psychological viewpoint the idea of crisis is of interest especially as it may infer some kind of negative process which would be quite wrong. The idea of life crisis is a key concept in psychological thinking and is widely used. A life crisis is very much a personal situation which arises when well-tried structures of adaptation and defence are no longer adequate to absorb new demands, which make an impact from within and from outside a person. When this happens there is a peculiar loosening or loss of cohesion of thought and feeling. In common everyday language we both feel and say we think we are going mad. This partial disintegration of thought and feeling is accompanied by a measure of anxiety and perplexity, and often by impulsive action and sometimes primitive fantasy intrudes. However, it is a necessary healthy process. When it happens the person concerned is able to test out the new situation and discover new ways of thought and action to meet his own needs and those of the external world (Caplan 1964, Mayerson 1975). For some adolescents it may be a time with hardly noticeable distress and for a few it may even be an enjoyed experience. It does seem, however, that for the crises of adolescence to be resolved, the steps we have outlined have to be passed through in some degree or other.

When describing adolescence some workers take ego identity as a central theme (Erikson 1968). According to the basis of this approach, the individual, as he progresses through various developmental stages, meets with some degree of life crisis. The crisis of adolescence is seen as one of identity formation. At this time the various differing self-perceptions and aspirations previously acquired have to be integrated satisfactorily. The adolescent is neither a child, nor the possession of his parents, nor is he an adult. He is not yet someone with a set appearance or with an identity which has been tested in society. He may identify with conflicting personalities and therefore suffer with identity diffusion as he attempts to develop a well-knit self-image, by dropping some and adopting other characteristics from the people who form his various models. The individual can sometimes suffer if too early a chosen identity is taken on. He needs to experiment with a number of roles if he is to develop the type of identity for adulthood which will support him in later life.

We can summarise adolescence by saying that the central theme is seen to be self-discovery taking place during a period of rapid physical growth and rousing sexual activity. There is a desire for greater independence from parents and an element of resultant conflict brought about by the lack of defined status. Although related to puberty, the characteristic behaviour patterns of adolescence seem also to be culturally determined, varying very much with social demands and individual experience. It is a time of social learning.

The development of a social self entails an awareness of one's self in relation to others and this includes understanding duties as well as privileges. The development of a sexual self involves relationships with those of the opposite sex, ranging from friendly indifference to deep involvement, leading to marriage and the founding of and caring for a family. There is also the development of a working self which involves the idea of vocational adjustment which is also related to avocational interests. Finally there is an element of life interpretation both philosophically, religiously and politically.

The Contribution of Maturity

With the adult, change takes place in a much more individual manner. The sequence of development is spread over many years with each person going through highly personal and complex development as part of the whole process of life. Recognising that personality is peculiarly individual, we may however say that, by and large, adult personality is characterised by a greater consistency than that of children or adolescents, and that it tends to be markedly channelled in the direction of family, work and leisure interests. Conservatism becomes very much the underlying rule for many people. Adult personality seems to change only very slowly and most people, unless constantly stimulated by environmental or other change, become well settled in a steady way of living.

For most adults the finding of a satisfactory work identity, especially if it can be chosen, can be a remarkably satisfying experience. As a person in our culture finds assurance and self-sufficiency he is then able to take on the commitment of shared love. A great deal of the testing of ourselves in the adult world concerns the effective contributions we are able to make to others and to life itself. Adult status and maturity presupposes the contributions a person can make to others and the recognition for them (Storr 1960). In the work setting the adult finds varying degrees of repetition, together with some opportunity for creativity and responsibility. Unfortunately much repetitive work largely excludes any choice of action and the means by which people seek variety are well known. However, for many people work requires a degree of choice and here more skill is required. In the more creative job a person is able to use formal thinking and imagination to conduct some new ordering of things or ideas that were not present before. Creative activity is one of the most deeply enjoyable human experiences. Choice of course or activity entails a measure of uncertainty and anxiety about performing a task. This involves the idea of responsibility for the completion of the task concerned and responsibility for others in the process. In being responsible a person has to use his feelings in such a way that they are a motivating force, but on the other hand they must not be allowed to overwhelm him. Work provides its own peculiar problems and anxieties, and some people are able to take on more responsibility than others.

Although the idea of work responsibility carries a measure of seriousness we must also remember that it can none the less provide deeply satisfying experiences. When we find a personal patterning of roles which give satisfaction we experience a sense of wholeness. This satisfying integration of adult identity is centred on the self, and is very much private to the individual concerned (Erikson 1963, 1968). Adult identity takes in the idea of integrity as a person evaluates and balances the responsibility of his own enjoyment with that of others. In order to maintain the integrity of his personality so that he has a sense of the integration of his desires, his conscience, and also the demands of the outside world, a person has to make compromises. Adult life is particularly marked by a pattern of compromise. As a new situation arises, so the individual is called upon to re-evaluate the position and to develop new patterns of thought, and to find new compromises which will maintain his own integrity and that of others (Storr 1960).

In mid-life there is a changing awareness of the time a person has ahead of him. This is affected by the development which has gone before and by the early forties one begins to look equally back and forward with an awareness of middle age. Ideas of mortality set a boundary to the conception of oneself and begin to control the sense of identity. The recognition that life is finite provides the individual with positive ideas of reality, which enable him to assess what he would like still to do in life. We are all aware of the menopause crisis with its marked hormonal changes, but we need to view this as symptomatic of the older woman's identity crisis. It may well be that the disintegration of sexual centredness in middle age is not just a biological necessity but much more a psychological artefact. Even though the identity crisis for women may not be fundamentally linked to the change of life it is still linked to biological ageing. This time of life probably affects every woman in some degree with its depressive feeling of loss. It is a sadness, however, which should be used to herald new freedoms.

The external pressures on a man in our society will depend largely in mid-life on his work commitment. There is some question of whether men go through a change of life in any sense comparable with that experienced by women. Change in men is gradual, and not marked by any obvious physiological sign. Although the midde aged man's slower body functioning must play a part in a tendency to conservatism, it is probably much more connected with emotion and attitude than we realise. There is a tendency for a man to cling to the adult identity discovered long before, whereas he should be fundamentally changing his way of life and learning to enjoy what life now offers. For both men and women the mid-life crisis is at root a very normal condition arising out of the inevitable ageing process. Although it is essentially a crisis involving loss and renunciation it also involves future change. Mid-life and later life can in fact be a time of great creative energy with a heightened sense of purpose. Innovation and change does not come only from those who are young, but frequently from individuals in later maturity and beyond (Jacques 1970).

The Passing Years and Old Age

Attitudes and expectations towards human ageing are conditioned to some extent by society. Many people become old because they and the world around them have accepted the idea that because a person has reached a certain age, receives a pension or no longer works he must be old. Slowly there has been a move away from the work role as a mark of ageing to viewing old age more and more by a broad social competence. This is a move in the right direction for there appears to be little reduction in social competence for very many people between the forties and the seventies. In the industrialised countries the old have a prolonged expectation of life within a highly developed economy which can adequately support them. It is expected that by the end of the century the over-seventy-fives will make up something like 10 per cent of the population of most countries in Western Europe and North America. The percentage of people living closer to their life potential is now greater than ever before, mainly as a result of medical advances and improved nutrition. Women, living longer than men, constitute a large part of the older population. The average life expectancy of a man is into the early seventies and for a woman something like five years beyond this point. Men marry later in life than women and they die earlier. As a result of living longer, and sometimes of wars, women are more often widowed than are men.

There may be old rich people but by and large the old are poor. In the main the aged constitute a large segment of the poor in the overall population. They have more chronic diseases than the young and medical expenditure on the old is often three or four times as high. The killer diseases of old age are diseases of the heart, cancer and cerebrovascular problems such as strokes and diabetes.

Old people are as various and as individual as those who are younger. We should not think of the elderly as a homogeneous entity, for old people seem even more varied than other age groups (Huyck 1974). Old age is a time of both decline and development. The behavioural changes taking place are very much consequential both of changes going on in the body and the pressures of people and circumstances in society (Townsend 1963). The success of ageing is found in the way a person responds to these internal and external pressures and the cultivation of positive attitudes throughout life may help with this adjustment. Success in ageing comes about as a person makes the most of the opportunities which still lie ahead. Threatened with deterioration of bodily functions and social expectations that he will become useless and unwanted, irrespective of real capacities, it is not surprising that for some people old age is a very significant crisis of life. With retirement or reduction of work new functions have to be developed and integrated for life to continue with meaning and satisfaction. For many people identity will have largely centred around working capacity and with retirement this identity is removed, together with some considerable part of income. No matter how positively it is received, ageing is marked inevitably by a measure of depressive feelings. Physical deterioration means that there is a depletion in ego functioning and a shrinkage of the sense of self with feelings of smallness and helplessness. In some degree or other every individual as he grows older, however fit and active he may be, has to deal with background feelings of depression and anxiety. So long as a person can think and move he can maintain a great deal of his independence of judgement and hence his individuality. The progress of shrinkage is inevitable and many an old person is forced into dependence upon others. Where there is mutual recognition of each other's dignity the care of the aged may still be rewarding for all concerned.

In recent years gerontology, the study of human behaviour in adult life and old age, has become increasingly important. This scientific study of the processes of growing old takes in a vast area reaching into the biological and medical sciences, the social and behavioural sciences and even to technological innovation and the natural sciences. Gerontology looks at the complex sequences of change in which the organs and functions of the body become impaired, the changes in sensory and motor capacities, central mental processing and the nervous system. People's beliefs, attitudes and personal qualities are also part of this process of change (Bromley 1966). Gerontology seeks to look at human ageing in three ways, namely the theoretical, methodological and applied aspects. The theoretical aspect is concerned with the conceptual basis and the explanation of observed facts of ageing; the methodological aspect seeks to develop research procedures and to consider the logic of the arguments developed; finally the applied or practical aspect is concerned with prevention and reduction of the adverse effects of ageing. The applied aspect of gerontology is probably the most interesting area to those within the helping professions, with its concern to retard and ameliorate the process of ageing.

For many people old age is marked by aspects of death. Our industrial society with its enhanced opportunities for individuality has increased the possibility of loneliness, so that even dying tends to be hidden and often solitary (Gorer 1965). In the recent past at least, taboos have grown up directed at hiding death away and allowing the living almost to deny it, whereas awareness of death and its recognition by those around can mean that a person ends life with dignity and peace and will be remembered for this by those remaining (Kubler-Ross 1970). Greater openness about death also helps with the problem of bereavement. Acute distress marks bereavement but none the less it is a normal state. Distress is at its height in the first few days after death with the body in a state of biological arousal. Sleep may be disturbed and there is often subdued hyperactivity and hallucinatory perception in otherwise normal people. As the loss is recognised there comes a phase of searching for an answer, perhaps marked by periods of weeping and depression. Then come some times of calmness which help to mitigate the loss and slowly the person begins to come alive again and look outwards. Sadness at the loss but some feeling of being glad to be alive marks a person at this time (Parkes 1972). Bereavement is not only a time of distress, it is also an acute depressive crisis, which involves the breaking of old patterns of behaviour and the slow discovery and testing of a partially new identity. Slowly the grieving person finds new ways for distribution of his energies. He now has a sense of the dead loved one much more as he was when alive. The cumulative experience of mourning reaches a final stage as the mourner slowly but quite naturally comes alive again. The mourner himself is now more ready to carry on living, and although still fearful, a little more prepared to face death himself one day.

In adapting to both biological and social changes, the aged person continues to draw upon that which he has been as well as that which he is now. So we are brought full circle in our concern with some of the predominant experiences of human beings as they are born, grow up, mature, age and eventually die. The ending of life cannot be separated from the beginning.

This brief synoptic psychological framework concerned with some of the central features of human development and communication hardly does justice to such a wide and fascinating subject. It does, however, challenge us to strive not just to love but to understand human beings. Learning to understand other human beings and their individual experiences takes place primarily through an increasing awareness of oneself and of others. To be effective, the practice of any art concerned with people, such as aural rehabilitation carried out by hearing therapists, needs to be firmly grounded on knowledge of the nature of human nature (Watts 1980). The human life path has a beginning and an end, and no part of it has reality except in relation to the whole (Venables 1971).

References

Bromley, D.B. (1966) *The Psychology of Human Ageing*, Penguin Books, Harmondsworth.

Bruner, J. (1975) 'The Ontogenesis of Speech Acts', *J Child Language*, 2, 1-19

Caplan, G. (1964) *Principles of Preventive Psychiatry*, Tavistock, London

Chamberlain, G. (1969) *The Safety of the Unborn Child*, Penguin Books, Harmondsworth

Chomsky, N. (1957) *Syntactic Structure*, Mouton, The Hague

Chomsky, N. (1965) *Aspects of the Theory of Syntax*, MIT Press, Cambridge, Mass

Erikson, E.H. (1963) *Childhood and Society*, Penguin Books, Harmondsworth

Fleming, C.M. (1951) *The Social Psychology of Education: An Introduction and Guide to its Study*, Routledge and Kegan Paul, London

Furth, H.G. (1963a) 'Classification Transfer with Disjunctive Concepts as a function of Verbal Training and Set', *J. Psychol.*, 55, 447-85

Furth, H.G. (1963b) 'Conceptual Discovery and Control on a Pictorial Part Whole Task as a Function of Age, Intelligence and Language', *J Educational Psychol*, 54, 191-6

Furth, H.G. (1966) *Thinking without Language: Psychological Implications of Deafness*, The Free Press, New York; Macmillan, London

Furth, H.G. (1973) *Deafness and Learning: A Psychological Approach*, Wadsworth, Belmont, California

Gorer, G. (1965) *Death, Grief and Mourning in Contemporary Britain*, Cresset, London

Halliday, M.A.H. (1975) *Learning How to Mean*, Arnold, London

Huyck, M.H. (1974) *Growing Older. What you need to know about Ageing*, Prentice Hall, Englewood Cliffs

Jacques, E. (1970) *Work Creativity and Social Justice*, IUP, New York

Kubler-Ross, E. (1970) *On Death and Dying*, Tavistock, London

Lewin, R. (ed) (1975) *Child Alive*, Temple Smith, London

Lewis, M.M. (1963) *Language, Thought and Personality in Infancy and Childhood*, Harrap, London

Mayerson, S. (ed) (1975) *Adolescence and the Crisis of Adjustment*, Allen and Unwin, London

Murphy, K.P. (1964) 'Development of Normal Vocalisation and Speech in the Child who does not Talk' in Renfrew, C. and Murphy, K.P. (eds), Spastics Society Medical and Information Unit in association with Heinemann, London

Murphy, K.P. (1968) 'Language and Learning – Learning and Language', Spastics Society Conference Paper published in *The Child with Delayed Speech, Clin Dev Med No. 43*, Spastics International Medical Publications and Heinemann, London

Parkes, M. (1972) *Bereavement*, Penguin Books, Harmondsworth

Piaget, J. (1950) *The Psychology of Intelligence*, Routledge and Kegan Paul, London

Piaget, J. (1951) *Play, Dreams and Imitation in Childhood*, Routledge and Kegan Paul, London

Piaget, J. (1954) *The Construction of Reality in the Child*, Basic Books, New York

Piaget, J. and Inhelder, B. (1969) *The Psychology of the Child*, Routledge and Kegan Paul, London

Schow, R.L. and Norbonne, M.A. (eds) (1980) *Introduction to Aural Rehabilitation*, University Park Press, Baltimore

Segal, H. (1973) *An Introduction to the Work of Melanie Klein*, Hogarth, London

Sheridan, M. (1964) 'Development of Auditory Attention and the Use of Language Symbols in the Child who does not Talk', in Renfrew, C. and Murphy, K.P. (eds), Spastics Society Medical and Information Unit in association with Heinemann, London

Sinclair, H. (1967) *Langage et Operations: Sous-systemes Linguistiques et Operations Concretes*, Dunod, Paris

Storr, A. (1960) *The Integrity of the Personality*, Penguin Books, Harmondsworth

Townsend, P. (1963) *The Family Life of Old People*, Penguin Books, Harmondsworth

Venables, E. (1971) *Counselling*, National Marriage Guidance Council, Rugby

Watts, W.J. (1980) 'Hearing Therapy', *Hearing* (March/April), Royal National Institute for the Deaf, London, 58-61

3 EXPERIENCES OF ACQUIRED DEAFNESS

Kenneth S. Pegg

Why yet another article about acquired deafness? When I was asked to contribute to this book, I felt a certain reluctance. After all, much has been written about the problem from both professional and personal points of view, and while circumstances may alter cases, a fairly general picture has emerged regarding the effect of the handicap. It was then pointed out that there might be some advantage in looking at the effect of acquired deafness upon a teacher whose working life has been spent with both the pre-lingually deaf and adults with acquired deafness.

This then is acquired deafness as experienced by one individual who has had the good fortune to be employed in the education of the deaf, has seen the problem from many angles, and has enjoyed the association of professional workers in related disciplines.

No matter how one views the problem of acquired deafness it is, to put it mildly, a nuisance not only to the sufferer but also to those with whom he comes into contact. Why should this be so? After all, tremendous advances have been made in the medical and surgical treatment of deafness and great improvements have been made in the development of hearing aids of all kinds. Nevertheless, it would seem that the acceptance and management of a hearing impairment still leaves much to be desired. It is often said that deafness is a hidden handicap, the implication being that the general public is not instantly aware that there is something amiss. Might it not also be argued that the hearing-impaired themselves do much of the hiding? In the early days this was certainly true in my case, and I strongly suspect it to be true of many other adults with acquired deafness whom I have met professionally and socially over the years.

It is impossible for those who have been brought up in a hearing and speaking society to imagine what it would be like to be born deaf. We can, however, try to put ourselves in the position of an adult who has suffered an impairment of hearing and we can imagine passing from the stage when people no longer speak as clearly as they once did, to the stage when we are forced to accept that there is something wrong with our hearing. On seeking medical help we could find that there is no treatment appropriate in our case, but that we can have a hearing aid.

Up to this point we have probably been feeling isolated and depressed, but we are now likely to feel a little happier because we are going to be given an instrument which will restore our hearing. It could be, however, that we will be disappointed. We could well find that while sounds generally are made much louder by the hearing aid the sounds of speech are no clearer, and we are quite unprepared for this. If, however, we are among the fortunate ones, we will be given instruction in how to use the instrument to the best advantage, and may be told that it would be advisable to learn to speechread and also told where to go for instruction. The chances in so many cases are that we will not be given this information, but will be left to work out our own salvation, often with tragic social results. If we are fortunate we will be shown how to use the hearing aid and told what it will do and what it will not do, where it will work most effectively and where it will not. We practise speechreading and find that our ability to communicate is improving, but we also find that even when using hearing and speechreading combined, we become tired much more quickly than in the past. We also become aware that speechreading is ambiguous and we make mistakes, and that while some people are easy to speechread others are almost impossible.

So practical living problems are increasing. We begin to find that leisure-time activities are curtailed and that we can get little pleasure from the radio or record player and only a limited amount of information from television. We try to keep going with visits to friends. We are likely to be resentful if, after arranging with our wives beforehand to rephrase conversation, or repeat the missed punch line of a joke, we are told 'Oh, it wasn't important' or 'I'll tell you later'. We shall certainly be disinclined to accept an invitation to dinner when we know that our hostess is keen on dining by candlelight and speechreading is impossible. If we have problems with our friends and family, *what is likely to happen at work?* It may have taken us many years to reach our present position in whatever type of employment we are engaged in, but can we still manage? It is imperative that we do, because if we fail it will almost inevitably mean a financial loss, with a debilitating effect upon our self-esteem and a change in the standard of living of our family.

So we have many things to remember and practise if we are to overcome our handicap. We have to try not to strain to hear or see speech, but when we are tired this is far easier said than done. We must try to remain relaxed but at the same time alert and 'tuned in'. We know that we are not going to get every word, but must be looking constantly for key words. We have to stage-manage every situation to our advantage, but we also have to remember that conversation is a two-way affair, so that in any attempt to direct and control it we must not monopolise it. Some or all of these difficulties are part of the everyday experiences of hard of hearing adults. They occur in spite of long-established mental habits that condition and facilitate the comprehension of speech and the use of words in the expression of thought. It is small wonder that some hard of hearing people suffer from depression, isolation, self-consciousness and lack of confidence, and that they need rehabilitative help.

It is one thing to be aware of the problem academically, to have learnt from others in such a situation, but it is quite another thing to experience the problem at first hand. It might be expected that one would learn by experience of the problems of others and therefore be adequately prepared to deal with the new situation. Initially this was not so in my case. At first I was embarrassed by the situation and experienced a certain feeling almost of shame. This was not because I had acquired a severe hearing impairment: after all, I had reached an age when such an occurrence should not cause too much surprise. Nor did I experience the feeling of why should it happen to me; but I was, for the first week or so, totally unable to understand why I could not manage to deal more effectively with the problem of communication. There was then a sense of mounting frustration and certainly a shortening of temper. I had a job that I thoroughly enjoyed which involved meeting single or groups of individuals, attending staff and management meetings, and going to committee meetings at national level and I did not want to give anything up. The inability to hear properly often causes a withdrawal from threatening communication situations and in the early days this is what happened to me when I was not monopolising the situation. By talking and talking and talking you are less likely to be put in a position of asking the speaker to repeat what he has said. I am making no excuses for this, because I should have known better. After all, if you have no hearing impairment you have no hesitation in asking people to repeat something but you are less inclined to do so if you cannot hear properly.

It has become fashionable in certain quarters to decry the teaching of speechreading, the implications being that this cannot be taught, that in any case everyone can speechread to a lesser or greater extent and that the only rehabilitation required is the issue of a hearing aid. A great deal has been written and said about this in recent years. So much so that even I began to question the validity of offering speechreading classes for hearing-impaired adults. I felt a great reluctance to abandon or modify teaching programmes which had apparently been so successful for many years. People attended classes and demands for additional classes increased, as did the necessity to train more teachers of speechreading.

In my experience there are wide variations in the ability to speechread. Some are born speechreaders, the majority have a reasonable ability in utilising visual clues but others find it most difficult. Some factors which make for good speechreading have been investigated, but there is reason to suppose that there may be other aspects of the process which are not fully understood. Speechreading skills can be improved with training, determination and practice but individual differences seem to persist despite training, at least the kind of training commonly employed today.

Most of us have learned that if we watch a speaker we do not have to listen quite so carefully. We obtain information more readily when we can both see and hear the speaker, and in a verbal exchange we watch intently, not only to enhance the message but also to take in the facial expressions, the gestures, the subtle postural changes, and the situational cues which convey so much information. Many situations are greatly dependent upon visual clues to enable us to communicate effectively. When it became necessary for me to supplement my severely diminished auditory ability by the more efficient use of speechreading, I was at a loss, in spite of all the experience I had gained over the years in teaching speechreading and in the problems of others in a similar situation. Why should I have experienced this difficulty? After all, I could still hear to some small extent, I knew about speechreading from the academic standpoint and I still possessed the average hearing person's ability to speechread. I can only conclude that the initial problem was connected with lack of confidence. I could not rely on my innate ability and I found myself doing all the things which I had spent years happily telling others not to do.

I was fortunate in having professional colleagues to whom I could turn for help, and this help was willingly given. I am told that I am now a good communicator. Be that as it may, I am convinced that without the patient instruction and help that I received I would still be floundering. I am also more certain than ever that the acquisition of an effective standard of speechreading to supplement residual hearing is essential if one wishes to remain a fully functioning member of society. It would be nonsense to suggest that all hearing-impaired adults require speechreading instruction but far more do need it than is commonly supposed. The modern hearing aid is in many ways a very effective instrument but it cannot restore hearing to normal, and I would strongly advise those who are experiencing difficulty in communication to consider having instruction in speechreading. Together with very many others, they will find it to be a lifeline in communication.

I have said nothing about the use of hearing aids, mainly because for various reasons I have been unable to use one effectively. Nevertheless, even without the use of an individual hearing aid it has been possible, by the use of existing techniques, to train my residual hearing and to make the fullest possible use of the sounds I am still able to discriminate.

My own personal experiences have significantly confirmed my long-held belief in the necessity for the teaching of speechreading and for the provision of auditory rehabilitation and informed counselling. I must express again my gratitude to all those whose skill and patience have been of such value. I am encouraged in the belief that many more adults with acquired deafness will, in the future, receive similar help from teachers of speechreading and members of the new profession of hearing therapists.

4 DENMARK AS A CONTEMPORARY EUROPEAN MODEL OF AURAL REHABILITATION

Andreas Markides

When this book was planned it was the intention to include a brief account of the world situation of aural rehabilitation. However, as has already been pointed out, there is a serious lack of reliable information of this nature. It was therefore decided that it would be very useful to present a detailed model of the most successful contemporary European example, as found in Denmark.

Denmark is a lowland country and in addition to the Jutland peninsula it consists of 490 islands covering an area of 43,000 square kilometres. It has a population of 5m people of whom nearly 30 per cent live in rural areas. Twenty-five per cent of the population are under 15 years old and 11 per cent are over 65.

Legislative Basis of Danish Audiological Services

The remarkable audiometric, educational, technical and rehabilitational services for hearing-impaired people (both children and adults) in Denmark owe their development primarily to three recent Acts of Parliament introduced in the last 30 years. Tribute must be paid, however, to the role of the voluntary associations for the deaf (established in the early nineteenth century) and to the Danish National Association for Better Hearing (established in 1912) which played a leading and decisive role in bringing about and influencing the contents of these legislative Acts. During the last 30-35 years, the state, through the Ministry of Social Affairs, has exhibited a highly commendable interest in audiology. Without this interest, the present organisation and service would not have been reached, a status which includes complete financial responsibility by the state.

The acts providing for audiological treatment of all categories of hearing impairment (hard of hearing and deaf children as well as hard of hearing and deaf adults) are the following:

(1) The Act of 1950 providing for hard of hearing and deaf persons

(preceded by Amendments to the National Insurance Act of 1933).
(2) The Rehabilitation Act of 1960.
(3) The Education Act of 1958.

The last act (Education Act 1958) deals mainly with the education of deaf children and, therefore, its implications are outside the scope of this report.

The Act of 1950 Providing for Hard of Hearing and Deaf Persons

This Act among other things led to the establishment of:

(i) Three state hearing centres — Copenhagen, Odense and Aarhus (established in 1951-52,
(The two state hearing institutes for deafened adults — Copenhagen, Fredericia — had already been established.)
(ii) A national vocational guidance service for hearing-impaired adults.

The inter-related functions of these services will be presented and discussed later on.

The Rehabilitation Act of 1960 (Preceded by Amendments to the National Insurance Act of 1950)

This act dealt mainly with the provision, dispensation and maintenance of hearing aids and with subsequent follow-up services for hearing-impaired adults. It reiterated that every Danish citizen, including other people with a permanent address in Denmark, is entitled to free audiological treatment and it stipulated that hearing aids, although remaining state property, should be issued to patients free of charge. It set up a joint state hearing aid purchasing committee, including doctors, engineers and hearing pedagogues (teachers) whose function is the purchasing of hearing aids in bulk, following tenders, from commercial Danish and foreign hearing aid manufacturers. The far-reaching effects of this act will be made clear as this chapter progresses.

Organisation of Services for Deafened Adults

The organisation of audiological and follow-up services for deafened adults in Denmark are summarised in a diagrammatical form in Figure

Figure 4.1: Organisation of Audiological and Follow-up Services in Denmark

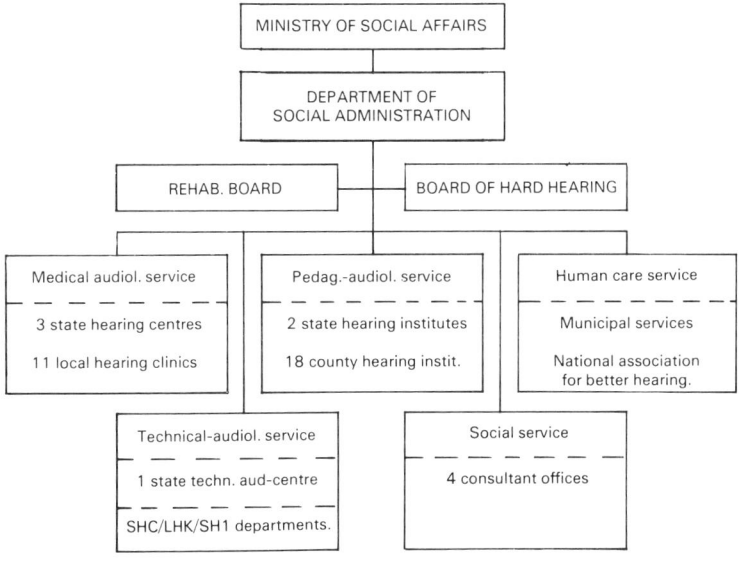

SHC = State hearing centre
LHK = Local hearing clinic
SHI = State hearing institute.

4.1. In practice the functions of these services are closely interwoven.

The comprehensive services provided for deafened adults in Denmark can be divided into five areas: the medical-audiological service; the technical-audiological service; the pedagogical (educational)-audiological service (rehabilitation); the social service (vocational guidance); the local (municipal) human care service (including the Danish National Association for Better Hearing).

This report is primarily concerned with the medical-audiological service and the pedagogical (educational)-audiological service (rehabilitation) and their functions will be dealt with in detail later on. The functions of the other services are mentioned first.

The Technical-Audiological Service

The main function of this service is to carry out research on the electro-acoustic properties of hearing aids and earmoulds; to develop and evaluate new audiovisual and audiometric equipment and to provide national guidance and advice to all technical departments situated within the state hearing centres and/or local hearing clinics, state hearing institutes and state schools for the deaf. The headquarters of this national service is housed next to the state hearing centre at Odense (which is within a teaching hospital) and is headed by a graduate engineer and staffed with engineers, physicists, and technical staff trained in electronics. They work in close collaboration with medical and educational professionals.

The Social Service (vocational guidance)

At present Denmark is divided up into four areas with each area being served by a central office with travelling vocational consultants. It is the duty of these consultants to give the patients the right vocational placing and also to assist them in their social problems, if any. In addition to this there are five similar offices which deal primarily with ex-pupils from the state schools of the deaf and hard of hearing.

The Local (municipal) Human Care Service

These are local organisations, both state and voluntary, and their main function is to look after the welfare (housing, pensions, home helps, etc) of those in need including deafened adults.

The Medical-Audiological Service

As stated, the Act of 1950 brought about the establishment of three state hearing centres – the Copenhagen state hearing centre which serves one half of the country lying east of the Great Belt, with a population of 2.3 million people, and the Odense and Aarhus state hearing centres which serve a population of 2.6 m people living in the part of Denmark lying west of the Great Belt. In addition to this, the Odense centre serves Greenland, Denmark's Arctic county. These state hearing centres are attached to large general hospitals (university teaching hospitals) and they are headed by doctors who have specialised both in otology and audiology. Owing to the large number of people seeking audiological treatment, however, there has been a movement towards decentralisation and at present there are eleven local hearing clinics in the country. These hearing clinics are headed by audiologically trained otologists and they form (except one) an integral part of the ENT department of the hospital in which they are situated. The 14 hearing centres and clinics are scattered all over the country and as a result of this very few patients need travel more than 30 miles for audiological treatment. (Future plans include the establishment of an additional four local hearing clinics, one in each county (each one serving a population of around 300,000 people).)

The function of the state hearing centres and of the local hearing clinics is (a) to provide a comprehensive audiological service for all hearing-impaired people in their respective area, (b) to initiate and assist in prophylactic work both in the community, in schools and in industry, and (c) to carry out research in this field. In summary, their function is diagrammatically shown in Figure 4.2.

Before embarking on a detailed description of their various activities, however, it is pertinent at this stage to comment on the referral procedures followed. Half of the patients (be it children or adults) referred to the state hearing centres and/or the local hearing clinics come mainly through their family doctor or local otologists. In addition to this there exists a self-referral system which entails a formal application by the patient to the state hearing centres for audiological treatment. This formal application is available to all Danish citizens and can be acquired from local health centres, local social welfare offices, schools, libraries and factories.

Waiting periods for treatment vary according to the category of the patient. For adult patients who are out of a job and/or elderly patients (over 65) the waiting period is around eight weeks; for adults in employment the waiting period is four weeks and for children the waiting period is only two-and-a-half weeks.

In detail the activities of the state hearing centres can be divided into ten sections:
(1) Medical section
(2) Audiometric section
(3) Technical section
(4) Hearing aid section
(5) Earmould construction section
(6) Aural rehabilitation section
(7) Inpatient section
(8) Research
(9) Administration
(10) Referrals

Figure 4.2: Function of State Hearing Centres and Local Hearing Clinics in Denmark

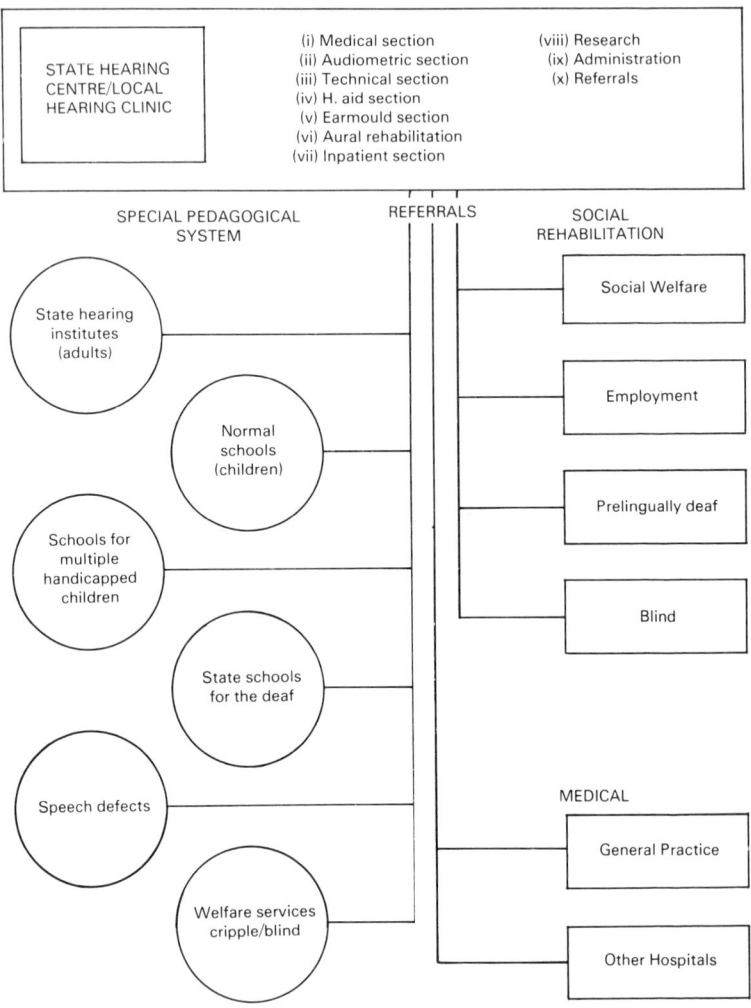

Medical Section

A new patient, on arrival at the state hearing centre, is first seen by an interviewer, a doctor (usually the audiology physician or a doctor under supervision by an audiology physician) who takes his/her medical and social history and gives him/her a medical and otological examination.

(This varies from place to place.) As a result of this interview, coupled with the medical and otological examination, the doctor initiates the audiometric examination of the patient. On the completion of this examination, the doctor makes a diagnosis and in consultation with the hearing pedagogue (aural rehabilitation) and the audiology assistant (technician), prescribes treatment, be it medical, surgical or hearing aid and follow-up rehabilitation in speechreading, auditory training, environmental aids, etc. The training of these audiology physicians will be dealt with later on.

Audiometric Section

Having seen the doctor, each patient is passed on to an audiology assistant for tests of hearing. The training of the audiology assistants will be dealt with later on.

Hearing Tests. Each patient, as a routine procedure, is given the following tests of hearing:

(1) pure tone tests of hearing by air conduction with masking when necessary,
(2) pure tone tests of hearing by bone conduction with masking when necessary,
(3) tests of recruitment (alternate loudness balance test/short increment sensitivity index (SISI)/uncomfortable loudness level (ULL),
(4) earphone speech audiometry,
(5) impedance measurments.

Two important points, one relating to speech audiometry and the other to impedance measurements, need to be made here. In all three state hearing centres, speech tests of hearing (monosyllables, spondees, sentences, low redundancy speech stimuli — without and with background noise) are centrally recorded and delivered continuously to each testing room through a multi-channel arrangement, a procedure which enables several patients to be tested separately at the same time. Impedance measurements are in most of the centres the sole concern of the doctors who on medical grounds consider it inappropriate for audiology assistants to be involved!

Once these tests are carried out, if there are any problems, the doctor, the audiology assistants and the hearing pedagogue come together and decide on subsequent treatment which may involve:

(1) Additional tests of hearing and vestibulometry, such as binaural speech audiometry, sensitised speech audiometry (low redundancy speech tests of hearing useful in the diagnosis of central lesions), delayed speech tests (for diagnosis of psychogenic hearing impairment), evoked response audiometry (ERA) and Electrocochleography;

(2) Medical and/or surgical intervention. The patient, together with his records, is referred to the appropriate medical department for treatment; and

(3) Issuing of hearing aid(s) and subsequent follow-up rehabilitative treatment. This area will be treated more thoroughly later on.

Technical Section

This section is staffed with electro-technicians working under the supervision of graduates in engineering. Their functions are the following:

(1) Testing of hearing aids before being issued.
(2) Carrying out minor repairs to hearing aids (major repairs are carried out by authorised commercial firms).
(3) Assisting in hearing aid evaluation, and
(4) Calibrating and repairing audiometric equipment.

Hearing Aid Section

The number of different models and types of individual wearable hearing aids available free of charge to hearing-impaired people in Denmark varies slightly from year to year but generally speaking there are 40 different types and models of hearing aids available. The hearing aids available have been selected following a tender system and after satisfying strict criteria pertaining to their cost, electro-acoustic and mechanical properties, aesthetic qualities, battery consumption, durability and facilities for repair and maintenance.

Initial Selection. The initial selection and issuing of a hearing aid to a patient is based on the decision of a team (this varies from place to place) consisting primarily of a hearing pedagogue, an audiology assistant and an audiology physician. Before reaching a decision as to which hearing aid(s) should be issued to a particular patient, the team takes into consideration the following:

(1) Electro-acoustic properties of the hearing aid
   – frequency characteristics
   – maximum amplification

- maximum output
- compression amplification
- peak clipping, etc.
(2) Audiometric findings
- type and pattern of pure tone audiogram configuration
- recruitment
- amplification needed
- speech discrimination
(3) Other factors concerning
- otologic findings, diagnosis
- secretion, atresia
- body or ear-level aid
- monaural/binaural treatment
- earmould type (people with average hearing losses 30-40 dB are fitted with open earmoulds)
(4) Psychological factors
- cosmetic
- surgical possibilities
- age
- habituation, etc.
(5) Economic factors
- price
- battery consumption
- guarantee and repair service.
(6) On the basis of the above information the team selects two or three different models of hearing aids, those most likely to meet the needs of the particular patient, and the audiology assistant tests the patient with each hearing aid by speech tests of hearing delivered in the presence of a competing message, usually random noise. The results of these tests, although not entirely conclusive, provide additional information which influences the initial section of a hearing aid.

Having decided on the initial selection of a hearing aid the patient receives guidance on its proper use by the hearing pedagogue. The patient is informed that the hearing aid has been issued to him/her on a trial basis for three months during which period he/she can undergo intensive education in its proper use, limitations and maintenance by the local hearing pedagogue. At the end of the three months period the local pedagogue reports back to the state hearing centre on the suitability of the patient's hearing aid and/or on any other relevant problems arising. The local hearing pedagogue has the power to recommend a new hearing aid on trial for a patient if in his/her opinion the patient needs a different one. In most cases (nearly 95 per cent) this action is not necessary as the initial hearing aid selected, followed by intensive guidance, proves to be effective.

Ear-level versus Bodyworn. The decision as to whether a patient needs an ear-level or a bodyworn hearing aid is based primarily on the degree of the hearing impairment of the patient and on his/her fine motor co-ordination abilities. People with a hearing impairment ranging from 30 dB to 80 dB (averaged across 500, 1000, 2000 and 4000 Hz) with fine motor co-ordination abilities are candidates for post-aural hearing aids, be it behind-the-ear or in spectacle frames. People with more severe hearing impairments and/or patients with difficulties in fine manipulation (very elderly people) are issued with bodyworn hearing aids.

Monaural vs. Binaural. This is a controversial subject in Denmark. The state hearing centre at Aarhus issues binaural hearing aids to cover 75 per cent of the patients. The state hearing centre in Copenhagen and the one in Odense issue binaural hearing aids to only 35 per cent and 20-25 per cent of their patients respectively. The Aarhus centre issues binaural hearing aids as a matter of policy (except to very elderly people with severe difficulties in fine manipulation and, of course, to unilaterally deaf people). The Copenhagen and Odense centres issue binaural hearing aids mainly to people with symmetrical bilateral hearing impairments ranging from 30 dB to 90 dB (averaged across the main speech frequencies, 250 Hz-4000 Hz). They exclude people with
    (1) Asymmetrical hearing impairment (more than 40 dB between the ears approximately)
    (2) Difficulties in fine motor co-ordination (mainly elderly people)
    (3) Central hearing lesions, and
    (4) People with unilateral hearing impairment.

Hearing Aids for Unilaterally Deaf People. People with aidable unilateral hearing impairment (nearly 2 per cent of all patients attending) are issued, on a trial basis, with a hearing aid fitted in their affected ear. People with unaidable unilateral hearing impairment are entitled to the CROS (Contralateral Routing of Signals) hearing aid system but no reliable figures on this were available.

Hearing Aids for People with Conductive Hearing Impairment. In Denmark, as a matter of policy (except in the Gentofte clinic), a patient with a conductive hearing impairment at present is first given the chance to use hearing aid amplification and only afterwards decides whether he/she is willing to undergo surgical treatment. As a result of this policy the number of conductively hearing-impaired people requesting surgical treatment has been reduced considerably.

Consumption of Hearing Aids. The present consumption of hearing aids in Denmark is around 35,000 per year. Most of these are of the ear-level type (55 per cent); 25 per cent are in spectacle frames and only the remaining 20 per cent are of the bodyworn type (10 per cent of the latter are issued with 'Y' lead). Although the State of Denmark provides a wide variety (40 types) of hearing aids (all with telephone coils), a considerable number of the 35,000 hearing aids issued each year are covered by six main types (two models of bodyworn hearing aids, two models of post-aural hearing aids and two models of hearing aids in spectacle frames) each type being equipped with a tone control (normal setting, low and high frequency settings) and with telephone coils.

According to official statistics nearly 3 per cent of the population of Denmark (150,000 people) are at present fitted with hearing aid amplification and a further 3 per cent are suffering from slight hearing impairment not as yet requiring hearing aid treatment. Nearly 60-65 per cent of these patients (females slightly more than males) are elderly people (65 and over).

Repair of Hearing Aids. A new hearing aid is guaranteed by the manufacturers for the first 15 months and this covers all repair costs. Subsequent repairs are carried out by authorised workshops owned by the hearing aid manufacturers, most of the major repairs being routed through the state hearing centres. Repairs costing less than £4.00 (approximately) are met by the user. Higher repair costs are refunded to the user by the state provided an application is made to the local state hearing centre which first ascertains the nature of the repairs needed and afterwards verifies the adequacy of the repairs carried out. During the repair period the patient is issued temporarily with a reconditioned secondhand hearing aid(s) from a pool of used hearing aids kept by the state hearing centres and/or state hearing institutes.

Renewal of Hearing Aids. By law each patient is entitled to a new hearing aid(s) if needed every five years or sooner if this is indicated.

Batteries. The cost of batteries for hearing aids is met by the patients themselves except in cases where the patient uses a high powered hearing aid with excessive battery consumption. For these patients the batteries are provided free of charge by the state which distributes them through a battery department in Copenhagen. This affects only adult patients. All hearing-impaired children receive batteries free of charge.

Earmould Construction Section

Once it has been decided that the patient requires amplification through hearing aid(s) and once a hearing aid(s) has been selected, he or she is passed on to the earmould laboratory. This section is staffed by two to three earmould technicians who take the impressions, make the moulds, cast them and construct the individual earmould. On average it takes three to four days before individual earmoulds are ready. Each state hearing centre (and local hearing clinic) has its own earmould laboratory and the final earmould product is of high quality. Only 4-5 per cent of the earmoulds made are found to be unsatisfactory.

Aural Rehabilitation Section

This section is staffed by professionals referred to as hearing pedagogues or teachers of deafened adults or audio-educators. Basically these professionals are qualified teachers with additional training in the education of the hard of hearing and/or deaf children and adults. The background and training of these people will be dealt with in detail later on.

Each state hearing centre employs at least two hearing pedagogues who work in close co-operation with locally based hearing pedagogues who are employed by the state hearing institutes. All local hearing clinics are served by the local hearing pedagogues. Not only are the hearing pedagogues involved in the diagnostic work of the hearing centres and clinics but they also provide the following specific services within these establishments.

(1) Hearing aid selection (assisted by audiology assistants, earmould technicians, engineers and doctors – Aarhus and Gentofte).
(2) Hearing aid fitting (Aarhus and Gentofte).
(3) Initial guidance regarding the use of the hearing aid.
(4) Information on the use and demonstration of the potentials of environmental aids.
(5) Initial information on the following

- hearing aid repairs
- local contacts
- local state hearing institute and its activities.
- vocational training (re-training)
- local social workers
- social benefits
- voluntary associations, etc, and
(6) Initial evaluation of
- speechreading (evaluation with and without the use of hearing aids).

Of all the members of the audiological team it is the hearing pedagogue who is in most frequent touch with the patient and for this reason this expert carries considerable responsibility within the Danish audiological organisation. His/her therapeutic efforts are not only geared to teaching, guiding and advising the patient but also to evaluating both the personal, family and social status of the patient and to initiating other relevant treatment such as vocational guidance, employment, social help, etc.

It is pointed out that the great majority of the hearing pedagogues for deafened adults in Denmark are employed by the two state hearing institutes. Even the small number of hearing pedagogies (N = 5) employed by the state hearing centres come to a certain extent under the supervision of the state hearing institutes.

By agreement all adult patients issued with a hearing aid(s) and/or adult patients suffering from a hearing impairment which is likely to affect their social and emotional life adversely are referred to the state hearing institutes for rehabilitation and follow-up (if this is required). This continuity of service between the state hearing centres and the state hearing institutes is primarily maintained by the hearing pedagogues. There is a mutual exchange of services, with the hearing pedagogues in the state hearing centres being involved in local activities and with the local hearing pedagogues employed by the state hearing institutes working part of their time in the state hearing centres and local hearing clinics. This bond is additionally strengthened by regular meetings and conferences.

Inpatient Section and Domiciliary Visits

The state hearing centres are also involved in the diagnosis of patients with neurological and psychiatric problems and they also run a peripatetic audiology service (a team consisting of audiology physician, audiology assistant, earmould technician and hearing pedagogue) for immobile patients who live either in their homes or in institutions such as geriatric hospitals, old people's homes, etc.

Research

Research activities in the state hearing centres are extensive and they encompass most audiological aspects and especially as follows: in Copenhagen, aural rehabilitation (hearing aid selection, hearing aid use, audiovisual communication, evaluation of therapeutic techniques, etc). In Odense, hearing aids (selection, use, electro-acoustic properties, earmoulds), diagnostic audiometric procedures and epidemiology of deafness. In Aarhus, binaural hearing aids, cochlear otosclerosis. In addition, evoked response audiometry and electrocochleography are studied in the Copenhagen local hearing clinic, the University ENT clinic at Copenhagen and in the SHC in Odense.

The research which is at present generating quite a lot of interest in Denmark is a project entitled 'operation effect' which is being carried out at the state hearing centre in Copenhagen. This project basically attempts to evaluate the effectiveness of the audiological-rehabilitational services provided.

Administration

The overall administration of each state hearing centre and/or local hearing clinic lies in the hands of a doctor who is qualified both in otology and audiology and referred to as audiology physician. He is the chief co-ordinator of all activities within the hearing centre or clinic and mainly through daily staff conferences (morning tea time, lasting 15-20 minutes) keeps all members of his staff informed of developments both in policy, patient treatment and research. Major decisions affecting policy are team decisions (doctors, hearing pedagogues and technical staff). New appointments, reception of patients, paying of travelling costs to patients and staff, writing and keeping of records, correspondence, telephones, budget, etc, are dealt with by a team of administrators and secretaries.

Referrals

A hearing-impaired person, after attending a hearing centre or a hearing clinic, is referred to other specialised agencies for specific help as the case of each particular patient may require. For example, as stated, all hearing-impaired persons with acquired deafness in adulthood are referred to staff of the state hearing institutes for aural rehabilitation and follow-up. Adult patients needing specialised professional and/or vocational training, further medical examination, etc, are referred to the appropriate local services for advice, training and/or treatment. Hearing-impaired children are referred to the appropriate educational authority for placement in either ordinary schools, special classes, state schools for the deaf, depending on the individual abilities and aptitudes of each child.

Staffing. The number of staff at the time of visits to the three state hearing centres and to one local hearing clinic is shown in Table 4.1.

Table 4.1: Staffing Levels at Three State Hearing Centres and One Local Hearing Clinic in Denmark

		Copen-hagen	Odense	Aarhus	Copen-hagen District Clinic
(i)	Director	1	1	1	1
(ii)	Medical section				
	Audiology physicians (and trainees)	5	3	4	3
(iii)	Technical section				
	Engineer	1	1	1	1
	Electro-technicians	1	2	2	1
	Radio-technicians	3	—	—	—
	Assistants	2	1	1	—
(iv)	Earmould section				
	Technicians — fulltime	4	3	2	2
	— parttime	3	1	1	—
(v)	Pedagogical section				
	Hearing pedagogues — fulltime	2	2	1	2
	— parttime	3	2	2	1
	— secretary	1	1	1	2
(vi)	Batteries				
	Dispenser	1	1	1	—
(vii)	Audiometric section				
	Audiology assistants — fulltime	6	6	5	6
	— parttime	2	2	2	3
(viii)	Administration				
	Head	1	1	1	—
	Assistants	4	5	3	—
	Secretaries — fulltime	3	2	2	3
	— parttime	1	1	—	—
	Housemother	1	1	1	1
Total		45	36	31	26

Table 4.2: Workload of Some of the Major State Hearing Centres and Local Hearing Clinics in Denmark

State Hearing Centre — Copenhagen (1974-75)			State Hearing Centre — Odense (1973-74)		
A. Examinations			A. Examinations		
(i)	New adults	2,242	(i)	New patients	1,883
(ii)	Complete re-examination of adults	1,962	(ii)	Re-examinations	1,616
(iii)	Control (borderline cases) examination of adults	315	(iii)	Controls (under observation)	50
(iv)	Partial examination — adults	1,008	(iv)	Partial examinations	2,248
(v)	New babies	142	(v)	In-patients	3,897
(vi)	Complete re-examination of babies	347	(vi)	Consultation — pedagogical 75% — technical 15% — medical 10%	5,077
(vii)	New school children	239		Total	14,781
(viii)	Complete re-examintion of school children	1,195			
(ix)	In-patients — adults — children	870 1,101	Sex distribution: 55% males; 45% females		
(x)	Consultation — pedagogical 80% — technical 15% — medical 5%	12,046	Age distribution of referrals (excluding in-patients) 0-14 years 15-64 years 65 years +		9% 37% 54%
(xi)	Prophylactic examination	327	Waiting List: 1,000 patients approximately		
	Total	21,794	B. Issues of Hearing Aids Bodyworn hearing aids Ear-level hearing aids — behind the ear — in spectacle form		714 2,120 720
Sex distribution: 49% males; 51% females				Total	3,554
Age distribution of referrals (excluding in-patients) 0-14 years 15-64 years 65 years + Waiting List: 31.3.1975		3% 44% 53% 1,377 patients	C. Earmoulds Ordinary Special (open, skeleton, vented, hooks)		1,245 pieces 3,400 pieces
B. Issue of Hearing Aids Bodyworn hearing aids Ear-level hearing aids		1,140 5,300		Total	5,643
	Total	6,440			
C. Repairs Switch defects Volume control defects Ear-phone defects Other defects		822 186 1,023 12,069			
	Total	14,100			
D. Construction of Earmoulds Ordinary (whole meatus Special (open, vented, hooks, etc)		1,418 pieces 7,247 pieces			
	Total	8,665 pieces			

Physical Accommodation. The three state hearing centres visited are housed in excellent physical accommodation consisting of at least six independent sound-treated audiometric units (two rooms, one for observation and one for testing, in each unit with a closed circuit TV and intercommunication system, 25 × 40 ft each unit); earmould construction unit (two to three rooms, each one 15 × 20 ft); pedagogical unit (two to three rooms, each one 15 × 20 ft); waiting room and reception area (20 × 30 ft); lecture hall; medical examination rooms (at least two); and offices. All rooms, including corridors are adequately sound-treated.

Workload. The figures in Table 4.2 reflect the considerable bulk of the workload being carried out in the state hearing centres and in the major local hearing clinics.

Audiological Diagnosis. The information on audiological diagnosis received from the state hearing centres is shown in Table 4.3.

Table 4.3: Audiological Diagnosis in State Hearing Centres

(i) Conductive hearing impairment — 25-30% of all cases
    2- 3% — congenital and traumatic malformations
    75-80% — middle ear infections
    15-20% — otosclerosis.
(ii) Sensorineural hearing impairment — 70-75% of all cases
    45-55% — presbyacusis (35-40% of all patients)
    15-20% — congenital
    10-15% — traumatic
    10-15% — postinfection / toxic / vascular / Ménière's
    5-10% — unknown.
(iii) Retrocochlear hearing impairment — 2-3% of all cases
    3- 5% — acoustic neurinoma
    5-10% — psychogenic
    85-90% — other central cases.

The Pedagogical Service — Aural Rehabilitation for Deafened Adults

The organisation of aural rehabilitation for deafened adults in Denmark is shown diagrammatically in Figure 4.3. The country is divided into

72 Denmark as a Model of Aural Rehabilitation

Figure 4.3: Organisation of Aural Rehabilitation in State Hearing Institutes

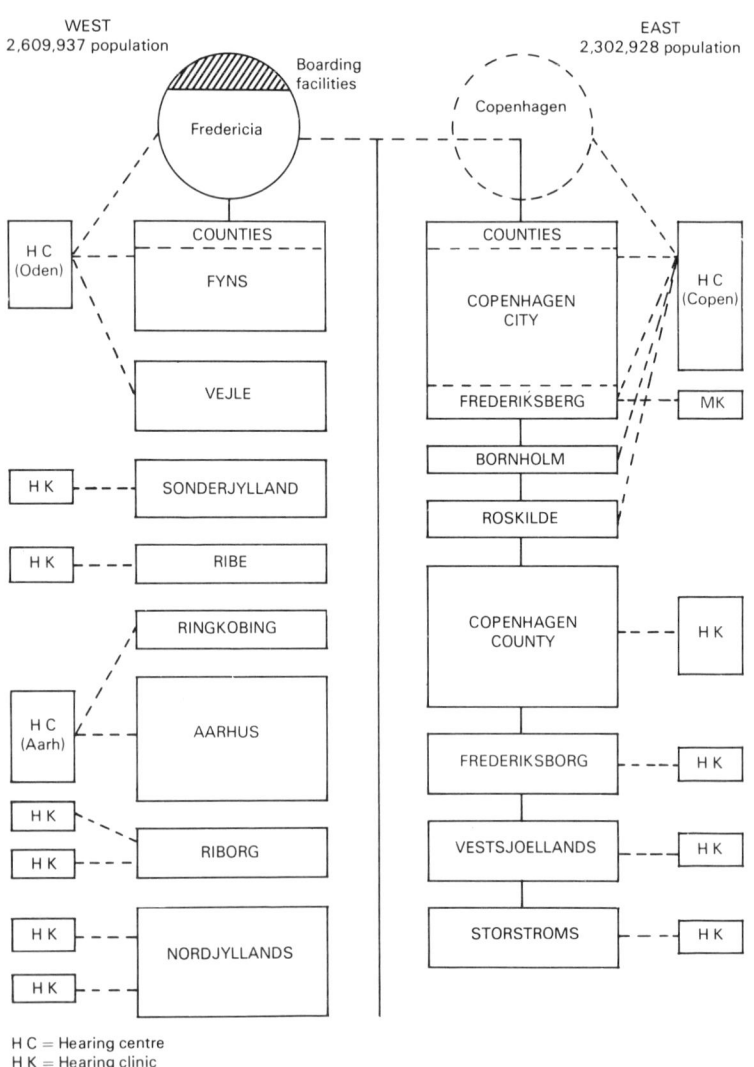

H C = Hearing centre
H K = Hearing clinic

two main regions — the West Region (population 2,600,000) and the East Region (2,300,000). The West Region is divided into ten counties, the East Region into eight. Each county has its own team of peripatetic hearing pedagogues for deafened adults who operate from a central place (local hearing institutes) and cover the whole of the country. All hearing pedagogues for deafened adults in the West Region of the country are employed by and come under the control and supervision of the state hearing institute at Fredericia. Those in the East Region are under the administration of the state hearing institute at Copenhagen. Both state hearing institutes are headed by directors who are qualified hearing pedagogues.

Staff

The basic professional training of the hearing pedagogues employed by the state hearing institutes will be discussed in detail later on.

The total number of full-time hearing pedagogues for deafened adults employed in the whole of the country is 50; 30 of them are employed by the Fredericia state hearing institute and the remaining 20 are employed by the Copenhagen state hearing institute. In addition to these 50 full-time professionals, the state hearing institutes employ nearly 150 teachers of the deaf and/or hard of hearing pupils on a part-time basis mainly for evening group work. In addition to this, the work of the hearing pedagogues is backed up by technical laboratories and audiometric services which form integral parts of the Institutes.

According to the chairman of the Danish Society of Hearing Pedagogues for Deafened Adults (Mr Niels Skamris) the number of full-time hearing pedagogues actually needed to provide a national comprehensive service is in the region of 70-80, that is one hearing pedagogue for every 60-70,000 people.

Workload and Services Provided

At present each full-time hearing pedagogue supervises 3,000-4,000 deafened adults (not all active cases) and generally speaking the services provided are summarised in Figure 4.4.

Referrals

All new patients referred to the state hearing institutes come directly from the state hearing centres and/or the local hearing clinics. The patients referred are always provided with a summary of their medical and audiological records and it is up to the state hearing institutes in consultation with the patient to decide the content and duration of the aural rehabilitative treatment for each particular patient.

The state hearing institutes with their county centres and their countrywide peripatetic services provide both central training for

74 *Denmark as a Model of Aural Rehabilitation*

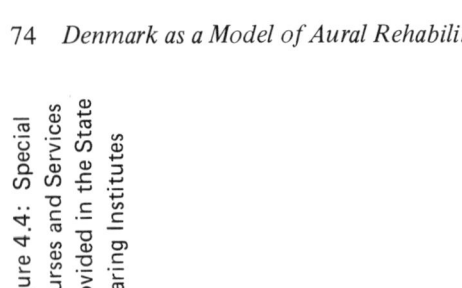

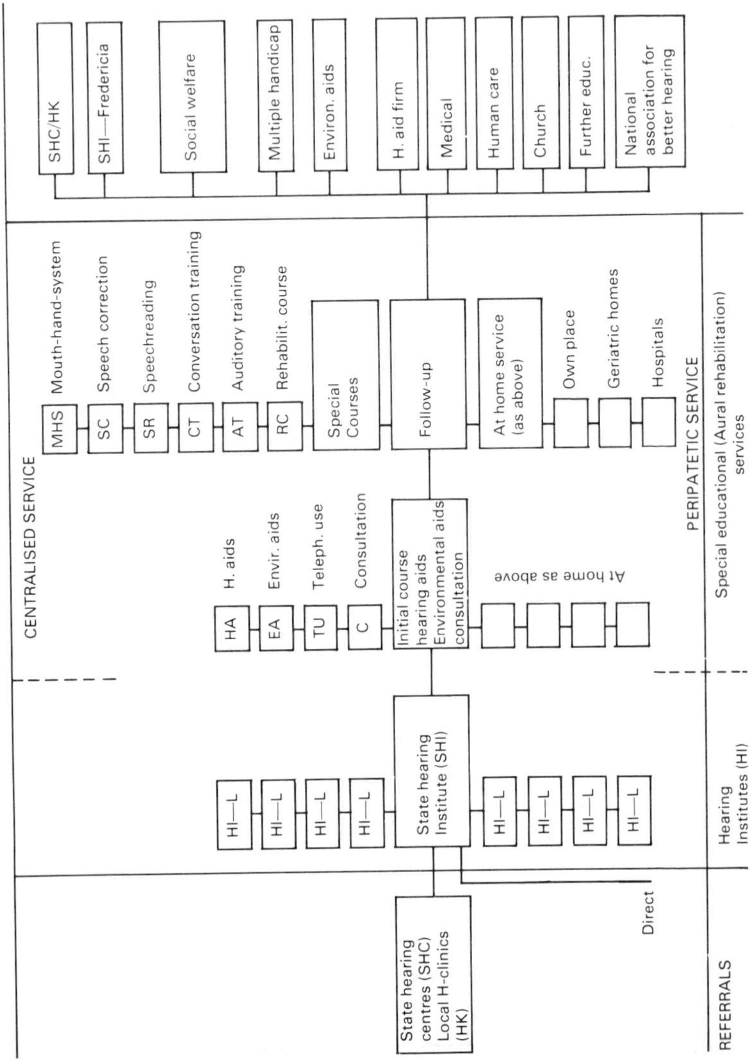

Figure 4.4: Special Courses and Services Provided in the State Hearing Institutes

those patients who are mobile and a domiciliary service for those patients who for one reason or another are unable to travel.

Courses

All new patients are given an initial course consisting of four two-hour sessions over a period of four weeks. The chief aim of this course is to help the patient to make maximum use of his/her hearing aid and to acquaint the patient with the use and potential of environmental aids. At the end of this initial course (which is available to all people issued with a government hearing aid(s)) the patient is left to use his/her hearing aid experimentally for a period of three months and then report back to the hearing pedagogue on any problems or queries arising. The hearing pedagogue in turn has to report to the state hearing centre on the suitability of the particular aid issued, on progress being made and on any other problems arising. If the patient is not satisfied with his/her hearing aid a new model of hearing aid is issued on a trial basis.

Nearly 80 per cent of the new patients are discharged following this initial course. They are, however, encouraged to keep in touch with their local hearing pedagogue and seek his/her guidance and advice if and when required.

However, 20 per cent of the new patients are found to require more extensive and specialised help. For these patients the state hearing institutes, their county headquarters and their peripatetic service provide the following courses.

Mouth-Hand-System Course (MHS). All deafened adults, especially those with severe hearing impairment, are encouraged to learn this system which, it is maintained, can help them considerably with speech-reading. Not only are the patients encouraged to learn this system but also their families, friends and neighbours. Teaching facilities for the MHS are available all over the country and its use is widespread. The hand movements involved and the basic rationale of the MHS are very easy and it takes only 15-20 minutes for an adult with average intelligence to learn them. Considerably more time and practice, however (a few weeks), is required before a person becomes fluent in the use and interpretation of the system.

Speech Correction Courses (SCC). These courses can last from a few weeks to as long as 12 months. The people selected for these courses are deafened adults with very severe hearing impairments who find the use of a hearing aid of limited benefit. As a result of their severe deafness these patients tend to develop both articulatory and voice quality problems and the aim of these courses is to remedy these speech deficiencies. The methods followed are similar to those developed for hearing-impaired children and they consist primarily of helping the patient to monitor his/her speech by combining all clues available from audition, vision, vibro-tactile and kinaesthetic sensations. Both individual and group tuition for speech correction is provided and the lessons are carried out by using the patients' individual hearing aids, speech training units and group hearing aids. During these lessons the patients receive extensive training in the control of the loudness of their speech under various environmental conditions.

Speechreading courses (SRC). These courses are available all over the country and they are geared to meet the individual needs of each particular patient. Owing to the large number of people attending, the classes are finely graded according to the abilities and needs of the patients. Speechreading courses are planned on a 3 monthly/6 monthly/9 monthly/yearly basis, and each patient is assigned to one of these courses depending on his/her abilities and needs. Speechreading lessons are given

(1) with and without the use of individual hearing aids.
(2) with and without the use of group hearing aids,
(3) using filmed material,
(4) with and without background noises,
(5) at various angles and distances,
(6) by a number of hearing pedagogues

so that the patient can have practice in speechreading as many people as possible under semisheltered conditions.

The aim of these lessons is primarily to teach the patient to become more aware of speechreading and to combine speechreading clues with auditory clues (audiovisual approach). Speechreading is not looked upon as a complete entity by itself (as it is commonly considered to be), but instead it is treated as a vital part in the communicative process which encompasses audition (primarily) and vibro-tactile and kinaesthetic sensation.

Progress in speechreading ability is periodically assessed by using filmed speechreading tests consisting of random monosyllables, phrases and short sentences. Some of these tests, however, have not as yet been standardised (apart from those in use at the SHC, Copenhagen) for wider application and for research purposes, and therefore their scientific usefulness is very limited and of dubious quality.

Conversation Training Courses (CTC). Conversation training courses are run side by side and/or in conjunction with speechreading and auditory training courses, their main purpose being to train the hearing-impaired person to acquire basic strategies, regarding positioning, sitting arrangements, concentration, etc, which are conducive to better functioning within a group situation. In addition to this the hearing-impaired person is given experience of participation in conversation in groups of various sizes and under diverse listening conditions. During these courses, members of the patient's families, friends, neighbours and other people are invited to attend and participate under the guidance of the hearing pedagogue.

Auditory Training Courses (ATC). The purpose of these courses is to help the patients to maximise the use of their residual hearing by listening to graded material ranging from simple sounds – syllables – words – phrases – sentences – stories, etc. – presented under various listening conditions and situations.

These lessons are often carried out in combination with speechreading (reinforcing the rationale of audio-visual approach to communication) but in many instances the patients are required to try and discriminate the presented message by relying solely on auditory clues. The patients are always encouraged to use their individual hearing aids during auditory training lessons but they are also given intensive training through speech training units and group hearing aids.

Rehabilitation Courses (RC). These courses consist of 48 one-hour sessions spread over a period of three months, and their main aim is to educate the patient on the effects of deafness and to help him/her develop the necessary attitudes to cope and live with the handicap.

These courses are run and co-ordinated by the hearing pedagogues but a large number of other professionals such as family doctors, social workers, the clergy, psychiatrists, employers, etc, are invited to take part.

Most of these sessions are carried out with groups of people although individual work with patients is often undertaken.

Referrals

The hearing pedagogue, depending on the individual needs of the patient, can make and/or initiate referrals to the following specialised services:

(1) State hearing centre and/or local hearing clinic.
(2) Hearing institute at Fredericia.
(3) Social welfare (vocational training, re-training, employment, home helps, etc).
(4) Multiple handicaps (cripples, blind, mentally retarded, etc).
(5) Environmental aids. (All environmental aids are paid by the patient and information on these is available from SHC, LHC and SHI.)
(6) Hearing aid firms (repairs).
(7) Medical (removal of cerumen, for example).
(8) Human care (pensions, social benefits, housing, etc).
(9) Church (Denmark is divided into four ecclesiastical regions, each region having a comprehensive set up of churches with services specially designed to meet the needs of deafened adults).
(10) Further education (help at college, university and/or any other higher educational institution).
(11) National Association for Better Hearing (meetings, clubs, excursions, leisure activities for the whole of the family, etc).

The function of the state hearing centres and/or local hearing clinics has already been stated and the functions of the other services have already been summarised. Special mention, however, needs to be made of the function and activities of the state hearing institute at Fredericia, for it is a unique establishment (most probably in the world) and it plays the central role in the aural rehabilitation of deafened adults in Denmark.

State Hearing Institute — Fredericia

The Fredericia state hearing institute, as compared to the one in Copenhagen which is a day institute, has boarding facilities and caters for the following categories of people from all over Denmark who require help over and above that provided in their locality.

(1) Patients with acquired deafness or with a severe hearing handicap.

(2) Hard of hearing patients with special hearing aid problems.

(3) Hard of hearing patients with a demand for aural rehabilitational treatment which cannot be met locally.

(4) Hard of hearing persons affected mentally by their condition.

(5) Hard of hearing persons with social or occupational problems.

(6) Hard of hearing persons whose audiological status has to be evaluated with reference to disablement benefit or pension.

The patients attending (usually 30 at any one period) are often admitted together with their spouse or another family member. Only those patients are admitted who are mobile and can look after their physical wellbeing. Nearly 300 patients attend every year.

The Fredericia hearing institute provides the following facilities which are directed, planned and carried out by hearing pedagogues with collaboration from otologists, audiology assistants, engineers, social workers, psychologists, psychiatrists (a psychiatrist visits the institute once a week), clergy and other professionals whose services are deemed to be necessary depending on the needs of the individual patient.

Courses

Residential courses for 20-30 patients lasting from two weeks to 36 weeks. The majority of the patients, however, are admitted for a period of four weeks. During this course (five days a week from 7.00 am to 3.00 pm daily) the patients receive intensive tuition on the following:

(1) Use of hearing aids, their maintenance and limitations (Hearing aid tactics).

(2) Speechreading. This is carried out on an individual and group basis under a wide variety of environmental conditions and situations. The progress of the patients is regularly monitored by giving them a filmed speechreading test. The Institute has developed an impressive amount of graded speechreading materials, both on paper and on film, which are designed to highlight individual speechreading difficulties and to provide extensive remedial practice.

(3) Auditory training. Again this is carried out both on an individual and group basis under varying acoustic conditions and with different types of amplifying equipment (individual hearing aids, speech training units, group hearing aids, loop system, etc).

The institute has developed a comprehensive set of exercises on auditory training consisting of isolated sounds, syllables, monosyllabic words, disyllabic words, phrases, related sentences, unrelated sentences, short stories, long stories, dialogues, plays, etc, recorded under varying acoustic conditions and presented with varying degrees of background noise. These exercises can be presented live by the teacher but also can be controlled by a computer which has been programmed to monitor the responses of the patients. If the response of the patient to one particular stimulus word is correct then the computer proceeds to the next item; if the response is wrong, the patient is required to listen again more carefully until he or she responds correctly. This programmed self-teaching learning facility is available in each bedroom and each patient is required to spend at least one hour every day in the comfort of his/her bedroom listening and responding to these graded auditory training exercises. Their individual progress is self-monitored and also tabulated by the resident tutors who are always at hand to provide the necessary guidance.

(4) Speech correction and speech conservation training. As a result of acquired severe and/or total deafness in adulthood some patients develop both articulatory and voice quality speech defects. For these people, the Institute provides training in speech correction, the purpose of which is firstly to identify articulatory and voice defects and secondly to help the patient recognise these defects and by using his/her residual hearing, speechreading and vibrotactile and kinaesthetic sensations to develop as far as possible an effective multisensory feedback mechanism to control both the articulatory and aesthetic qualities of speech.

(5) Group conversation training. This is considered a very important training at the Institute, for most of the patients attending find difficulties in communicating, especially within a group situation. Each patient is given daily training in conversation, with groups of people varying in sizes between two and ten persons in each group.

(6) Basic information on deafness. Each patient attending the Institute is given substantial information on deafness (pathology of deafness, hearing mechanism, cause of deafness, psychological and social effects of deafness, etc), the purpose of which is to increase the patient's insight into their own handicap with a view to relieving anxiety which in some cases may be based on an incorrect or misinformed appraisal of the basic facts. This information is imparted both on an individual and group basis and the lessons are taken at a deliberately slow pace thus allowing the patients to ask as many questions as they like.

(7) Environmental aids course. The Institute provides daily tuition and practice in the use of the environmental aids available. Considerable emphasis is put on the proper use of the telephone, the loop system, and the various television adaptors. Each bedroom is wired with environmental aids thus providing for the patient's extensive practice.

(8) Group therapy. In addition to periodical individual therapy sessions (one tutor − one patient) the patients are divided into groups

and with the help of a leader (usually the hearing pedagogue) they talk about and discuss their mutual experiences and difficulties.

(9) Consultation. The institute arranges, depending on the individual needs of the patient, consultation with employment consultants, psychiatrists, psychologists, opthalmologists (all patients have their eyesight tested on admittance), social workers, clergy and other professionals as the case may be.

In additional to the above courses the Institute provides advanced audiometric examinations and carries out hearing aid selection and evaluation, including the construction of earmoulds. Furthermore the laboratory staff evaluate and suggest other technical aids which may be helpful such as flash light and other alarm signals, radio, TV and telephone aids. The laboratory also has a limited out-patient function. Two otologists specialising in audiology (the directors of the state hearing centres at Odense and Aarhus) frequently visit the Institute and give expert advice and assistance.

In addition to the hard-of-hearing patients, the Institute also treats patients who have undergone laryngectomy and who cannot receive adequate speech training in their own district. Four to five in-patients are continually receiving speech instruction. The consultant for the laryngectomised patients covering the whole of the country is attached to the Institute, and aids and advises patients with social and occupational problems.

This institute also runs short courses for home helps, psychiatric nurses, social workers, etc.

In addition to the internal activities the institute is also responsible for all aural rehabilitational services for deafened adults in the Western Region of Denmark.

Staffing

The permanent internal staff of the institute consists of a principal, a superintendent and five teachers, all qualified hearing pedagogues. One of the teachers is head of the laboratory (two audiology assistants), another is vocational and social counsellor. The office staff consists of a head clerk and three assistants. There is a matron and a caretaker living at the Institute, plus a staff of eight in the kitchen. There is also a part-time occupational therapist (there is a workshop where the patients can enjoy certain hobbies — painting, sewing, woodwork, etc).

Internal Administration

There is a close co-operation between the staff. Weekly staff meetings are held with all the staff being present. Here the treatment of each patient is discussed. There is also a weekly meeting of the teaching staff and a close liaison is kept between the internal and external services of the Institute.

Finance

Residence as well as treatment and travelling expenses to and from the institute (each patient is encouraged to go home during weekends) are paid by the Ministry of Social Affairs. In 1974/75 a total of 6,365,500 D. Kr. was spent: 4,286,000 D. Kr. on external services and 2,078,800 D. Kr. on internal services. For each resident hearing-impaired patient the average cost was 4,500 D. Kr. and for each hearing-impaired outpatient it was 370 D. Kr. (£1 is equal to approximately 12.34 D. Kr.)

Professional Training

Otologists

All otologists in Denmark before qualifying as such are expected to work full-time for a period of three months within one of the state hearing centres.

Audiology Physicians

These are otologists with substantial experience in audiology. Before qualifying as audiology physicians they are required
   (1) to work full-time for two years under supervision within one of the State Hearing Centres, and
   (2) to publish papers concerning audiological research.

Audiology Assistants

At present there is no formal training for audiology assistants (technicians) in Denmark. The people working in this field receive one year's in-service training in audiology (five centres are designated for this) after which they are considered as qualified audiology assistants. Ninety-six (12 males – 84 females) audiology assistants are at present employed in the country and every year 10 more assistants are trained. According to the Chairman of the Danish Society of Audiology Assistants, there are plans in hand to start, in collaboration with other

Scandinavian countries (Sweden and Norway), a joint training scheme for audiology assistants most probably lasting for a period of two years.

Earmould Technicians

Most of the earmould technicians in Denmark are basically trained as dental technicians (two years full-time training), and as such are highly-trained prosthetists commanding a relatively high salary. This is reflected in their work since nearly all hearing aid earmoulds, covering a wide range of types and materials are made by them (rather than by some central commercial laboratory). They are always given information on the medical condition of the ear.

Hearing Pedagogues

These persons are all qualified teachers (four year college training and/or university education) with additional 14 months specialised training in the education of hard-of-hearing (partially hearing) children. During their specialised training, which is undertaken in Copenhagen at the Royal Danish School of Educational Studies and/or in Aarhus (under the same college), the prospective hearing pedagogues receive academic and practical training in teaching both hard-of-hearing children and deafened adults. If they desire to teach in a school for the deaf, however, they must undergo additional training lasting for three months in a school for the deaf.

Additional Benefits to Patients

These are as follows, and are referred to as 'invalid pension':

(1) For hearing-impaired pupils over 15 years old — 400 D.Kr. per month tax-free

(2) For hearing-impaired adults (speech reception threshold higher than 80 dB and aided optimum speech discrimination ability — PB word lists — less than 70 per cent) — 500 D. Kr. per month tax-free. All retired deafened adults are entitled to this, as are working deafened adults also, but the amount varies according to income.

Finances: National Audiological Care and Treatment

A comprehensive analysis of the cost of the national audiological services in Denmark was carried out by the state hearing centre at Odense and the figures (financial year 1971/72) are shown in Table 4.4.

Table 4.4: Cost of the National Audiological Services in Denmark in the Financial Year 1971/72

(i)	Working costs of hearing centres and branch clinics (27,126 patients exam., 140,000 under treatment)	D.Kr. 7.83 million	22%
(ii)	State technical-audiological laboratory	D.Kr. 0.52 million	1.5%
(iii)	Aural rehabilitation (external services of the state hearing institutes)	D.Kr. 6.50 million	24%
(iv)	State hearing institute (internal service)	D.Kr. 1.85 million	
(v)	Vocational counselling offices	D.Kr. 0.63 million	2%
(vi)	Hearing aids (34,890 pieces)	D.Kr. 15.42 million	44%
(vii)	Batteries for central distribution	D.Kr. 1.04 million	6.5%
(viii)	Repairs of hearing aids	D.Kr. 1.26 million	
Total		D.Kr. 35.05 million	

The more recent comprehensive national statistics on the cost of the audiological services come from the state hearing centre at Copenhagen. These statistics (1973/74 costs) relate to the average cost per examined patient, as shown in Table 4.5. (In Figure 4.5 the cost of audiology is illustrated in another way.)

Table 4.5: Average Cost per Examined Patient, State Hearing Centre at Copenhagen, 1973/74

(i)	Medical examination, audiological and hearing aid investigation2	300 D.Kr.
(ii)	Two earmoulds	100 D.Kr.
(iii)	Two hearing aids	900 D.Kr.
(iv)	Refund of fares	50 D.Kr.
(v)	Aural rehabilitation (pedagogical treatment)	300 D.Kr.
(vi)	Administrative cost	100 D.Kr.
Total		1,750 D.Kr.

Note: £1 = approximately 12.34 D.Kr.

Summary

The audiological services for adults in Denmark are remarkably well organised, homogeneous, very comprehensive and highly professional. According to the professionals involved, this achievement has been brought about mainly because the chief components of the service —

Figure 4.5: The Cost of Audiology

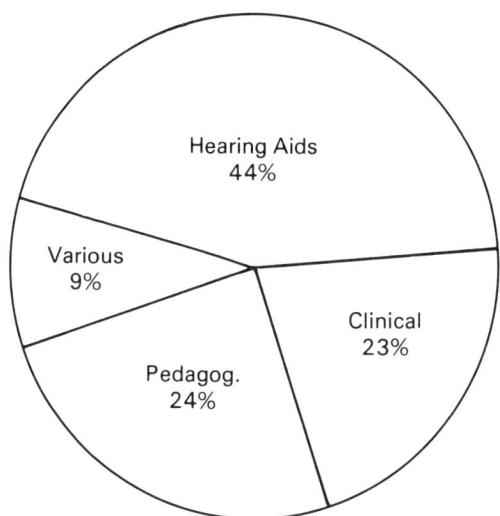

7.00 D.Kr. per inhabitant annually
250.00 D.Kr per patient annually
1305.00 D.Kr. per examined patient annually

Note: £1 = approximately 12.34 D.Kr.

medical, technical, pedagogical — have been planned and allowed to develop as separate entities and directed and staffed by their own professionals with strong interconnecting links which are safeguarded by legislation. This arrangement has brought about a mutual respect between the professionals involved, a situation which enhances co-operation. Having said this, however, it is pointed out that there are also shortcomings in the services provided. For example, there are shortages of trained staff; audiological training is informal and at present it is considered to be the sole prerogative of the medical profession; there is a state of uneasiness among the professionals in this field because of impending reorganisation; and recently financial limitations are a perpetual source of anxiety both for the professionals and for the patients.

Acknowledgements

This chapter could not have been written without extensive help from a large number of Danish professional people, especially Dr H.W.

Ewertsen MD, Director, State Hearing Centre, Bispebjerg Hospital, Copenhagen and Dr C. Rojskjaer MD, Director, State Hearing Centre, University Hospital, Odense. The Figures included in the chapter are based on the work of Mr Poulsen Vad, Director, State Hearing Institute, Copenhagen. The writer is more than grateful to their colleagues and associates for all the help and hospitality extended to him.

Originally this chapter was produced in the form of a Supplement by the *British Journal of Audiology* and it appears in its present form by kind permission of the editor concerned.

(Markides, A. (1977) 'Rehabilitation of People with Acquired Deafness in Adulthood', *Br J Audiol, Suppl. No. 1, March*.)

5 THE ROLE OF THE OTOLOGIST

John Groves

Doctors specialising in the ear, nose and throat (ENT) have for many generations confined their work to these anatomical regions. Basically, the ENT specialist is seen, and sees himself, as a surgeon. He is trained after qualifying in medicine to master the surgical skills involved in, for example, the microsurgery of the ear, operations on the nasal sinuses, and everything inside the throat from a tonsillectomy to a laryngectomy. The universal availability in many countries of primary care at the level of the family doctor provides for the non-surgical treatment of simpler ENT diseases such as acute otitis, tonsillitis, laryngitis and so on. It might be thought surprising therefore that by far the greater part of an ENT man's life is spent in the out-patient department, not in the operating theatre. This is largely because of his otological expertise — otology being 'the sum of what is known regarding the ear', and an otologist being 'a physician versed in otology' (*Saunders' Medical Dictionary*). To put things plainly the majority of ear disease is not remedied by operation. For this reason the physician's attention must be given to the whole patient and his predicament, not merely to his ear and its treatment.

Obviously every ENT surgeon will strive to be as good an otologist as possible, and his necessary training in aural surgery has always given him a privileged position in relation to the deaf and hard of hearing. Indeed, the respect for his expertise is well demonstrated by the regulation in Britain that only an otologist or his supervised deputy may authorise the fitting of a hearing aid under the National Health Service. Surgeons practising otology in its best sense have for many generations given their energy and experience not only to the diagnosis and sometimes treatment of hearing losses, but also to the counselling and rehabilitation of the great numbers of irremediably deaf people of all ages presenting in out-patient clinics.

It is very important indeed for aural surgeons to continue to play their part as physicians counsellors to the hard of hearing, not only as members of a busy and versatile team, but especially because it is this part of their work which should educate and permeate their surgical judgement. The time must soon be coming, however, when the growing complexity of surgical techniques in the ear may demand another change in the pattern of specialisation. In order to provide the necessary operative skills it may be necessary for the next generation of otologists to give up doing laryngology and rhinology. This is obviously a controversial matter and some people will of course see it differently. It seems that an otologist would do well to sustain his long-term involvement with his deaf patients both before and after surgery, rather than to resign their care entirely to other disciplines, while he turns his other energies to nose and throat work.

Things are changing all the time, never suddenly, always slowly by degrees. In the nineteenth century ears were treated by surgeons and throats always by physicians. In the first half of the twentieth century ENT as a one-man specialty gradually came together and established its boundaries. In many countries and centres ophthalmology was also part of this more than taxing repertoire, and eye work had later to be 'off-loaded' to enable both it and ENT work to be practised at an acceptable standard. Today's otologists are rapidly becoming more and more occupied with the advances which have been made in the past ten years in so-called objective audiometry — electrocochleography and brain-stem responses, for example, evoked response audiometry or ERA. These are at last solving the problems of diagnosis and evaluation of hearing losses in very young children as well as adults, which even ten years ago were beyond our reach. This field of work has fascinating overlaps with the disciplines of neurology, neurophysiology (especially vestibular function) and audiology. Overall we have therefore a complex matrix of disciplines in the centre of which the popular figure of the ENT man, complete with head mirror, must try to be all things to a great many people. Should he write his own job description or should it be determined by the needs of his patients?

Either way, he can do nothing useful without colleagues. In both his medical and surgical activities nursing care of the patient is paramount. Anaesthetics are too often taken for granted, but anaesthetists are not always readily available and in ENT work they encounter some of their trickiest problems. Physiological measurement technicians (PMTs) are as indispensable in otology as are technicians in cardiology, neurology, or any other discipline. The fitting and dispensing of hearing aids has become a time-honoured part of their work, and growing out of this in some degree the counselling and rehabilitation of the deaf passed into their hands. Now the arrival of hearing therapists will bring a further very necessary expansion of these activities, and where they are available, it seems probable that the PMTs will now turn some of their attention towards a more active role in ERA work and vestibulometry. The hearing therapists, meanwhile, will probably reach out to a broader interface with social services and with adult education.

The otologist writing this chapter is acutely aware of his central role as the only medical specialist in his team, and wonders how, in his expensive hospital environment, he could usefully share the medical element of care with the patient's general practitioner. It probably cannot be done within the present organisational framework but it would surely be a great improvement if the rehabilitation, as distinct from the treatment, of people with hearing impairment could be concentrated geographically into non-clinical environments.

The Otologist at Work

Many people reading this book will find themselves working closely with an otologist and must have a natural curiosity about what he really does, and specifically what does he do to patients? As we have already seen, he wears a head mirror or headlight much of the time. (Some of us can hardly wait to get it off, others seem to live permanently with it on — this is a matter of personal idiosyncracy.) It is required only because the otologist has to be able to see with bright light far into the depths of the ear (or nose or throat) and still have both hands free for use of instruments. In all other respects the otologist or ENT surgeon follows the same clinical methods which all other doctors follow. He must establish a rapport with his patient and while doing this he must elucidate a history of the patient's complaint and write it down in note form.

All doctors know that however crucial a specific abnormality found on examination of the patient may be, its interpretation, in diagnosis, prognosis, and treatment depend entirely upon the history. That is the most important evidence and that is what doctors most skilfully extract from patients and carefully evaluate. The history is followed by examination — visual inspection of all the relevants parts of the body, in our case usually confined to head and neck, and palpation — feeling with the finger tips the mastoids, the neck, the jaws and sometimes the floor of the mouth.

Otoscopy is usually the most important part of the otological examination. Always a speculum — a funnel-shaped device in metal or plastic — is required, the narrow end fitting accurately the diameter of the patient's ear canal. It may be used with the head mirror and naked eye, especially if there is wax to be hooked out with fine probes or forceps, or it may be fitted to an otoscope, which has built-in illumination and a magnifying lens. The otoscope is excellent for seeing the deep canal and the tympanic membrane but it is no use at all when wax or debris have to be removed because it requires both hands just to use it. The best of all ways to look into an ear is with an operating microscope which provides greater magnification, stereoscopic viewing and much brighter illumination. This is EUM, or examination under microscope. (Job jargon is an essential part of interdisciplinary communication, and while EUA (examination under anaesthetics), CSOM (chronic suppurative otitis media), SMR (sub mucous resection) and so on may all be deplorable abbreviations, nothing can eradicate them from our workaday language. The more we can grasp the lingua used by our colleagues, the greater is our comprehension and ability to co-operate.)

Hearing Assessment

Talking with the patient should usually lead to a fairly accurate estimate of an hearing loss. Usually the otologist will, almost without thinking about it, talk to the patient at varying voice levels including whispering, and will soon find out what the patient does and does not hear. He will next do simple tuning fork tests to find out whether any hearing loss is due to defective sound conduction (external or middle ear disorders) or to defective inner ear or auditory nerve function. These tests are called the Rinne and Weber tests and it is assumed that most readers will be familiar with them. To the otologist they are as basically practical as the use of a saw or a spirit level is to other skilled craftsmen.

Audiometry is invariably the next otological requirement. Very few otological problems can receive further investigation or treatment before this has been done. So the patient goes to the audiology technician having talked about his problem, having been examined, his ear drums seen, and having suffered no pain or indignity. This is important to emphasise: we are in this and in other ways a privileged specialty because most of our medical work does not, nor need not, terrify or wound the patient. The sooner the patient realises this and relaxes the better it is for all.

Further Investigations

These may be necessary but of course the investigative process ends as soon as the otologist is satisfied that he has a well-defined diagnosis and enough information for making a plan of action.

X-Ray Examination

An X-ray examination is often necessary and in submitting to this the patient will suffer nothing worse than the tedium of keeping still for a rather long time, with his head stabilised between padded clamps. In a very few cases the most modern X-ray techniques of computerised tomography (CT) scanning may be necessary, sometimes with an intravenous injection of 'enhancing' medium. These are painless and harmless procedures, just time-consuming and very expensive. In all this activity the otologist is usually trying to exclude rare causes such as tumours, or common symptoms like sensorineural deafness or vertigo. He must exercise great care and judgement in deciding how far each patient needs to go down this road of detailed work-out. The otologist's decisions in this area become more and more intuitive in the more obscure cases, and towards the last stages it may well be that the patient himself may call the next move, either by opting out or sometimes by demanding a 'scan'. At this stage even the thought of possible litigation for medical negligence can influence how much more investigation is deemed necessary.

Besides X-rays, various blood tests are commonly carried out, particularly to rule out syphilitic causes of deafness, and further to clarify diagnosis. In Menière's disease or suspected acoustic neuroma, tests of vestibular function may well be indicated. In this part of the discipline it is the equilibratory functions of the inner ear which are scrutinised, by observation of reactions to different positions and movements of the head and to thermal stimulation of the semicircular canals. The thermal reactions, usually referred to as 'caloric responses', are observed by recording the reflex eye movements (nystagmus) caused by irrigating the external auditory canals with water at temperatures slightly above, and slightly below, normal body temperature (44°C and 30°C).

For good measure, there are also in reserve such tests as electrocochleography and/or the brain-stem test ERA (evoked response audiometry) which must be used for the most difficult cases. Especially with investigations of this kind, we must all realise how much strain and tedium the patients may suffer from such protracted procedures; and if all these investigations are really necessary, then we must take great pains to make things easy and acceptable for those who undergo them. The patient's co-operation can be obtained by considerate planning of appointments to fit in with work or household commitments, and the reasons for everything that has to be done must be explained sympathetically again and again. We must realise that the patient is expecting us to find out what is wrong, and if we are busy trying to exclude what is not wrong, we must make this clear and tell him why it is important.

The Situation

If the patient has a remediable hearing loss the otologist is very much in his element. If, as is all too often the case, no medical or surgical treatment can prevail he is, in the popular phrase, 'on a hiding to nothing'. His professional pride is humbled and his patient's hopes are dashed. His human compassion is aroused but it encounters the barriers of helplessness and hopelessness. Good humour and gentle philosophy can gloss over slight to moderate hearing losses. Profound deafness leaves little scope for comfort, acceptance or consolation. This is the depth of despondency plumbed by the patient, meeting the realisation of his misfortune when his hopes crash and his greatest fears are confirmed by what appears to be the otologist's failure. None of us with hearing can imagine the reality of such a situation, nor can we cope with the challenge of usefully communicating without the natural spontaneity which only speech reception can provide.

Of course, most patients with hearing losses have a gradual onset of their problem which encroaches slowly over months or years. These people usually reach the otologist in a calm frame of mind. Already some of the everyday sounds they can no longer hear have faded away into forgetfulness so that they are not even missed. The presenting problem is often related to some specific difficulty in social or working life which has at last reached the point where it can no longer be ignored. For these patients, just as for those in the acute severe emotional distress of sudden incurable deafness, the otologist's consultation is a crisis point, where facts and fears have to be assimilated and faced. It is the turning point, the end of uncertainty, and it may be the beginning of rehabilitation.

6 THE TREATMENT AND PREVENTION OF DEAFNESS IN ADULTS

John C. Ballantyne

The sense organ of hearing (the organ of Corti) is situated in the *cochlea*, so named from its resemblance to a snail shell (see Figure 6.1). The organ of Corti consists essentially of some 20,000 microscopic structures, the hair-cells, the bases of which make contact with fibres of the auditory nerve. The hair-cells form the sensory part, the nerve forms the neural part, of the sensorineural apparatus. Sounds are transmitted or conducted to the inner ear from their source by way of the outer ear canal, the drumhead (*tympanic membrane*) and the chain of ossicles (the *malleus*, the *incus* and the *stapes*). These constitute the conducting apparatus. Between the air in the middle ear and the fluids in the inner ear are two windows: an upper *oval window* sealed by the footplate of the stapes and a *round window* closed by a movable membrane.

Types of Deafness

Anything which affects the functioning of the sensory or neural parts of the inner ear will give rise to a sensorineural hearing loss. Conductive deafness will be caused by anything which prevents the normal transmission of sound from its source to the inner ear, for example, anything which obstructs the outer ear canal, anything which prevents normal movement of the drumhead or anything which interferes with the normal functioning of the ossicles.

Causes of Conductive Deafness

When it fills the outer ear canal completely, wax will prevent the normal passage of sound waves towards the drumhead; anything which prevents the normal periodic opening of the Eustachian tube (with swallowing or yawning) will cause the tympanic membrane to be drawn in towards the middle ear. In adults this may happen rather rarely with malignant growths at the lower end of the tube (in the nasopharynx at the back of the nose) or much more commonly after flying or diving, and the middle ear may fill with fluid. The drumhead may be perforated by infection or injury and the ossicles may be disrupted or fixed by infection, injury or bony disease. Of particular interest is the condition of otosclerosis, in which the movement of the footplate of the stapes becomes progressively restricted by its invasion with this bony disease from the margins of the oval window. Any of these conditions will cause a conductive deafness.

Causes of Sensorineural Hearing Loss

In adults, the sensory and neural parts of the inner ear and its nerve connections may be affected, either separately or together, by a wide variety of conditions. The commonest cause is the 'wear and tear' of ageing. Ototoxic drugs, notably the aminoglycoside antibiotics (such as neomycin, kanamycin and gentamicin) may damage the hair cells, with subsequent degeneration in the auditory nerve fibres; exposure to excessive noise or certain specific infections (such as syphilis) may cause a progressive deterioration in hearing; sudden deafness may result from direct injuries to the inner ear (as in fractures of the skull base), from the effects of violent pressure changes as in diving or sudden straining, from viral infections or meningitis or from vascular conditions which interfere with the blood supply to the inner ear. All of these conditions will cause a sensorineural hearing loss, often profound, sometimes total; some conditions affect both ears, others only one.

The Medical and Surgical Treatment of Conductive Deafness

Great advances have been made in the treatment of conductive deafness since the end of the Second World War. Many of these have been made possible and practicable only by the development of antibiotic drugs, the operating microscope and modern anaesthetic agents. Wax can be removed by syringing or with probes or suction, acute infections of the middle ear (acute otitis media) can be treated effectively with antibiotics, fluid in the middle ear can be drained surgically and even tumours in the nasopharynx can often be treated successfully by radiotherapy, provided that the correct diagnosis is established without delay. In all such cases, the restoration of normal hearing is to be expected. However, the most rewarding results of treatment are to be seen in the surgical restoration of hearing in the conditions of otosclerosis, chronic otitis media and the rather rare traumatic lesions of the auditory ossicles.

Stapedectomy

Removal of the stapes, in whole or in part, has an interesting modern history. For those who prefer an operation to a hearing aid, stapedectomy is now the method of choice in the treatment of otosclerosis, in which the gradual fixation of the stapes by the bony disease (Figure 6.1) leads to a progressive conductive deafness, usually in both ears, in a patient with an otherwise healthy ear. In 1958, Dr John Shea of Memphis, Tennessee, described several cases in which he had removed the whole stapes, closed the oval window with a vein graft and bridged the gap between the incus and the window with a tiny piece of plastic (polythene) tubing; in one of his earliest reports, he claimed the successful restoration of hearing in 94 out of 100 consecutive operations. Two years later, Professor Schuknecht, now in Boston, described a modification of Shea's technique in which he used fat from the ear

Figure 6.1: Otosclerosis

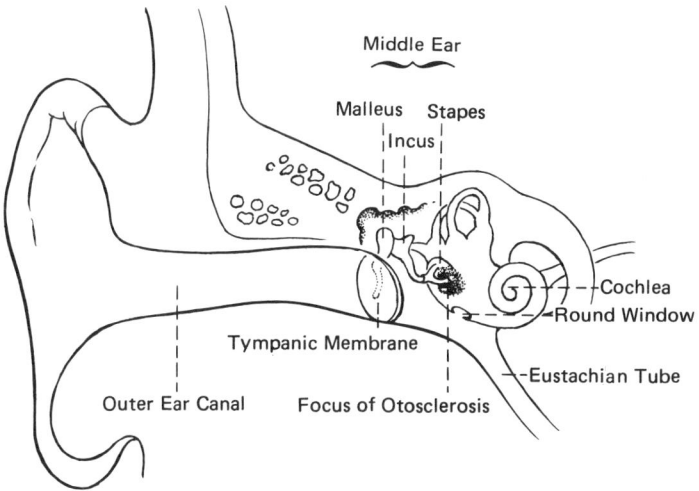

Figure 6.2: Stapedectomy

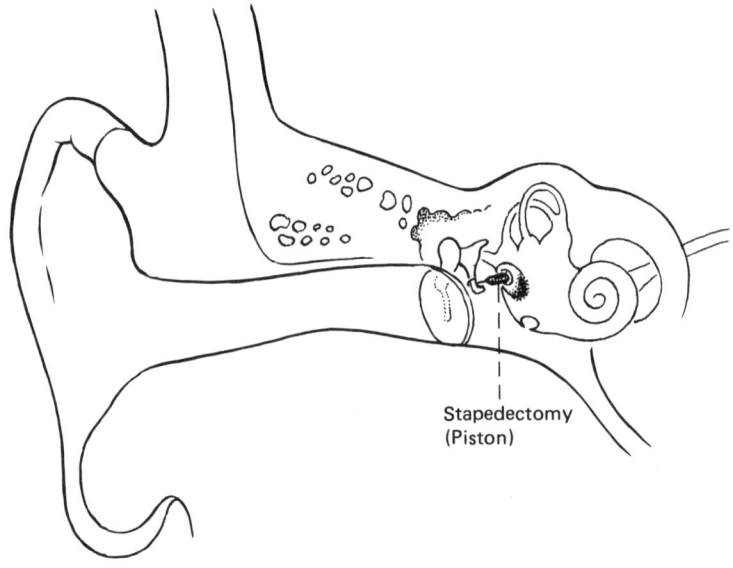

lobe and fine stainless steel wire, the fat sealing the oval window, the wire being crimped over the incus for extra security.

Nowadays, the most widely used techniques of stapedectomy are so-called 'small hole' techniques, in which most of the fixed footplate of the stapes is left in its normal position and a small hole is made in the footplate just big enough to admit a piston of stainless steel or plastic material or both which is crimped on to the incus (Figure 6.2). Stapedectomy is not without its problems and the greatest of these is the 'dead ear', in which all hearing may be lost permanently sometimes months or even years after the operation and often for no apparent reason. Because of the ever-present risk of this complication, however infrequently it occurs, it is customary to operate on the worse hearing ear in the first instance and, in the United Kingdom at least, there are few ear surgeons who operate routinely on the second ear, however successful the result may be in the first. Nevertheless, the overall results of stapedectomy have been very gratifying, in the majority of cases, over a period of 25 years and it represents one of the most dramatic advances in surgery in the last quarter of a century.

Tympanoplasty

This is the name given to the plastic reconstruction of the tympanic apparatus, i.e. the tympanic membrane and ossicles, in cases in which either or both have been damaged, most commonly as a result of chronic infective disease in the middle ear, less commonly as a result of injury. In either of these conditions the tympanic membrane may be perforated, or some part of the ossicular chain — most commonly the incus — is eroded by the disease or by injury so that the continuity between the ossicles is disrupted. Although surgical attempts to close perforations were made over 100 years ago by Dr E. Berthold, a German otologist, the modern history of sympanoplasty started in 1953, when another German otologist, Professor Horst Wullstein, introduced new techniques at the Fifth International Congress of Oto-Rhino-Laryngology in Amsterdam. Tympanoplasty consists of two essential procedures: when the tympanic membrane is perforated, it can usually be closed. This is referred to as myringoplasty; when the ossicular chain is disrupted, its continuity can often be restored. This is known as ossiculoplasty. Hence, tympanoplasty = myringoplasty + ossiculoplasty.

Myringoplasty

Recent perforations of the tympanic membrane may heal spontaneously. Other perforations of longer standing, especially when they are small, may be prompted to heal by the application of a small amount of caustic material to its healed edges but larger perforations (Figure 6.3) or perforations of longer standing — after, say, six months or a year — are much less likely to heal naturally. It is in such cases that myringoplasty may be indicated. When a perforation has been present for a long time, its edges are healed — so firmly healed, in fact, that they must be 'freshened' before there can be any reasonable hope of closing it. This means that the edges of a perforation must be carefully removed, through an operating microscope, with either a sharp needle or 'sickle knife' and fine aural forceps, as the first stage of any form of myringoplasty. The material used to close the perforation will then depend upon the preference and personal experience of the particular surgeon. The most popular material currently used for this purpose is 'fascia', the tissue which surrounds and binds all muscles, and because it is readily accessible the fascia most commonly used is that which covers the temporal muscle just above the ear.

There are several ways in which the fascia can be applied to the

Figure 6.3: Perforation of Tympanic Membrane

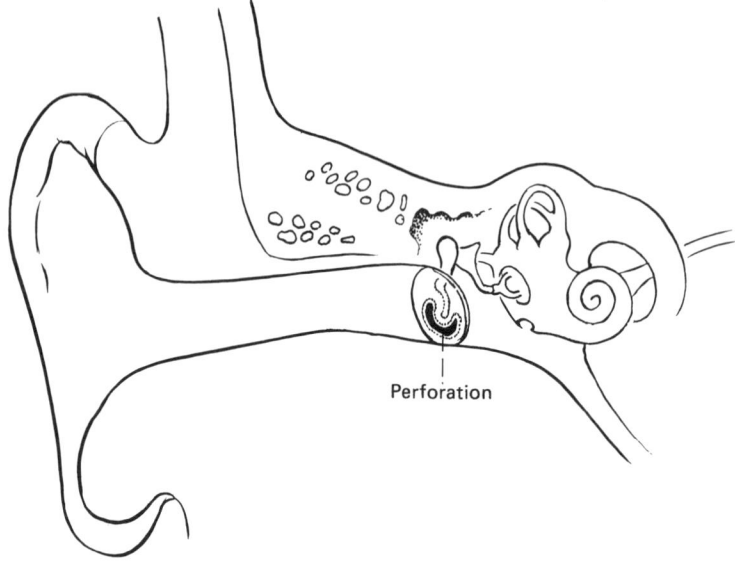

Figure 6.4: Myringoplasty

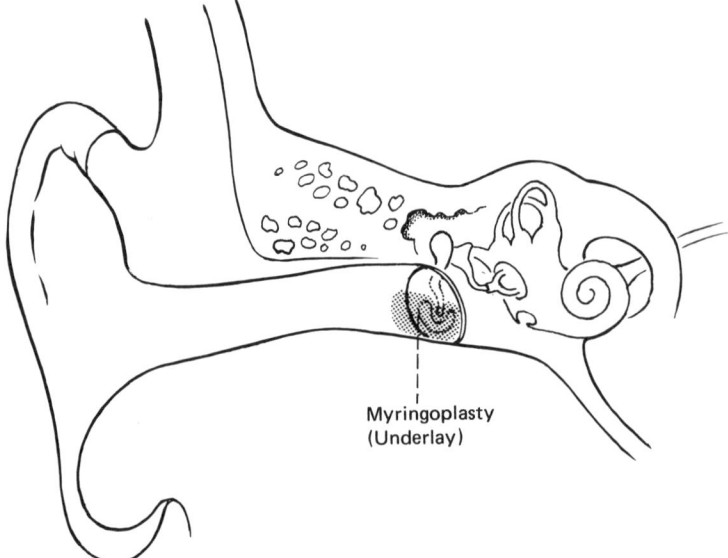

prepared tympanic membrane, but basically there are two: in one, the fascia is placed up against the under-surface of the membrane (i.e. the surface facing the middle ear). This is the 'underlay' technique (see Figure 6.4). In the other method, the fascia is placed over the outer surface of the drumhead (i.e. the one facing the outer ear canal). This is the 'overlay' technique. There are also several combinations of 'underlay' and 'overlay' techniques. A 'take' rate of over 90 per cent is claimed by many ear surgeons, though this is an optimistic estimate in the long term. Nevertheless, it is possible to close the majority of perforations, with careful preparation and a careful technique, especially in cases of traumatic perforation.

Ossiculoplasty

The reconstruction of a disrupted ossicular chain is more difficult and less successful than the closure of a perforation, and the long-term results of ossiculoplasty are not infrequently disappointing, though sometimes highly gratifying. The precise technique used will depend in the first place on the state of the ossicles. To take the most common lesion, in which the incus has been eroded (Figure 6.5), it will depend

Figure 6.5: Necrosis of Incus

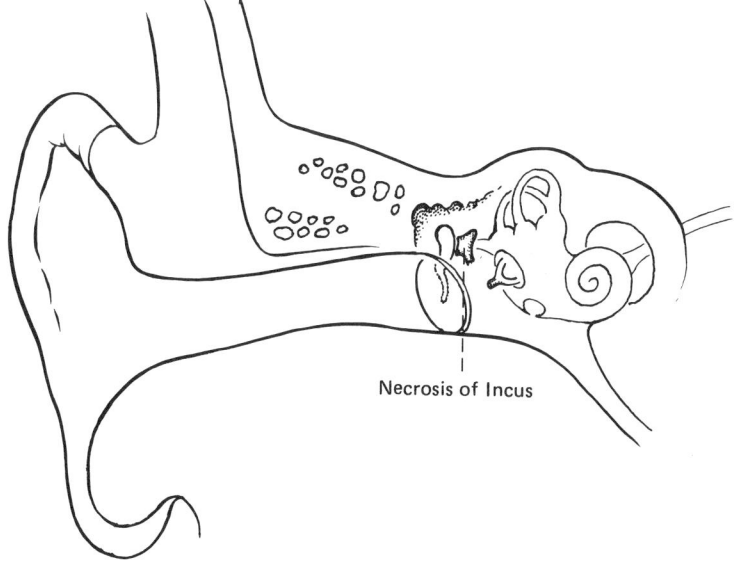

Figure 6.6: Ossiculoplasty: Incus Interposition (to Head of Stapes)

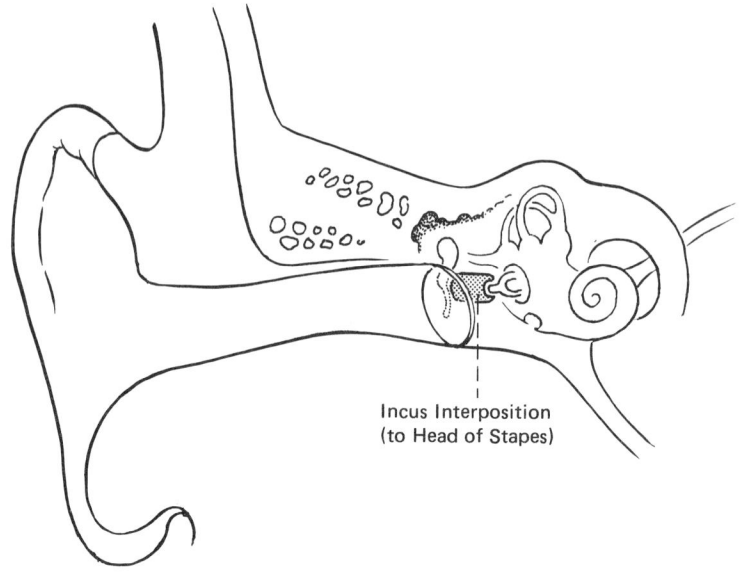

Incus Interposition
(to Head of Stapes)

upon the state of the stapes: if it is intact and mobile, some tissue may be interposed between the malleus and/or tympanic membrane and the head of the stapes (Figure 6.6). If the 'superstructure' of the stapes has also been eroded, some tissue must be interposed between the malleus and/or tympanic membrane and the mobile foot plate of the stapes (Figure 6.7).

The principles of myringoplasty and ossiculoplasty have been described separately but in practice they are often done together in a single surgical procedure; alternatively, the surgery may be 'staged' so that a myringoplasty is followed — usually months but sometimes years later — by ossiculoplasty. The most difficult cases are those in which the malleus also is eroded, for in such cases there is no firm 'anchorage' for the interposed material. It is in such instances that a middle ear transplant may have to be considered. In this type of transplant, the whole of the patient's tympanic membrane is removed, together with any remnants of malleus and incus, and replaced by a donor's (cadaver) membrane with the ossicles attached to it. These transplant techniques were originally developed by Professor Jean Marquet in Antwerp and Professor Christian Betow in Berlin and they are used by a limited number of otologists elsewhere.

Figure 6.7: Ossiculoplasty: Incus Interposition (to Footplate of Stapes)

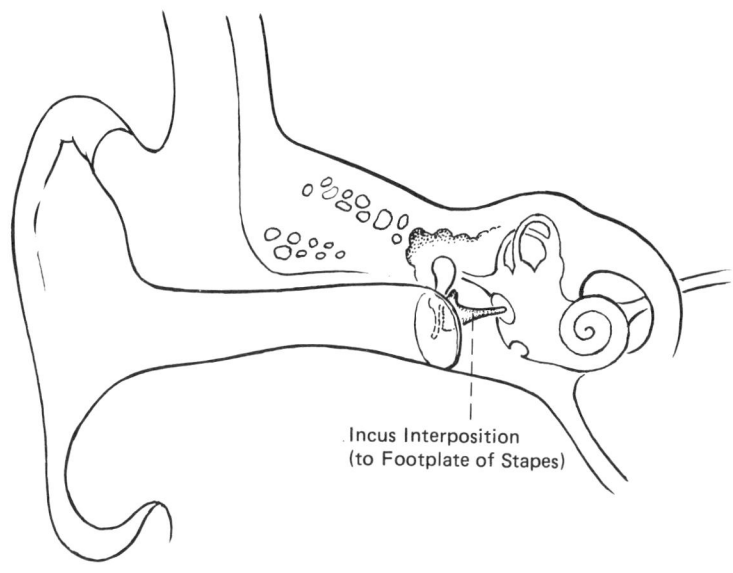

The various techniques of tympanoplasty and stapes surgery are also applicable to the surgical restoration of hearing in traumatic lesions of the ossicles. They are still developing and many ingenious variations have been devised, notably with the use of plastic materials and tissue 'glues', and there is reason to hope that the results of these procedures, too, will prove more reliable in time. They are, of course, mechanical solutions to mechanical problems but the treatment of sensorineural hearing loss is much more difficult.

The Treatment of Sensorineural Hearing Loss

There are still, regrettably, many cases of sensorineural hearing loss, especially those which progress relentlessly, for which no effective medical or surgical treatment can be offered. It is in such cases that one may have to rely entirely on the use of hearing aids combined with hearing therapy but it is essential to establish the cause whenever possible, for it is only when this has been done that rational treatment can be prescribed.

Some cases of deafness of sudden onset may be due to interruption of the blood supply to the inner ear and in a proportion of these cases it may be caused by vascular spasm. Energetic treatment with vasodilator drugs which relieve the spasm may be effective in a few cases. Such drugs include nicotinic acid, and occasionally an intravenous drip of histamine may restore the hearing. In syphilitic deafness, usually progressive, prompt diagnosis and aggressive treatment with antibiotics and steroids (cortisone derivatives) may prevent further deterioration and in some cases of atypical 'cochlear otosclerosis', treatment with sodium fluoride has been advocated by some authorities although there is no universal agreement about the existence of the condition or the usefulness of the therapy. There are, however, instances in which the hearing may be salvaged by surgical means; immediate surgical exploration of the ear is recommended when the otologist suspects a rupture of the labyrinthine windows, usually resulting from sudden pressure changes. A leakage of fluid may occur either from the round window or, less commonly, from the oval window, when sealing of the leak may be effected by fat or other tissues. If this procedure is carried out without delay, what hearing remains may be preserved or sometimes even improved.

There is no greater disability than the calamity of total deafness and the last fifteen years or so have witnessed the development of a programme of 'cochlear inplants' for a carefully selected number of those who can derive no help from the most powerful hearing aids available. Notable among the centres which have used these implants are those in Los Angeles, San Francisco and Stanford universities, all in California. There are other centres in Oklahoma, Paris, Vienna and Melbourne and there are also teams in London, one of them working in close association with Cambridge University.

In cases in which the ear cannot be stimulated acoustically it is sometimes possible to stimulate electrically whatever nerve fibres may remain. Not every patient who is totally deaf has surviving nerve fibres and one of the outstanding problems in selecting patients for cochlear implants is to determine whether there *are* any surviving neurones and, if there are, to find out *where* they are. It is known, however, from animal and human studies, that patients who have been deafened by ototoxic drugs usually retain between 5 and 10 per cent of their auditory nerve fibres and at present these patients are regarded as the ideal subjects for implantation. There is still much controversy

Figure 6.8: Cochlear Implant

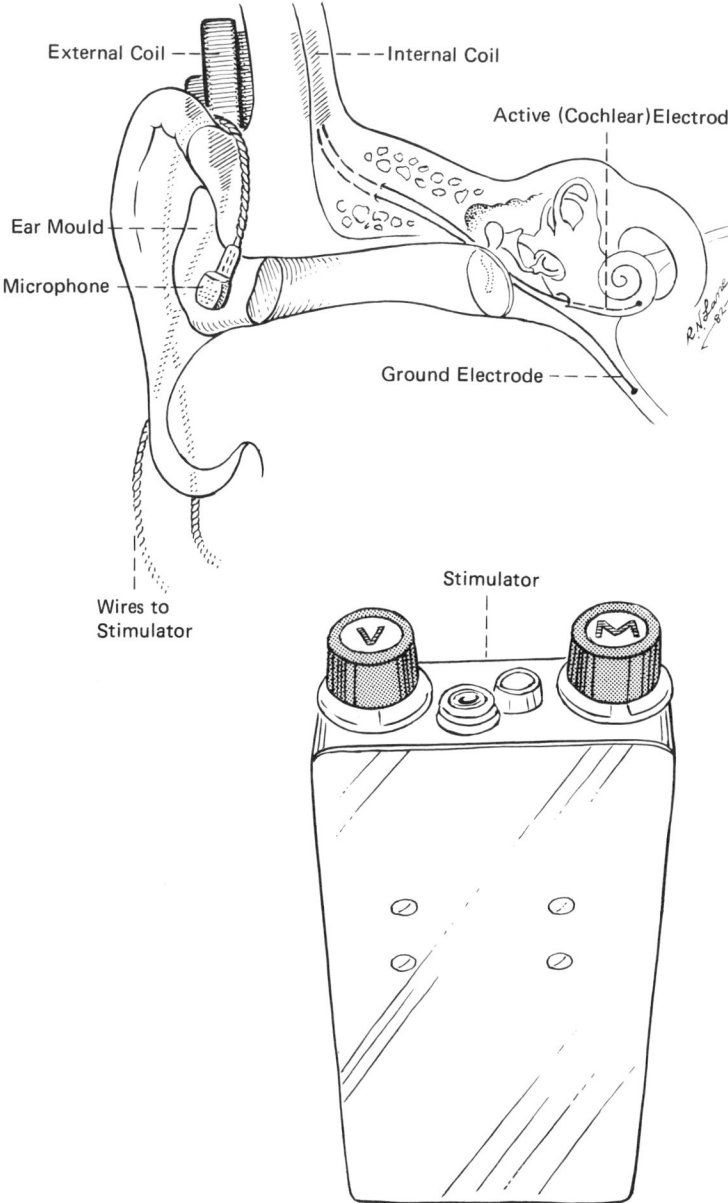

about the relative merits of single electrodes and multiple electrodes but in the type of implant which has so far been most extensively used in human subjects (in Los Angeles) a 'ground' electrode has been passed into the upper opening of the Eustachian tube and the active electrode has been introduced into the cochlea through the round window for a distance of about 14 mm (Figure 6.8). This places the ball tip of the electrode a little less than halfway round the basal turn of the cochlea. These electrodes lead to an internal magnetic induction coil, which is seated in a recess drilled into the bone above and behind the ear. Outside the skin, after the wound has healed, an external stimulator coil is fitted over the internal coil. The most effective way of holding the external coil in proper alignment over the implanted internal coil has been with a special coil holder attached to a spectacle frame.

The microphone can be attached to an ear mould, as shown in Figure 6.8, and this is connected by leads to the external electronic stimulator (consisting of a printed circuit board with associated components, a battery compartment and a contact strip), housed in a metal case, which has a volume control (V) and a modulation control (M). The microphone picks up acoustic stimuli (sounds) and transmits them to the external stimulator unit; the stimulator processes the signal and then transmits it to the external coil. The signal is magnetically induced across the skin barrier to the internal coil and thence down the active electrode into the cochlea. Current flows between the active and ground electrodes, thus stimulating the surviving nerve fibres and producing a sensation of sound. This is not to say that the patient will experience *normal* sounds but at least the sensation produced *is* one of sound, and many of those who have been satisfactorily implanted have been able to detect at least the 'prosodic' elements of speech — rhythms, cadences and some degree of intonation. Above all, many of these subjects have been enthusiastic about the transference from a world of total silence to a world of sound, with an awareness of their environment and assistance with their speechreading skills.

Cochlear implants are still in their relative infancy but they have now passed beyond the stage of experimental research into the category of a service provision for a limited number of selected patients for whom nothing otherwise can be offered at present. One of the incidental benefits which has been reported by several implanted subjects has been the relief of distressing tinnitus.

The Prevention of Deafness in Adults

Not all causes of sensorineural hearing loss are treatable but some are preventable; or, at least, once they have been detected further deterioration can often be avoided by taking appropriate measures. Chief among these are deafness due to noise and deafness due to drugs.

Deafness due to Noise

More than 150 years ago, in 1831, Dr J. Fosbroke first recorded deafness in blacksmiths. Then, almost a century ago, in 1890, Dr Barr recorded deafness in boilermakers and for many years 'boilermakers' deafness' remained the classical example of Industrial Noise-Induced Hearing Loss (INIHL). It also occurs in drop-forge workers, riveters, stampers and platers, welders and wormers, pneumatic drillers, aircraft workers, pop and rock and even classical orchestral musicians and occasionally in dentists who use high-speed drills. The onset of deafness in these people is usually insidious and susceptibility to noise varies considerably from one person to another. It is important that susceptible individuals should be detected as early as possible. The late Air Vice-Marshal E.D.D. Dickson believed that some idea of susceptibility could be gained if one knew the rate at which hearing recovered after a period of exposure to noise and it has been recommended that every workman engaged in a job in which the noise level exceeds 90 decibels above threshold for significant periods of time should have an audiogram before starting employment, and that he should be re-tested at regular intervals. Furthermore, any workman who complains of tinnitus after working in a noisy environment should also have his hearing monitored from time to time. The ideal remedy would be to eliminate injurious noise at its sources, and improvements in the design of machines and their mountings has already done something to help. Reduction of reflection and reverberation of noise by sound-proofing surfaces and baffle walls has also sometimes been effective but such measures are not always practicable.

Until quite recently, little attention has been paid to that other form of noise-induced deafness which occurs in those who use firearms and other weapons but perhaps the recent experiences in the Falkland Islands will focus more attention on the problems of 'acoustic trauma'. Even those who use small arms for sport or hunting tend sooner or later to suffer from acoustic trauma and in time the deafness may become very severe but the main sufferers are members of the armed forces, and the requirements of modern military equipment expose them to intense degrees of noise. The Wombat anti-tank gun, for example, produces exceptionally high sound pressure levels estimated at 187 dB; almost as noisy is the Carl Gustav anti-tank rocket launcher with an estimated level of 183 dB. There have been occasions when the blast from a Carl Gustav has actually sucked the glass out of the firer's wrist watch! Such weapons may cause severe hearing losses even from a single unprotected exposure.

Whether in industry or in military service, anyone exposed to damaging levels of noise should protect his ears, and several protective devices are available. Contrary to popular belief, in acoustic trauma there does not appear to be any substantial difference in the protection afforded by ear plugs, ear muffs and noise-excluding helmets. Whenever possible ear muffs should continue to be available for intense noise exposure but the necessity to use other head-protectors at the same time (on active service) makes this not always practicable. As has been said by Dr Michael Forrest of the Army Personnel Research Establishment, 'One is driven to the view that the human head is badly designed'. For infantry soldiers and for those who shoot for sport, ear plugs should be used. The EAR plug, which is made from a slowly-expanding resin foam, gives exceptionally good acoustic protection: it will fit any normal ear canal with a single size and it is comfortable to wear.

The most obvious defect in any hearing protector is that it may affect communication by speech, but this can be exaggerated. Indeed, in some circumstances, the use of hearing protectors may actually improve communication, especially in extremely noisy surroundings. A growing awareness of the hazards of noise has led to the development of hearing conservation programmes which should do much to reduce preventable loss of hearing from this cause.

Deafness due to Drugs

Many drugs may damage the hearing on occasion, and in the susceptible individual even such apparently innocent drugs as aspirin and quinine may be ototoxic; so too may many others but the worst offenders without a doubt are the so-called aminoglycoside antibiotics. These include streptomycin, neomycin, kanamycin, gentamicin, tobramycin and amikacin. They may be toxic not only when they are given by injection but also when they are taken by mouth or even when they are applied to extensive raw surfaces, as in burns. They should never be prescribed without very careful thought. However, that having been said, their use today is generally reserved for cases of serious illness such as septicaemia or liver failure in which to withhold them would be fatal. It is now customary for the levels of these drugs in the bloodstream to be carefully monitored throughout the period of their use, and they have been prescribed with greater caution since their potential toxicity became more widely appreciated. Constant search is being made for effective alternatives to the ototoxic drugs.

Summary

The last four decades have witnessed a veritable revolution in the otologist's attitude to deafness. The advent of antibiotic drugs, the optical perfection of the binocular operating microscope, and the remarkable development of safe anaesthetic agents have allowed him to turn his attention from the prevention of a fatal outcome in life-threatening ear infections to the preservation or restoration of hearing in cases of conductive deafness. A better understanding of the mechanisms of sensorineural hearing loss has led to more successful methods of treating it; and even in those desperate cases of total hearing loss, the cochlear implant holds promise of some hope for a select few. And in the case of deafness due to noise or drugs, both of them peculiar to the last forty years, a better understanding of the risks involved has led and will continue to lead to more effective methods of prevention.

7 AUDIOLOGICAL PROCEDURES IN DIFFERENTIAL DIAGNOSIS

John J. Knight and Peggy Chalmers

As has been described in previous chapters, the hearing chain commences at the external ear and proceeds through the stages of the tympanic membrane and ossicles of the air-filled middle ear (the eardrum) to the liquid-filled internal ear, the hearing nerve (VIIIth cranial nerve with the closely related VIIth nerve, the facial nerve) through the brain stem to the higher centres of the brain where sound stimuli are finally perceived. At each stage in the chain the acoustical, mechanical and finally electrical signals that result from a sound can be completely interrupted or distorted by disorders affecting one or more than one part of the complete system of the hearing chain. The effect of course varies between complete deafness and partial hearing loss, and a prerequisite to treatment of any form by whichever of the many specialists is involved (medical, surgical, scientific, technical or educational) is to identify the location of the main section of the chain that is causing the trouble. Next in importance is to identify the most likely nature of the disturbance in the section, for example, a deficiency normally expected to develop in old age (presbyacusis) or a growth affecting the hearing nerve close to the brain that can threaten life (acoustic nerve tumour). This is what is meant by differential diagnosis which today has reached an advanced state largely due to the development of standardised audiological procedures by physicists and electrical engineers working with their medical colleagues. (Audiology is defined as the science of hearing in all its aspects).

Fundamental to all these procedures is the capability to conduct hearing tests in a very quiet environment in which a subject's response to a controlled sound stimulus can be reliably identified with the stimulus unadulterated by other intrusive background noises such as speech or nearby traffic. Adequately quiet sound-treated rooms for these purposes are costly to construct but involve well-understood principles so that most modern audiology clinics are well-equipped in this respect. The next most important requirement is a calibrated instrument such as an audiometer, used to determine the subject's hearing threshold at a number of discrete frequencies, or an acoustic impedance bridge with which the functioning of the middle ear can be explored without the subject's active co-operation. For most purposes related to these audiological procedures, national or preferably international standards for the performance of the test instruments have been agreed and are maintained in the audiology clinics by physical scientists and technicians. The skilled operators of the equipment who have to explain to the subject the aims of the procedures and the required response from the subject are usually the audiology technicians. They are responsible for taking the measurements and reporting them so that the departure from normal can be quantified and the characteristic patterns that result from the different disorders identified, that is the differential diagnosis. On a windless day, away from the sea on a remote and uninhabited desert island, the most common hearing disorders are capable of being diagnosed on the basis of a simple series of tests with calibrated tuning forks of different frequencies. They have the unrivalled advantages of being cheap, easy to operate and not easily broken; they also maintain their calibration indefinitely. In the modern clinic their use is supplemented by sophisticated electro-acoustical instrumentation, the foremost of which is the diagnostic pure tone audiometer.

Pure Tone Audiometry

Pure tone audiometry (see Figures 7.1, 7.2, 7.3, 7.4, 7.5, 7.6) enables the subject's hearing sensitivity to be compared with that of average healthy young normals for a series of single frequency sounds (pure tones), one ear at a time through earphones. Other fundamental diagnostic information is readily achieved by connecting the same electrical signals to a bone vibrator on a headband instead of to the earphones. The hearing thresholds for air-conducted sounds (earphone listening) are compared with those for bone conduction (sounds transmitted through the skull directly to the internal ear from the externally applied vibrator held on the mastoid bone). Calibration of the audiometer is arranged so that the hearing loss dial reading for the normal air-conduction threshold is the same as that for normal bone-conduction, that is zero decibels hearing level, or 0 dB HL. Complete deafness is rare but profound hearing losses range from 90 dB upwards, while people do not usually seek help, say regarding initial use of a hearing aid, until their average loss exceeds 25 decibels. An average difference of more than 5 to 10 decibels between the air-conduction and the bone-conduction thresholds (with the bone reading necessarily being the more sensitive) implies an impediment to sound transmission somewhere in the chain before the internal ear (cochlea). A plug of wax in the external ear would cause this effect as would a disorder of the middle ear. These are known as *conductive* hearing losses. Most conductive hearing losses today can be remedied by medical or surgical treatment or, alternatively, they can be alleviated by any good quality hearing aid.

When the hearing thresholds are depressed and are approximately equal for air and bone-conducted sound, the defect is difficult to treat because it is then known to lie in the microscopic structures of the internal ear (for example presbyacusis), in the hearing nerve (nerve tumour) or in more central structures of the brain (for example as a result of a stroke). The result is termed *sensorineural* hearing loss and further audiological tests often enable a differentiation to be obtained between *sensory* and *neural* (or nerve fibre) hearing loss. In some quarters, sensorineural hearing loss is divided instead into *cochlear* and *retrocochlear* hearing loss. A combination of conductive and sensorineural hearing loss is called *mixed* hearing loss.

After determination of the hearing thresholds in a sensorineural hearing loss, the next step in ascertaining whether the defect lies in the cochlea is to apply tests for recruitment of loudness. Recruitment is a name for an abnormal growth of loudness with increasing intensity of a sound. It is evidenced by an intolerance to the noise tolerated by normally-hearing people and, if only one ear is affected, its presence is found by the alternate binaural loudness balance test. If both ears are affected, self-recording audiometry often reveals it as Type II audiograms or by acoustic reflex threshold measurements. Retrocochlear disorders are frequently differentiated by tone decay (abnormal auditory adaptation) tests. In these cases, difficulty is experienced in hearing a continuously-presented quiet tone at the mid and lower test frequencies for as long as one minute. The tone is presented at 5 decibels above threshold and is increased in steps, as required for continued audibility; the decay (or adaptation) is measured as the increase in decibels required for it to be heard for 60 seconds. Simple but accurate, pure tone audiometry is required as a routine in large numbers of cases and the procedure can become tedious during a long and busy out-patient clinic. The tedium is greatly relieved in self-recording audiometry which achieves the same objects, with every decision by the subject as to whether he hears a signal or not, being recorded on a chart as he presses and releases a signal switch.

The originator of self-recording audiometry was Békésy and it was first made available commercially nearly 30 years ago. Instead of the usual series of tests at frequencies one octave apart employed for manual pure tone audiometry, Békésy audiometers offer a continuous frequency sweep from 100 to 10,000 Hz. Simplified versions, however, as used widely in industry for hearing conservation programmes, automatically present six frequencies for 30 seconds each to the two ears in sequence. Much valuable diagnostic information is obtained from Békésy audiometry using a test tone first in a pulsed form in which the signal is interrupted twice a second to overcome any adaptation; with the same earphone placement, the subject then repeats the test with a continuous signal and the threshold is charted in a different colour. Comparison of the two results for the one ear enable the audiogram to be placed in one of five categories, each with a special diagnostic significance, as:

Type I   Present in normal hearing and conductive hearing loss
Type II Present in cochlear hearing loss (for example Menière's disease)
Type III Present in nerve fibre lesion (for example tumours on the hearing nerve)
Type IV Present in nerve fibre lesion (for example tumours on the hearing nerve)
Type V   Characteristic of non-organic hearing loss (for example malingering and psychogenic)

In many cases, investigation of hearing loss results in several components of the disorder being identified, such as the effect of age (the man is 85 years old), of noise (he served in the infantry in World War I) and of ear disease (he remembers having running ears as a child). Generally, audiometry has not previously been performed. It is easy to assess the present hearing loss and separate the middle ear component by the air-bone gap in the audiogram. Assessment of the effect of ageing relative to the damage of the noise of warfare and to a possible noisy occupation becomes a matter of probabilities. A complication which arises in all audiometric tests when there is more than 40 dB difference in the air-conduction thresholds, or when the two air conduction thresholds are similarly depressed but the bone conduction is almost normal, is that the test signals may travel through the skull to be perceived by the opposite ear. Special 'masking' procedures are applied in these cases, effectively to incapacitate the ear not being tested by occupying it with a rushing sound.

Speech Audiometry

While pure tone tests give a good indication of the hearing deficit in many cases, it is a fact that pure tones rarely occur in everyday circumstances. Any hearing handicap lies in difficulty in understanding the spoken word. Stroke cases and patients with acoustic nerve tumours sometimes give pure tone audiograms that are within normal limits, yet their understanding of speech can be minimal due to deficiencies in their central nervous system. Speech audiometry is diagnostically significant in such cases as it is also in the detection of 'non-organic' hearing loss, where a near-normal speech audiogram can be obtained from a subject with an apparent pure tone averaging 40 decibels or more. Obviously no significant hearing defect exists in such cases. For speech audiometry, specially prepared lists of everyday English words are reproduced, usually through an earphone at intervals of a few seconds at a series of controlled intensities; the subject is encouraged to repeat only what he thinks he heard, or even to guess. The resulting speech audiogram shows more realistically such measurements as the hearing loss for speech (in decibels) and the maximum word score (as a percentage) under the most favourable conditions. The deliberate introduction of controlled amounts of background noise degrade the subject's performance depending upon the hearing structures that are affected and simulate more exactly the real-life situation. Speech audiometry according to these principles is also of value in determining the relative value of different hearing aids.

Acoustic Impedance Measurements of the Ear (see Figure 7.7)

The concept of electrical impedance as applied to alternating current circuits was transferred to the analogous acoustical situation for the alternating pressure of sound waves by acousticians over 50 years ago. It was a short step from acoustics to audiology and the first acoustic impedance bridge was used to measure the acoustic impedance of normal and disordered human ears by Metz during World War II. For most diagnostic purposes, the chief diagnostically important measure is that of the compliance of the middle ear, which is measured by insertion of a small probe with an airtight seal into the external ear canal. The compliance is an acoustical measure of the mobility of the eardrum. If for some reason, the tiny bones (ossicles) of the middle ear have become disconnected, the membrane of the eardrum will in consequence move more freely than normally under the influence of an alternating pressure as from a sound, that is the acoustic impedance measurements will show a compliance higher than normal. In otosclerosis where the third ossicle becomes fixed by a bony growth to the oval window, the movement of the membrane of the eardrum becomes more difficult than normal and a low compliance is measured. A similar result is found quickly and easily in a young child with hearing loss caused by glue ear (serous otitis media) in which the air in the middle ear has been replaced by a viscous liquid which also restricts the movement necessary for sound transmission.

A great advantage of these measurements is that the subject under investigation is relieved of having to make any judgements — all that is required is that the subject is co-operative to the extent of tolerating the soft-tipped probe to remain in the ear, often for less than 30 seconds. The probe contains three narrow tubes. One tube is used to feed a low frequency pure tone (typically 226 Hz) into the ear canal, where the sound pressure developed depends on the mobility, or compliance of the middle ear structures. The sound pressure is measured by a miniature microphone connected to the second tube. A third tube in the probe sealed in the ear canal is connected to a pump to enable static pressure in the canal to be varied. In some conditions the eustachian tube, which normally ventilates the middle ear cavity to the back of the nose, becomes blocked and causes the pressure of the air in the middle ear to fall below the atmospheric pressure. The membrane of the eardrum is then sucked in and it becomes less compliant. In the procedure called tympanometry, the pressure in the external ear canal is changed to balance the pressure in the middle ear and it is determined by the compliance reading reaching a maximum. Clearly the membrane will be most free to move under the influence of an alternating sound pressure when it is not subject to the tension caused by a difference of static pressure on the two sides. Tympanometry provides a unique and elegant means of measuring the middle ear pressure and hence leads to conclusions as to the functioning of the inaccessible eustachian tube.

Measurements of the acoustic impedance of the ear are also used to test the correct functioning of the two muscles in the middle ear called the tensor tympani and the stapedius muscle. Normally pure tones above about 80 dB more than the normal threshold (65 dB with wideband noise) cause the muscles in both ears to contract by reflex action if either ear is stimulated. At first, the technology permitted only the ear opposite to that in which the probe was fitted to have its reflex stimulated by a tone from an audiometer earphone. This contralateral stimulation proved extremely useful but now, as the technology has advanced, the inclusion of a fourth tube in the probe allows the possibility of ipsilateral stimulation of the acoustic reflex. Acoustic reflex measurements aid diagnosis in the following respects:

(1) In conductive hearing losses, the acoustic reflex is not obtained with an air bone gap of 15 dB or more.
(2) Recruitment of loudness (and hence a cochlear disorder) is indicated where there is less than 60 dB between the hearing threshold and the acoustic reflex threshold.
(3) In very young children, elicitation of the acoustic reflex with pure tones implies that the hearing threshold is at least 30 dB better.
(4) Detection of non-organic hearing loss where the true hearing threshold must be at least 30 dB more sensitive than the acoustic reflex.
(5) In paralysis of the facial nerve, the presence or absence of acoustic reflex is significant in locating the position of the lesion on the nerve.

Electrophysiological Hearing Tests

Attempts to measure a subject's response to sound by study of the electrical activity appearing at the scalp were made more than 30 years ago at the time when acoustic impedance measurements of the ear were first proving useful as an aid to diagnosis. However, it generally proved impossible to recognise the very small wave from sound stimulation in the mass of other electrical signals in the electroencephalogram (EEG) until low-cost averaging computers became available in the mid-1960s. These averagers then enabled the desired response from a large number of sound pulses to be separated from the random background activity, and soon 'cortical' evoked response audiometry (ERA) emerged as a clinical tool (see Figure 7.8). As in acoustic impedance measurements, the active co-operation of the subject is not required beyond allowing three electrodes to be attached to the scalp, the earlobe and the forehead. The procedure soon developed into a reliable means of obtaining the pure tone audiogram in adults who were difficult to test by other methods. It was hoped that it would be equally effective with children and especially with very young children suspected of having defective hearing. This hope was not realised because it proved difficult to trace the evoked response to within some 30 dB of the actual threshold, partly because of the greater background of electrical activity in the developing brain of a child. A similar response to sound stimulation is available in the electrical signals received by electrodes placed over muscles in various parts of the body. Again, averagers have been utilised to enhance the desired signals (this time produced by sound clicks) with respect to background activity and the result is known as the auditory myogenic response. When electrodes are placed behind the ear, it is called the post-auricular response. In an application as a crude screening test for hearing loss in young children, it has been termed the crossed-acoustic response (CAR).

Considerable progress has resulted from a subsequent development which took place some 10 years ago when electrical signals were examined from the bony wall of the internal ear by a needle electrode inserted through the external ear canal and the drum. Sound clicks, or short bursts of tone, are used as stimulus and the result after averaging is called the electrocochleogram (E Coch G) (see Figure 7.9). A whole series of electrical signals are picked up in this procedure from the different structures involved in the hearing process. There is the action potential (AP), the cochlear microphonic (CM) and the summating potential (SP). By various means, each is capable of separation and identification in normally-hearing subjects. Their absence, distortion or delay has special significance in diagnosing and evaluating hearing loss.

A light general anaesthetic is necessary for children who undergo an E Coch G investigation; with adults, a local anaesthetic is sometimes employed but often is not required. The subject lies on a couch in a sound-treated audiometric room while the response to one to five hundred acoustic clicks generated under carefully controlled conditions is recorded in order to study the resulting CM and the threshold of the AP. There is a close agreement between this AP threshold and the average pure tone thresholds between 1000 and 8000 Hz. The detail concerning the shape of this part of the audiogram is established by further tests using short bursts of tones at the audiometric frequencies above 1000 Hz, but it is found that the E Coch G procedure does not give reliable information about the sensitivity at 1000 Hz and below. An advantage of the test, however, is that with the electrode placement in direct contact with one internal ear, the results relate only to this particular ear and there are no effects from the opposite ear such as would require masking in other forms of hearing examination.

In the past five years much diagnostic use in audiological and neurological cases has been made of measurements of the electrical signals emanating from the brain stem in response to sound — brain stem electric responses (BSER) (see Figure 7.10). The same apparatus is employed as for E Coch G. Clicks and higher frequency bursts of tone are used as the sound stimulus which is often repeated 1000 times, at a rate of 10 or 20 per second. An advantage of the BSER is that surface electrodes are sufficient for picking up the desired signals in response to sound although this signal seldom exceeds one millionth of a volt. Consequently a high degree of amplification is needed up to one hundred thousand times, that is by 100 decibels. Six distinct waves are recognised in normally-hearing subjects in the first 10 thousandths (milliseconds) of a second following the sound stimulus. They mark the progress of the evoked response along the structures of the auditory pathway where they arrive with progressive delays as follows:—

		Delay (milliseconds)
Wave I	Auditory nerve AP	1.5 to 2.0
Wave II	Cochlear nucleus	approx. 3.0
Wave III	Superior olivary complex	,, 4.0
Wave IV	Lateral lemniscus	,, 5.0
Wave V	Inferior colliculus	,, 6.0
Wave VI	Unknown	,, 7.0 to 8.0

The BSER investigation is currently proving of great value in the assessment of hearing loss in children under 3 years old who can generally be relied upon to lie still during the short time the sounds are presented. For the next two years, a greater movement is difficult to control until the test again becomes feasible with children over 5. Wave V is often used for threshold estimation but the actual form of the pure tone audiogram cannot be determined by this method. The BSER investigation is also used extensively in adults with suspected neurological disorders such as multiple sclerosis, where the anatomical localisation of plaques is aided, and in tumours in regions which affect the brain stem such as those on the acoustic nerve. In all these cases, the delay (or latency) of Wave V is generally prolonged. Research is currently being directed to study of ipsilateral and bilateral recordings with respect to monaural sound stimulation; also to the effect of binaural versus monaural sound stimulation. The complete range of electrophysiological signals available for examinations of hearing is known to extend up to periods of 0.5 to 2 seconds after the stimulating sounds. These are occupied by the so-called cognitive potentials and include the contingent negative variation (CNV) all of which are of but limited clinical application at present. Most interest is centred on E Coch G (in the first 6 millisecs), BSER (in the first 10 millisecs) and the cortical evoked response ERA (from 60 to 300 millisecs).

The Present Clinical Situation

The use in diagnosis of all the hearing test procedures outlined above, from pure tone audiometry to BSER, has depended on the application of scientific principles to the study of hearing. This originated in the national telephony and physical laboratories where the pioneers in this field were electrical engineers and physicists including H. Fletcher of the Bell Telephone Laboratory in the USA, W. West of the UK Post Office Research Station, R.S. Dadson of the UK National Physical Laboratory, von Békésy in Europe and the USA and T.S. Littler in the UK. They refined the basic acoustical techniques and standardised the hearing measurements, so that the developments which followed, with acoustic impedance measurements and the application of averaging techniques and signal processing in electrophysiological measurement, were rapidly applied to the clinical situation. Not every audiological centre needs to be able to carry out all these techniques but the position has now been reached where they are available in regional centres of audiological expertise to which patients may be referred from peripheral clinics. Particularly in the regional centres, audiological scientists work with audiological physicians and surgeons to provide an effective diagnostic service in medical fields wherever there is an influence on hearing. The scientists are supported mainly by audiological technicians, who perform the tests with patients, and by medical physics technicians who calibrate and maintain the ever more sophisticated instrumentation.

118 *Audiological Procedures in Differential Diagnosis*

Figure 7.1: Pure Tone Audiograms of normally-hearing persons aged 18, 50 and 70, showing how the sensitivity for hearing the higher frequencies declines with age. Left ear only is shown for air conduction; bone-conduction sensitivities are similar to air conduction.

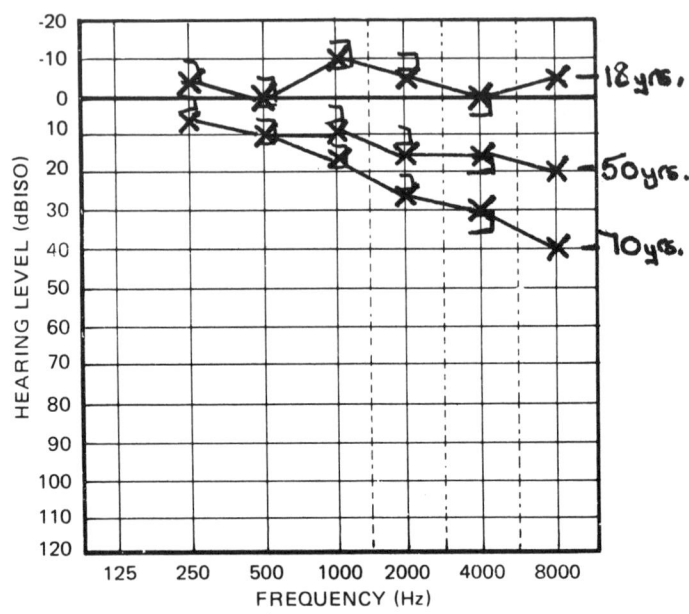

Audiological Procedures in Differential Diagnosis 119

Figure 7.2: Pure Tone Audiograms. Left ears only are shown. (a) An artificial conductive hearing loss produced in the 18-year-old person of Figure 7.1 by fitting an ear plug in the ear canal to protect the hearing from intense noise. It is seen that the hearing sensitivity for air-conducted sound is reduced particularly for higher frequencies while sensitivity for bone-conducted sounds is practically unaffected. (b) Child of 7 years of age with 'glue' ear (a conductive hearing loss produced by a viscous liquid filling the middle-ear space). Air conduction is reduced but bone conduction remains nearly normal. See also Figure 7.6(a)

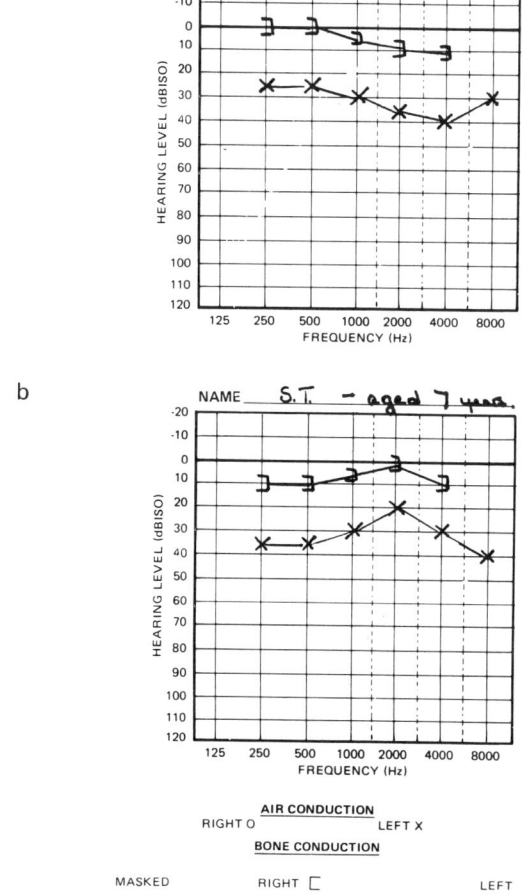

120 *Audiological Procedures in Differential Diagnosis*

Figure 7.3: Pure Tone Audiograms. Right ears only are shown. (a) Menière's disease affecting a 30-year-old person (a) sensorineural hearing loss produced by a disorder of the internal ear, the cochlea). Bone-conduction sensitivity is reduced approximately to the same degree as air conduction. (b) A 72-year-old man suffering from greater than average hearing loss due to ageing effects (presbyacusis). This is another type of sensorineural hearing loss where the bone-conduction loss approximately equals the air conduction

a
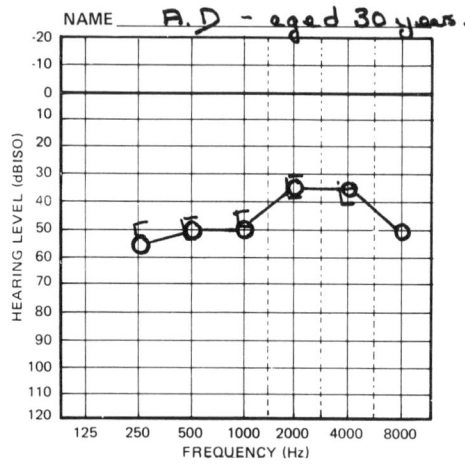

b
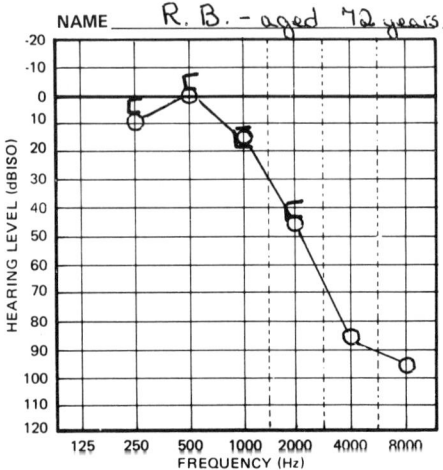

Figure 7.3 continued: (c) A 30-year-old rifleman exposed to firing approximately 10,000 rounds of Service rifle without ear protection. Permanent noise-induced hearing loss — sensorineural. (d) A 50-year-old shipyard worker after 34 years' exposure to rivetting, welding, and chipping hammer noise. Permanent, industrial noise-induced hearing loss — sensorineural.

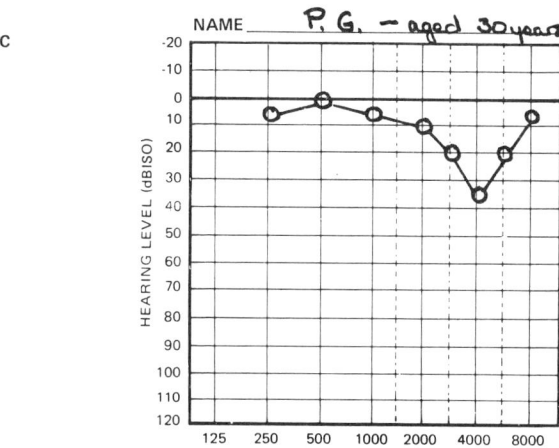

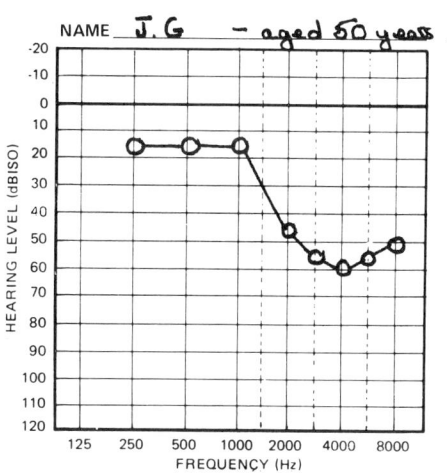

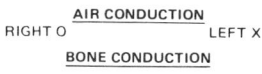

122 *Audiological Procedures in Differential Diagnosis*

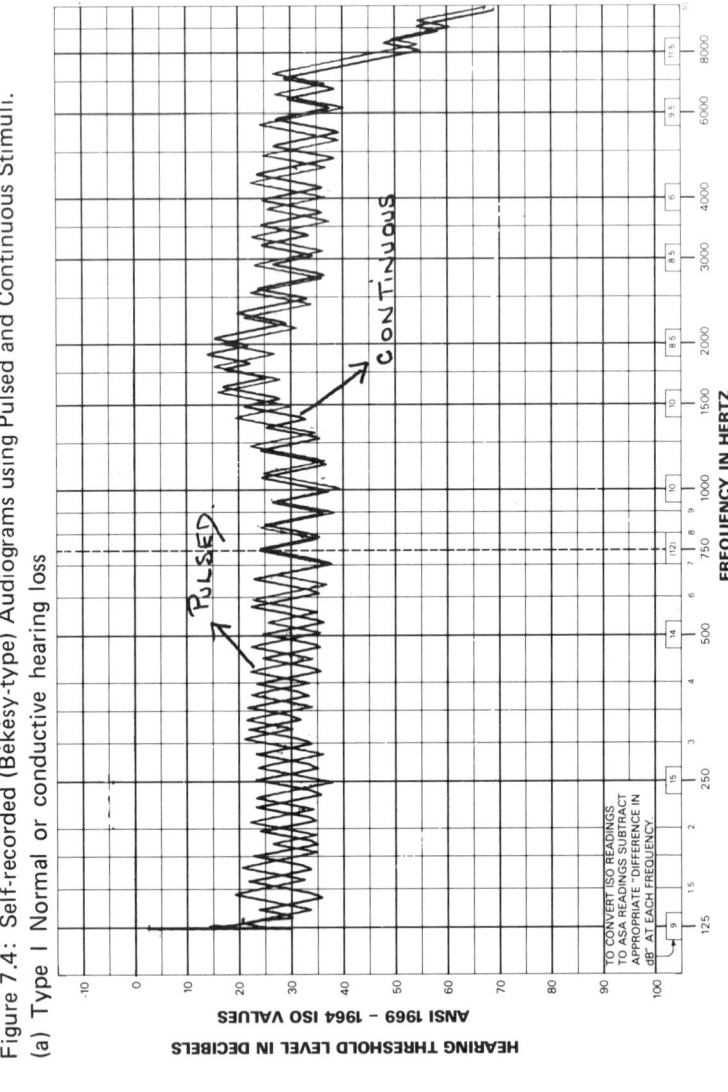

Figure 7.4: Self-recorded (Békésy-type) Audiograms using Pulsed and Continuous Stimuli. (a) Type I Normal or conductive hearing loss

Audiological Procedures in Differential Diagnosis 123

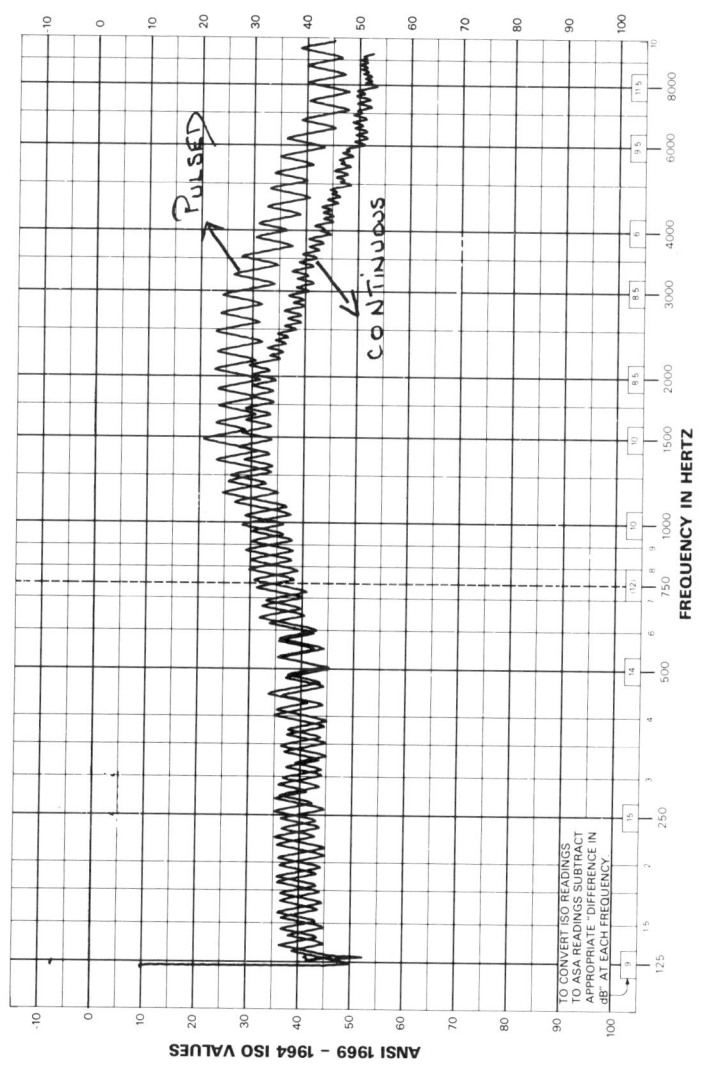

Figure 7.4 continued: (b) Type II Cochlear hearing loss

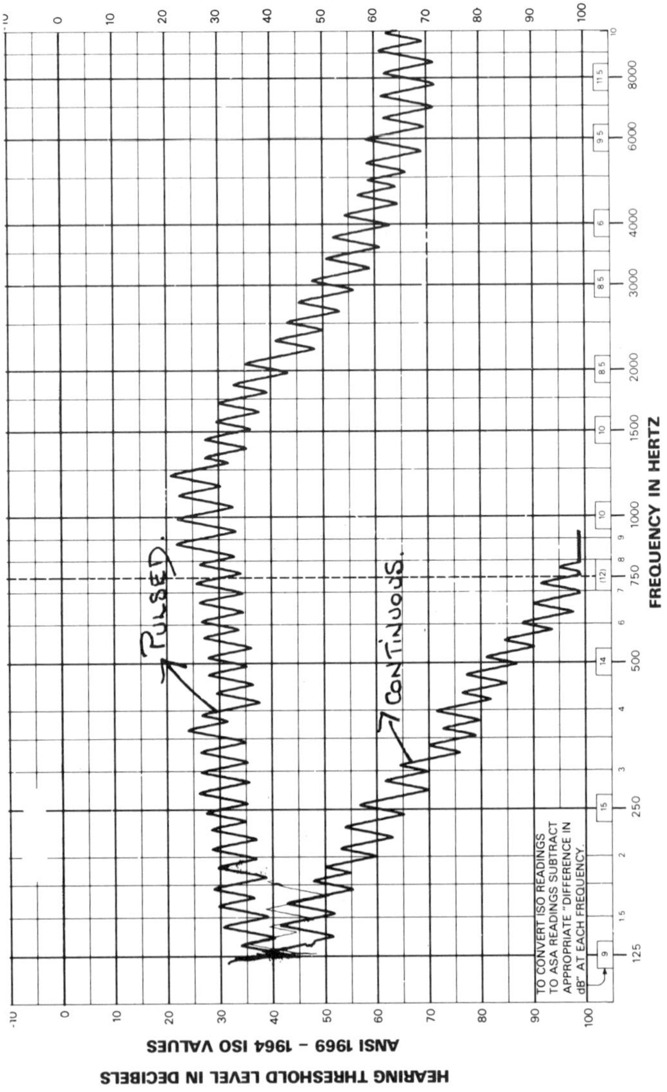

124 *Audiological Procedures in Differential Diagnosis*

Figure 7.4 continued: (c) Type III Retrocochlear hearing loss

Audiological Procedures in Differential Diagnosis 125

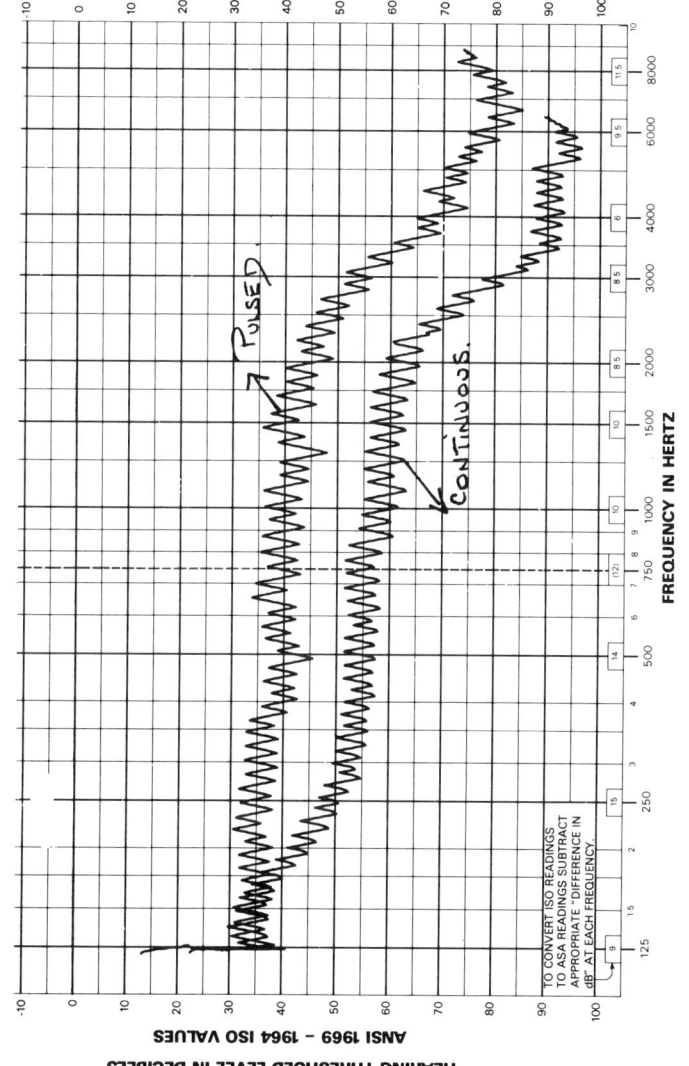

Figure 7.4 continued: (d) Type IV Retrocochlear hearing loss

Figure 7.4 continued: (e) Type V Non-organic hearing loss

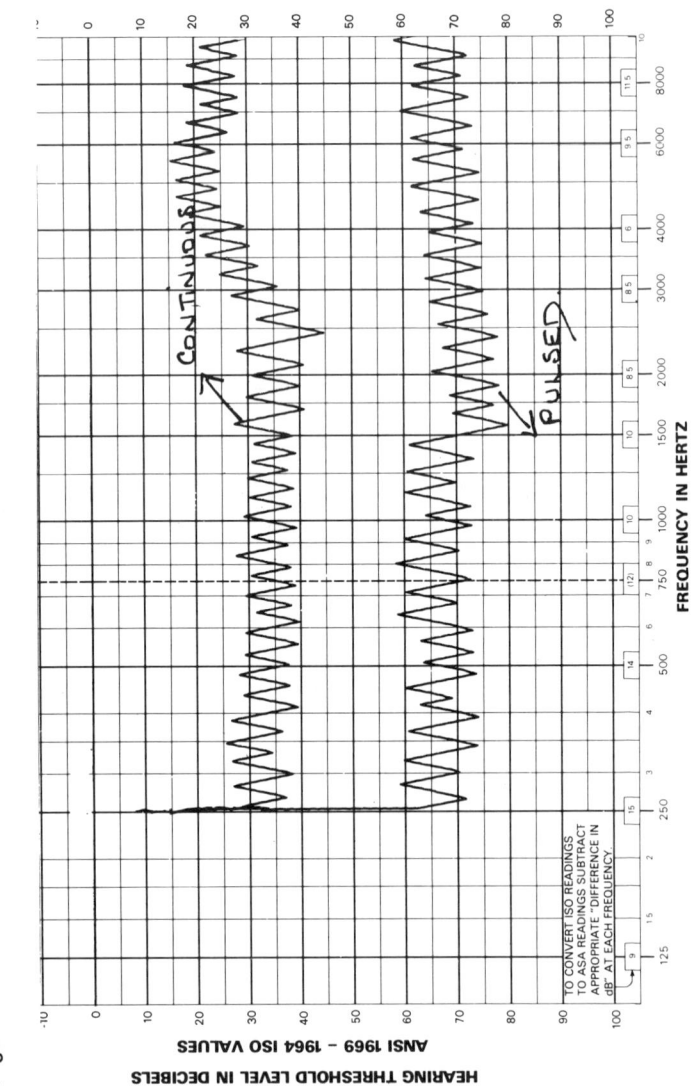

Audiological Procedures in Differential Diagnosis 127

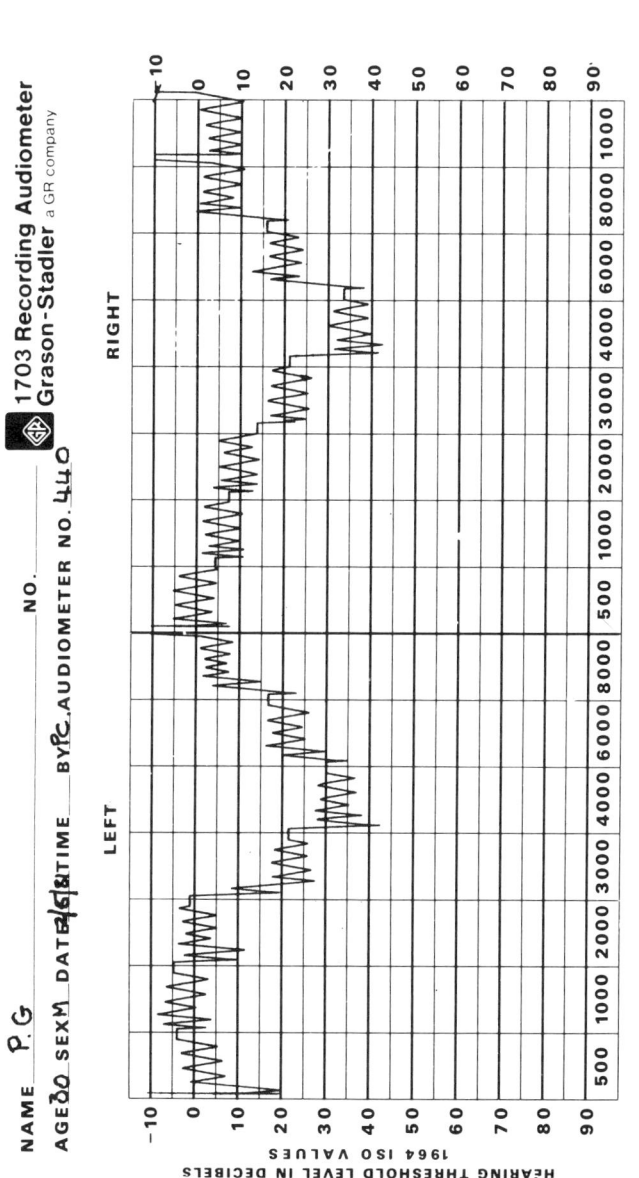

Figure 7.5: Simplified Self-recorded Audiogram using Fixed Frequencies and Pulsed Tones only. Noise-induced Hearing Loss. See also Figure 7.3(c)

Figure 7.6: Speech Audiogram. (a) Child aged 7 with Conductive Hearing Loss (relates to Figure 7.2(b)). Every word is repeated correctly providing the speech is sufficiently loud. (b) Shipyard Worker with Industrial Noise-induced Hearing Loss. Under the Best Conditions (a relative speech level of 50 dB), only 70% of the Words are repeated correctly. A Poorer Score results with Louder Speech (relates to Figure 7.3(d))

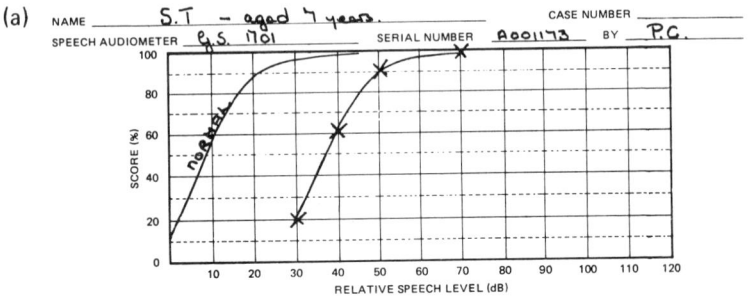

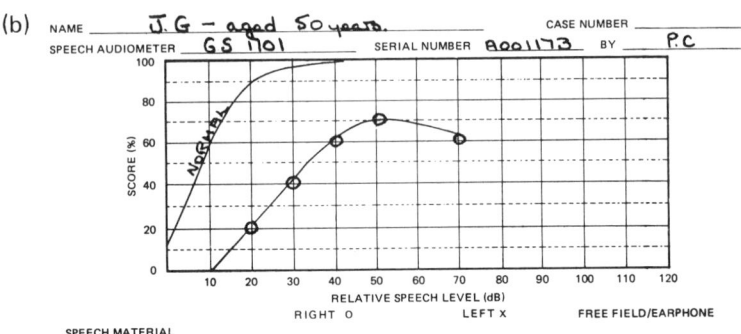

Figure 7.7: Acoustic Impedance Measurements — Tympanograms and Acoustic Reflex Measurements. (a) Normal subject. Tympanogram shows middle ear pressure of +15mms of water to be within normal limits; middle ear compliance of 0.8ml also in normal range. Reflex chart shows consistent reflexes at 1000 Hz 90 dB HL.

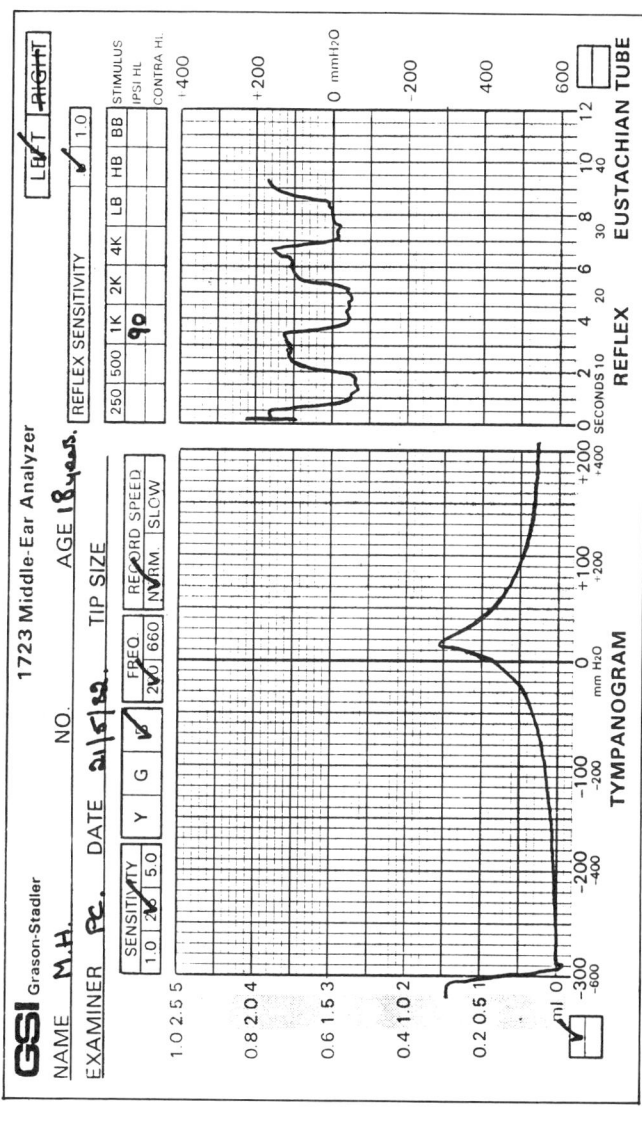

Figure 7.7 continued: (b) Child with 'glue ear' (See also Figure 7.2(b). Tympanogram shows no variation of middle ear compliance with change of pressure. Reflexes are absent

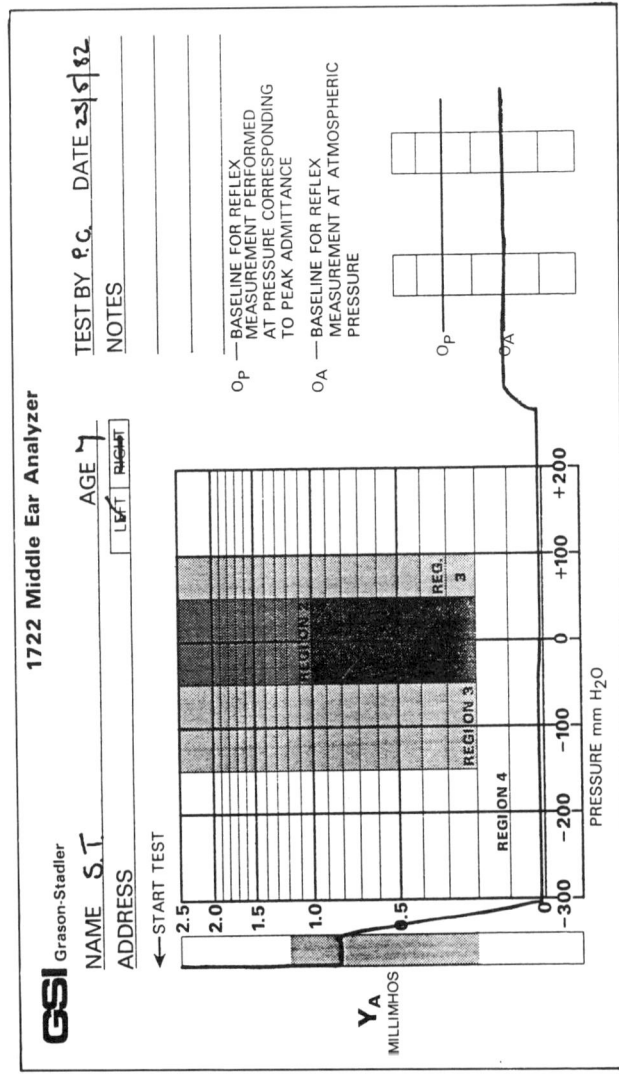

Figure 7.8: ERA Waveform of the Cortical Evoked Response in Normal Hearing averaged over 60 Presentations of a 100 millisecond Burst of 1000 Hz Tone at 50 dB above Threshold. The Characteristic Feature used for Threshold Assessment is the N_1/P_2 complex which disappears into the Background as the Intensity of the Stimulus is reduced. Its Latency (or delay) also increases as Hearing Threshold is approached

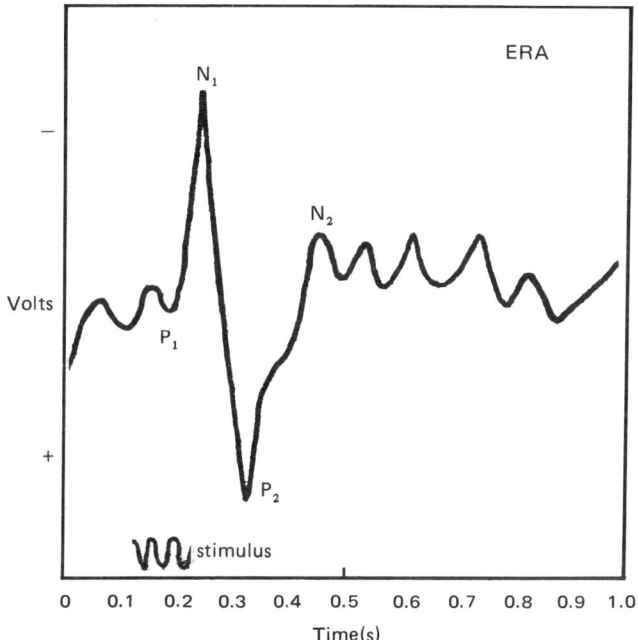

Figure 7.9: E. Coch. G. Waveform of the Action Potential AP and the Summating Potential SP (a) from a Normal Ear averaged over 50 presentations of clicks at a rate of 10 per second, at 70 dB above Threshold, (b) from an Ear with a tumour on the auditory nerve (acoustic neuroma) stimulated similarly. The characteristic feature here is the loss of the P_1 wave

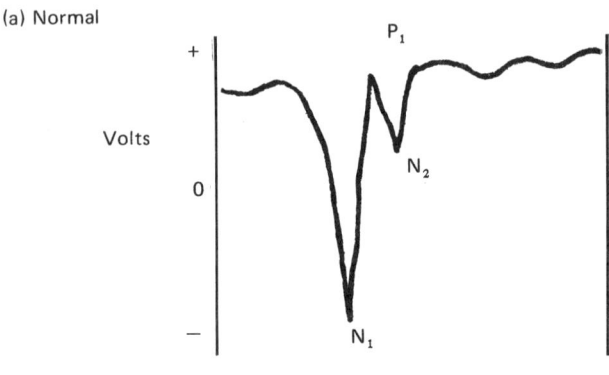

(a) Normal

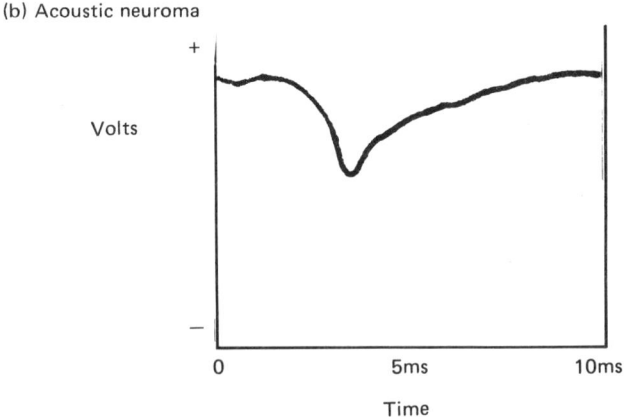

(b) Acoustic neuroma

Figure 7.10: BSER Waveform of the Brain Stem Electric Response in Normal Hearing averaged over 1000 clicks presented at a rate of 10 per second at 70 dB above threshold. Wave V is used for estimation of threshold and a prolonged latency indicates the possibility of a tumour

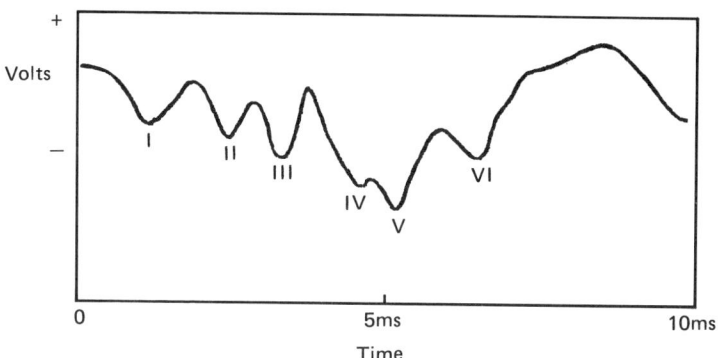

Further Reading

Beagley, H.A. (ed) (1979) *Auditory Investigation: The Scientific and Technological Basis*, Oxford University Press, Oxford
Beagley, H.A. (ed) (1981) *Audiology and Audiological Medicine*, Oxford University Press, Oxford
Department of Health and Social Security (1974) *Design Guide for E.N.T. Departments*. DHSS, London
Feldman, A.S. and Wilber, L.A. (eds) (1976) *Acoustic Impedance and Admittance: the Measurement of Middle Ear Function*, Williams and Wilkins, Baltimore
Hinchcliffe, R. and Harrison, D.F.N. (1976) *Scientific Foundations of Otolaryngology*, Heinemann, London
International Electrotechnical Commission (1979) *Audiometers, Publication 645* (Identical with British Standard (1980) Publication 5966).
International Organization for Standardization (1975) *Standard Reference Zero for the Calibration of Pure-Tone Audiometers. I.S.O. Recommendation R389*. (Also British Standard (1969-72) Publication 2497 Parts 1 to 4).

Note: British and International Standards are obtainable from the British Standards Institution, 101 Pentonville Road, London N1 9ND.

8 THE AUDIOLOGICAL PHYSICIAN

Larry Fisch

Significant developments have taken place in audiology during the past 15 years. The purely otological approach in the clinical investigation of hearing-impaired patients has proved to be inadequate in view of the better understanding of hearing impairment and vastly improved diagnostic facilities. Since it has been recognised that hearing impairment, as a communication disorder, has far-reaching social consequences and that it cannot be considered in isolation, and since the investigation of the needs of hearing-impaired people became more complex and more detailed, it has become apparent that it is impossible to deal with all requirements adequately even in the best-organised ear, nose and throat out-patients' department. Gradually it became obvious that special facilities were required. Those who deal with hearing-impaired people in this way must have wide knowledge of communication problems including all its social implications and they must have special training.

It became clear also that a single person was not able to perform adequately all the functions in connection with the rehabilitation of children, adults and elderly hearing-impaired people. All this experience led to the creation of a new specialty. Some ENT specialists gradually spent more and more time with hearing-impaired people and eventually they dedicated all their professional time to this subject. They became physicians rather than ear, nose and throat surgeons. Eventually, it was recognised that medical audiology should be practised by doctors who were specially trained for this work. At first many ENT surgeons understandably resented this splitting of a long-established specialty, particulary because they felt, quite rightly, that otology generally contributed so much to better understanding of the pathology, diagnosis, and treatment of various forms of deafness. On the other hand many ENT specialists today more fully appreciate the benefit of this development and value the help they can receive from a well-developed audiology department working in close co-operation with an ENT department.

Audiological medicine had also to evolve close co-operation with various other professions which previously did not have the opportunity to work closely with ENT surgeons. These include specialists in various problems of communication, social workers, teachers, organisations of hearing-impaired people, community health workers, and a variety of technicians and communication engineers. A busy ENT surgeon simply could not fulfil all these obligations because of inadequate time and lack of appropriate facilities. One of the best ways of presenting day-to-day work of the audiological physician is to reproduce a 'job description' of an authority advertising for such a person.

Job Description of the Audiological Physician

(1) The primary function of the audiological physician is to establish a differential diagnosis in a patient suspected of having a hearing loss, that is, providing an expert answer to the question: Has the patient a hearing loss or not? Once the audiological physician has established that the patient has a hearing loss he should be able to diagnose its nature, extent and causation. He should also be able to determine what treatment is possible or necessary.

(2) Following the diagnosis he should outline what further investigations are required in order to complete an all-round assessment of the patient with hearing impairment, and make all the necessary arrangements for various investigations to be carried out. He should be able to evaluate the results of these investigations and correlate them in a form which would provide an overall picture about the patient. Especially the audiological physician should carry out all the necessary investigations, or ask for these to be carried out, to find out whether the patient has other disabilities or abnormalities apart from the hearing impairment. These would include disturbance of balance, loudness perception abnormality or tinnitus.

(3) The audiological physician should be able to recommend, following the examination of the patient, the necessary steps in the patient's rehabilitation, training and improving or re-establishing his communication ability, in conjunction with the other members of the audiological team. He should co-ordinate all the efforts in the interest of the patient and make certain that these are as comprehensive as possible. He should be able to assess whether the patient can physically wear or use an applicance for amplification. For example, an elderly person with severe arthritis of fingers or hand may not be able to manipulate a post-aural aid.

(4) In order to achieve these aims, the audiological physician is

required to conduct regular clinics for examination of patients. He should be able to manage patients of all ages, including children, adults and the elderly. In the case of children, he should be able to carry out all the necessary tests of hearing in free field by behavioural observation or free field play audiometry and the various types of speech reception ability tests. He should determine which other special tests are required to complete the diagnosis. The audiological physician will then discuss the results with the members of the audiological team and also discuss with the parents all the relevant problems. He must then decide whether amplification can compensate for the loss of hearing and prescribe the most suitable hearing aid or other types of amplifiers. At this stage he should make arrangements with the hearing therapist or teacher of the deaf for training the person in its best use.

(5) The audiological physician will see patients affected by a great variety of disabilities and syndromes and is expected to recognise these syndromes, to have a detailed knowledge of them, and to be able to modify the examinations according to the patient's additional disability of behavioural disorder. He should understand the problems of the elderly and especially the effects of communication disability on their everyday life. He should carry out in due course a full otological examination of all patients.

(6) The audiological physician should obtain the history provided by the parents or relatives and by medical sources. Such a history should contain all the information necessary to make clear the possible cause of the hearing loss. A satisfactory explanation should be given to the parents, adult patients and their relatives so that they clearly understand. The physician should give detailed information to the hearing therapist or the teacher of the deaf about the nature of the clinical condition and its implications.

(7) In addition to the diagnostic work concerning new patients, the audiological physician should continue to reassess all patients with hearing impairment. Periodic reassessment must be an important part of the work. No patient should remain without appropriate reassessment for too long a period, and it should be the duty of the audiological physician to determine how often the patient should be reassessed and when the next examination should be carried out. When patients are reassessed the audiological physician should discuss the patient's progress with the hearing therapist or teacher of the deaf and should give them his expert opinion obtained from medical and other investigations. He should discuss in detail the patient's progress with the relatives, hearing therapist or teacher of the deaf.

(8) As part of the reassessment process the audiological physician should examine the patient's hearing aid and be able to judge whether the aid is adequate and used properly. He should consult the hearing therapist or teacher of the deaf about whether a better aid is required or available. He should carry out informal tests of discrimination with the aid and find out how the patient handles the instrument. He should then obtain more detailed tests of discrimination from his colleagues and tests of the performance of the aid from the technicians. He must be able then to evaluate the results of these tests. The audiological physician is expected to have a good technical knowledge of hearing aids and other types of amplifiers. Because of the rapid developments in this field, it must be part of his duties to keep this knowledge and information up to date. He should from time to time discuss this with the audiology technicians, hearing therapist or teacher of the deaf and see that up to date information is available and that his patients receive the best instruments to be had. Detailed attention must be paid to environmental aids especially in the case of the elderly. The audiological physician will rely to a great extent on the co-operation and reports of the hearing therapist who will assess the communication needs of the elderly hearing-impaired.

(9) The audiological physician should, as part of his routine work, prepare adequate records and ensure that the statistical aspect of recording is carried out. This is essential in order to be able to detect changing trends and also to plan for the future. He should be responsible for adequate statistical records of the rehabilitation work.

(10) The audiological physician should certainly be required to conduct research or investigative work, particularly into various problems which emerge as a result of routine practical work in the clinic. He should also encourage investigative work by the rest of the staff and should be able to give expert help and provide the necessary initiative to carry out such work. He should be able to judge how effective the rehabilitative work has been over a certain period of time.

(11) From time to time the audiological physician should inspect the equipment at the clinic and ensure that proper maintenance and calibration work is carried out. This should be done in conjunction with the audiology technician and the regional audiological scientist.

(12) The audiological physician should consider teaching as part of his routine work. The welfare of his patients depends to a great extent on a relatively large number of workers from various professions and they must be instructed adequately and provided with new information. Teaching, often of visiting staff, has to be carried out

frequently during routine clinics and the audiological physician must be prepared to do this. He should be prepared also to give lectures, conduct discussions and organise appropriate courses of instruction. As part of his routine work the audiological physician should reserve ample time for discussions with the rest of the staff concerning individual cases of patients and from time to time he should conduct case conferences.

(13) The audiological physician must co-operate closely especially with the hearing therapists and teachers attached to the clinic. They should be considered as integral members of the audiological team and people with whom the audiological physician co-operates very closely. He must therefore be fully conversant with the work of a hearing therapist or a teacher of the deaf. The audiological physician must do everything possible to help them in their work, and provide them with all the necessary information concerning the medical aspects of patients' abnormalities or difficulties.

(14) It is expected that the audiological physician will be well acquainted with the training, educational, social help and welfare facilities available in the region and the country as a whole, so that he should be better able to judge what the possibilities are for rehabilitation. From time to time he should visit special units or centres in his area and he should try to keep up his personal or indirect contacts with them.

(15) The audiological physician should call or organise from time to time meetings of all the staff to discuss current problems, deal with various difficulties that may emerge during the normal work of the clinic and discuss various plans for future requirements as regards equipment. He should discuss with them the new technical developments of communication aids.

(16) The audiological physician must be prepared to co-operate closely with all the other services concerned with the care of the hearing-impaired, that is, social, educational, hospital and general practitioner services, and he should provide all concerned with adequate information, which is essential for professionals whose work is concerned with hearing impairment.

(17) The audiological physician should from time to time examine the clinic facilities, especially to make sure that the environmental standards are maintained, such as acoustic conditions, general appearance and standards necessary for successful examination of patients.

Special Aspects of the Work of the Audiological Physician

It is most important for an audiological physician to extend his assessment beyond the immediate problem of the hearing loss as presented by the results of the various tests. First of all he should inquire into the general mental and physical health of the patient. Many physical conditions directly determine what kind of amplification systems are possible or unsuitable, as has already been pointed out. Severe arthritis of the hands for example, or any condition which considerably limits the fine movements, will be considered as a contra-indication to the use of a post-aural aid. It is important for any hearing-impaired person to be able to control the instrument for himself, otherwise he will depend on others, which is often impossible for many elderly people. Various physical conditions may also determine whether a body-worn aid should be used. Strenuous efforts should be made by the audiological physician to inform general practitioners about the problems of the elderly deaf and impress on them how much they can help. Details about the patient's health should be obtained from the GP or from hospitals when this is relevant to the communication problems caused by hearing loss. The audiological physician should discuss the clinical conditions in detail with the hearing therapist and explain their nature or consequences. A visit by the hearing therapist to the patient's home will make many problems clear and a report to the audiological physician will then provide a comprehensive picture of the patient's needs or difficulties which would otherwise be difficult to obtain.

The following are some of the special clinical conditions which are described in greater detail in order to illustrate in a practical form the complexities of the clinical work of the audiological physician. These examples show that close co-operation not only of the audiological team itself, but also of various other clinicians and other outside agencies, is essential.

Sudden Deafness

Sudden sensorineural hearing loss is relatively rare, but when it does occur prompt action needs to be taken. When a patient with this type of hearing loss is presented at the audiology clinic for examination by the audiological physician, he should make arrangements for such a patient to be investigated as an emergency in a neuro-otological unit, or better still he should ask for the patient to be admitted to a hospital where such a unit exists. It may be necessary to admit such a patient to a neurological unit. The reason for this is the fact that it may be one of the rare cases where the hearing could be restored, in spite of its being a sensorineural loss. Such cases may also need detailed investigation of the possible cause. It is most important that the audiological physician should remain in touch with the patient and that after release from the hospital, and especially if hearing has not been restored, he should take all the necessary action for rehabilitation. A patient who suddenly becomes deaf will almost certainly be seriously affected psychologically and socially. If he is still working, his occupation may be threatened and therefore co-operation with the hearing therapist and urgent measures for rehabilitation will be necessary. The co-operation of a psychologist may be required and if the hearing loss is so profound that it almost amounts to total deafness, it may be necessary to arrange for the patient to attend a course in a centre for rehabilitation of such patients. In England it would be the Link Centre in Eastbourne, which is the only centre of this kind. It is essential that the patient should be in continuous contact with the audiology clinic and be seen regularly by the hearing therapist.

Various types of modern communication aids may be required and some clinical tests may have to continue in order to detect any possible neurological complications which did not appear at the initial stages. The co-operation of many other organisations or agencies will be required and continuous reassessment is essential. The hearing therapist may have to investigate the problems of maintaining the present occupation of such a person, and what can be done from the point of view of modern communication aids. The audiological physician may want to refer the patient back later for further neurological investigation in order to detect possible complications and he may wish to consult several of his colleagues.

Disorders of Balance

The audiological physician should be able to deal with disorders of balance, especially when associated with a hearing loss. He should always make inquiries into possible symptoms of balance disorders and be able to determine whether the symptoms are due to vestibular abnormality (true vertigo) or 'fainting attacks', 'falling about', and so on, caused by some other physical non-vestibular disorder. Most audiology centres may not be equipped with the more sophisticated and complex apparatus for diagnosing vestibular disorders (electronystagmography, strictly regulated and controlled rotational tests, caloric tests, etc.) but even then the various simpler diagnostic procedures should be carried out. These may reliably indicate that the symptoms of disturbed balance are of vestibular origin and if necessary referral to a neuro-otological unit may be indicated for further more detailed investigation.

Neuro-Otology

When investigating hearing loss, the audiological physician should always be on the look-out for possible associated symptoms which may indicate more serious neurological involvement. This applies not only to bilateral hearing losses but to unilateral ones as well. An acquired or progressive unilateral loss will alert him to the possibility of the presence of an acoustic tumour and referral for detailed neuro-otological investigation will be an urgent matter. Newly acquired and quickly progressing hearing losses will alert him in the same manner. Examining the stapedius reflex in detail with the help of a modern impedance meter may lead to a differential diagnosis indicating urgent treatment. A well-trained audiological physician will be familiar with the neurological anatomy and physiology of the stapedius reflex and suspect or diagnose an acoustic tumour following the appropriate tests.

The Otological Examination

An audiological physician is trained in the examination of ears, diagnosing middle ear disease and reliably establishing the differential diagnosis between conductive and sensorineural hearing loss. He should be able to make a decision concerning referral to an ENT specialist. Close co-operation between the two specialties is essential. Many patients are examined by both the audiological physician and the ENT surgeon and an amicable relationship between the two is essential. It is a great advantage if they are able to elaborate a common policy and outlook. This is essential for a successful audiology service.

Hearing Loss from Noise Damage

Hearing loss from excessive noise, as a single or a contributory cause in an already existing sensorineural loss, should be remembered as a possibility and an inquiry about exposure to noise should be part of the history-taking. The audiological physician should be familiar with various conditions which produce an 'at risk' situation for a patient who already has a hearing loss when exposed to high noise levels. He should be able to explain the risk and the prognosis to the patient. In co-operation with the hearing therapist, he may have to discuss the social consequences of maintaining the patient's present occupation or the possibilities of reducing noise levels in the person's place of work. In this context the audiological physician must be fully aware of legal requirements as they now stand and of legislation relating to claims made as a result of noise damage. He may be asked to attend a court where such cases are being considered and therefore the audiological physician must be clear about how much of the hearing loss is due to noise effect and whether it contributed to the present level of loss. He should also be aware that he may be asked to give evidence concerning past hearing loss of the claimant, especially if the patient attended an audiology clinic for some time. He may even have to ask for the records of school screening audiometry, if available. If he can produce evidence that hearing loss was already present at a younger age, or before the person started work, it may be decisive as far as a claim is concerned. Such aspects of noise-induced deafness are of increasing importance in audiological medicine.

An important factor in connection with noise-induced deafness is the problem of prevention. In young persons with even a very moderate sensorineural loss, it is essential to warn them about the possibilities of noise damage. Persons with slight or very moderate sensorineural high-frequency losses should be considered 'at risk'. This should be explained to the young person when the question of selecting a future occupation is discussed and a careful record should be kept in the patient's case notes. These notes are confidential but may be used as a legal document in court proceedings.

Health education about noise prevention should be part of the audiological physician's work. Such education covers not only industrial noise, or noise connected with type of occupation, but also 'entertainment noise' created by the use of powerful amplifiers. Noise-induced deafness is on the increase. Its onset is insidious and in the initial stages it may remain symptomless for some time. Legislation as a result of accumulating experience is bound to change from time to time and the audiological physician should follow developments closely, from both the clinical and legal points of view.

Research and Epidemiology

It should be the responsibility of the audiological physician to arrange for proper statistical records to be kept. This is especially important for the purposes of epidemiological research. Detection of changes in the prevalance of hearing loss and in the structure of the hearing-impaired population, and detection of trends in the causation of hearing loss are important considerations when planning the future of services and estimating the resources that will be required. For example, special investigations may be initiated when it has been noticed that in particular districts the number of patients with hearing loss resulting from noise damage has increased. Special hearing problems may be detected in immigrant or ethnic groups. The genetic composition of the population may also change. Prevention of hearing loss should always be in the mind of the audiological physician, and without occasional epidemiological surveys such work would be difficult. In this context he may have to co-operate closely with the health and education departments of the various local authorities concerned. In fact, where hearing problems are concerned, health education should be considered an important part of the audiological physician's work and his co-operation with various other organisations will also be required. Hearing loss can never be considered in isolation and its social consequences are inevitable. This enlarges the scope of the work of the audiological physician who should consider the preparation of publications, or helping to prepare them in co-operation with the health and education authorities.

Research should be considered an essential part of the work. Hearing loss is not a static disorder in its social context. Continuous changes are taking place. Causes of deafness which were previously highly significant may become less important and new causes (for example from new drugs) may appear at any time. Monitoring these changes should be part and parcel of the work of an audiology clinic. Some of these changes may be local and therefore one cannot depend only on a nation-wide change in this respect. For this reason the audiological physician should be well acquainted with research methods, basic concepts of statistics and, to an increasing degree, with computer-processing and information. It is almost inevitable that the audiology clinic should have a close association with a computer centre. It would not be surprising if in due course a small computer should become an essential part of clinic equipment. If we are to progress and improve the quality of the work it will be essential for the audiological physician to be familiar with this aspect of research.

The Audiology Team and the Audiology Clinic

Because of the complexities of audiology it can never be practised properly by one person only. The very nature of the specialty dictates the need for team-work and the audiological physician should consider himself as part of a team without a notion of any hierarchy within such a team. Nobody should be considered more important than anybody else, although there must be one person who takes the final responsibility for the patient; the audiological physician is in the best position to do this.

It is essential that the members of the team should think in the same terms and share the same general philosophy of the nature of their work. They should be generally in agreement about the fundamental problems of rehabilitation, training, communication problems and social consequences of hearing loss. The audiological physician should consider it his responsibility to explain in detail the clinical aspects of the hearing loss of each patient to the members of the team. It is important that no serious divisions should exist within the team and if such divisions do exist it is the responsibility of the audiological physician either to resolve them or to re-organise the team. It is also his duty to make certain that all the information concerning the patient is confidential and must stay so, and all members of the team must be made fully aware of it. This is of prime importance because in some cases it could be the explicit wish of a patient that the fact that his hearing is impaired should remain confidential. Naturally, attempts will be made to convince such a person that it is much more advantageous to be open and not to hide the hearing loss, because this may make communication problems even more difficult. But this will have to remain the patient's decision. The stigma of 'deafness' in society (although to varying degrees in different countries) still prevails and the audiology team should try to help to overcome it as much as possible and alleviate its effects on the patient and his relatives.

First of all it is most important that the environment in which patients are examined should be suitable not only from the point of view of acoustics and satisfactory ventilation, but also from the point of view of reducing the natural anxieties of patients and their relatives. A friendly and relaxing atmosphere is absolutely essential. Unfortunately, this is often neglected in many centres. It should be emphasised that anxiety in a patient may not only prevent various examinations and tests being made but may directly produce false results. For example, in the case of children, if a child is extremely anxious, it is best not to attempt a test. In many ways, although not to the same degree, this also applies to elderly people, who can be extremely anxious. The manner of examination and the approach by the audiological physician and members of the team may be decisive. When the patient enters the examination room, this should be the first consideration and everything should be done to reduce the anxiety of the patient. One could say that if the patient leaves the centre more anxious than when he arrived, the audiological physician has failed in his duty.

The second important consideration is establishing communication with the patient. This may necessitate quick judgement (which is learnt by experience) in an audiological clinic for adults. Modern equipment should be installed so as to provide for direct person-to-person contact between doctor and patient. This can be achieved nowadays very satisfactorily and should be part and parcel of the equipment of the centre. Suitable communication aids could be almost built into the desk where the patient is interviewed. In the case of children, the parents will always be available, but elderly patients often come on their own and therefore they should be encouraged to bring their relatives on subsequent visits. Although the hearing therapist will provide all the necessary information as soon as possible, it is useful even after the first examination to give printed information in the form of leaflets explaining the various conditions and what is necessary for patients to do. Experience shows that patients may come away from the clinic after the first examination without understanding much of what the doctor said and may remain confused. Where a hearing therapist is available, the situation is much more favourable. Home visits may well provide conditions in which essential communication will be established. In this way everything can be explained in greater detail step by step, when the patient is more relaxed and less anxious. The process of rehabilitation can then start in earnest.

9 THE DESIGN AND USE OF HEARING AIDS

Michael C. Martin

Hearing aids of an acoustic type have been used for centuries and still have a place in modern society. Electrical aids of the carbon type were introduced at the turn of the century and electronic aids using thermionic valves were introduced in the mid-twenties. In 1953 the first hearing aid using transistors was introduced, which heralded the advent of the all-transistor body-worn aid, spectacle aids in 1954, aids worn behind the ear in 1956 and all-in-the-ear aids in 1957.

From the above it can be seen that two important technological steps have led to present-day aids. First, the introduction of thermionic valves and their subsequent development allowed body-worn hearing aids to be brought down to a size that still remains today. Secondly, the introduction of the transistor allowed the hearing aid to be run off one battery and in conjunction with the reduction in size of other components also allowed aids to be reduced sufficiently in size to be worn on the head and in the bowl of the ear. Consequently in terms of ease of wearing hearing aids the steps forward have been very significant. This is therefore seen by many people as the most significant development for the hearing-impaired and in certain respects this would not be denied. However, if one looks beyond the ease of wearing the hearing aid, the advances may be seen to be much less spectacular. Hearing aids will be worn only if they are socially acceptable or vital to a person's everyday life. Unfortunately hearing aids are still not socially acceptable in general and they are not vital to many people. A major public relations and educational problem therefore still exists to make people aware of the benefits that could be obtained from the use of aids.

In order to appreciate the advances it is important to understand what hearing aids can do in terms of acoustical performance and what hearing problems they are attempting to alleviate. This chapter will therefore be divided into two parts covering first the design and performance of hearing aids and then the perceptual problems of hearing impaired people.

Design and Performance of Hearing Aids

Basic Design

All hearing aids consist of four functional parts, i.e. microphone, amplifier, earphone and power supply. In the design of a hearing aid all four parts are of course highly relevant and the requirements of each section are discussed below.

Microphone. The microphone places the first limitation on performance, as the amplifier and earphone that follows the microphone can amplify only those signals that are passed through by the microphone. Microphones vary in terms of the manner in which sound is turned into electrical signals and whether they are directional or omnidirectional (respond equally to sound coming from all angles). Three types of microphone have been used in hearing aids and these are magnetic, piezo electric and electret designs.

The magnetic microphone is one where a coil and a magnet move in relation to each other in response to sound falling upon a diaphragm attached to either the coil or the magnet, depending upon the design. This type of microphone suffers the disadvantages of having a poor low-frequency response, a remaining somewhat irregular frequency response, and being susceptible to vibration and stray magnetic fields. It was, however, widely used in earlier transistor hearing aids and does have a low output impedance as well as being relatively inexpensive.

The piezo electric microphone consists of a bar of piezo electric material which if bent or deformed produces a voltage across its surface. This voltage is present at a high impedance and therefore has to be fed into an amplifier with an equivalent high input impedance. The old valve aids had the necessary high input impedance and therefore used this type of microphone which was then called a crystal microphone. Crystal microphones have very good low-frequency responses, providing they feed into a high impedance, but have a somewhat irregular high-frequency response. In recent years new piezo electric materials called Ceramics have been available and Ceramic microphones are used in hearing aids with the high impedance amplifier built into the case of the microphone. The older transistor amplifier originally had a low input impedance and therefore could not be easily used with crystal microphones. Piezo electric microphones are also prone to producing signals when vibrated and this manifests itself as noise to the listener.

In recent times the electret microphone has become widely used.

This microphone works as a condensor microphone but with the high polarising voltage of a condensor microphone being replaced by an electret foil. The electret microphone is basically a high impedance device and a preamplifier is built into the microphone housing to overcome this problem, as with the piezo electric microphone. The electret microphone has the advantages that it can be made very small and has a very wide flat frequency response; it is also relatively immune to producing noise when vibrated and hence is widely used in modern hearing aids.

Directional characteristics can be achieved with most types of microphone. It is important to note that the directional effects occur at low frequencies and are greatly modified when the aid is worn on the head. The directional effect itself is achieved by having two openings in the microphone which allow low-frequency sound to cancel out. It is very easy to identify a directional aid by looking for two microphone openings.

Amplifier. The amplifier of the hearing aid increases the size of the very small electrical signal from the microphone sufficiently to provide the earphone with sufficient power to produce the required sound output. The design of the amplifier has to ensure that it has sufficient gain to produce the required output power with minimum distortion and is electrically stable. In addition the amplifier will generate electrical noise which must be kept sufficiently low so that it is not discernible to the listener. The higher the output power of the amplifier the higher the drain will be from the battery which reflects on the hours of use. The amplifier will also be the means by which tone control is achieved as well as other features such as automatic gain control (AGC) and peak clipping (PC). These features will be discussed later.

Earphone. Hearing aid earphones of the button type used with body-worn aids have a very good low-frequency response but are strictly limited at high frequencies particularly when high output sound levels are required; the higher the output the more restricted the higher frequency response will be. Earphones used in head-worn aids have a sound outlet tube which goes into the ear canal. These earphones have a more restricted low-frequency response and are not capable of delivering such high outputs as the button type earphone. It must be remembered that the acoustic tube connecting the earphone to the ear canal can significantly alter the performance of the aid.

The Design and Use of Hearing Aids 149

Power Supply. The power supply for a hearing aid is very often a primary cell, often loosely called a battery. A battery is in fact a number of cells joined together. Primary cells are those that can only be used once, while secondary cells are the rechargeable type which can be used many times with appropriate recharging. Group hearing aids and auditory training units may well have mains-operated power supplies. Cells differ in four ways: first their size and shape, secondly the voltage they provide, thirdly the manner in which the voltage they provide changes as they are used, and finally the capacity of the cell

Figure 9.1(a): Average Discharge Curve for Cells Used in Hearing Aids (L = battery life)

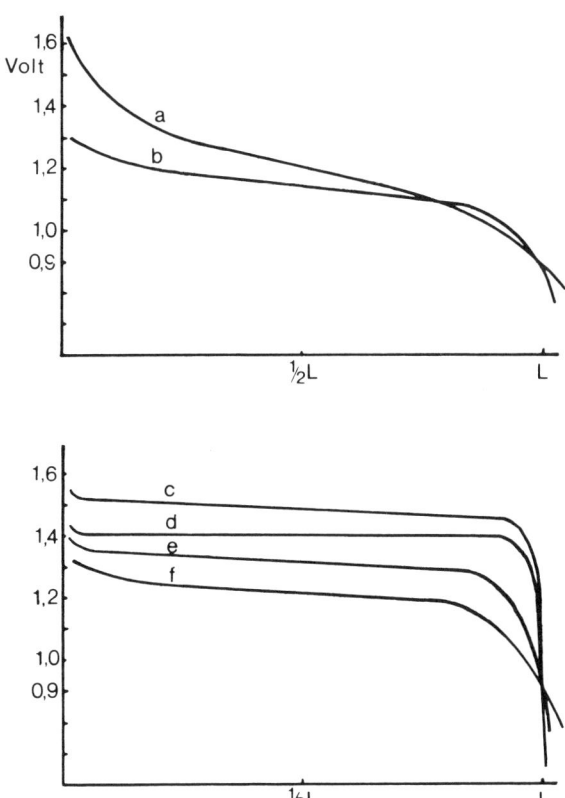

a R 6 carbon-zinc, b R 6 alkaline, c R 44 and R 48 silver oxide, d R 44 zinc-air, e R 44 and R 48 mercury oxide, f R 44 and R 48 nickel-cadmium (rechargeable)

Figure 9.1(b): Relative Change in dB From Maximum Amplification and Maximum Sound Intensity Caused by Changes in Battery Voltage. a. and b. Maximum amplification and sound intensity respectively in a modern Hearing Aid (AD 400 series, Phillips). c. and d. The same, but in an older type of Hearing Aid

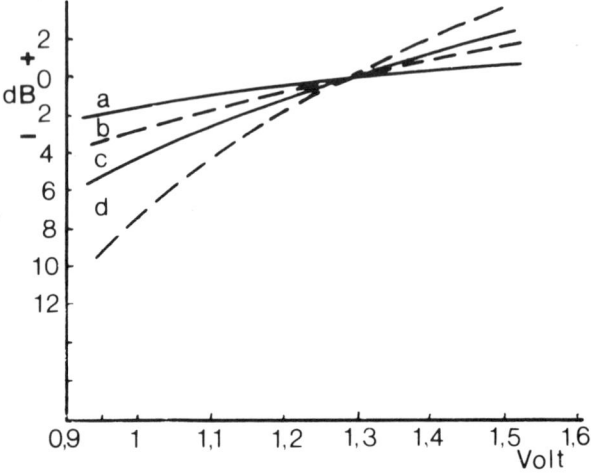

Note: Diagrams reproduced by courtesy of Phillips Product Information Service Hearing Aids.

i.e. the amount of energy it stores. Cells used in hearing aids are chosen to give a cost effective life with a minimum size. Figure 9.1 shows the characteristics of various types of cell used in hearing aids.

The capacity of a cell is described in terms of the ampere hours it will give. This means a cell that can deliver 5 amps for 1 hour will have a 5 ampere hour (5Ah) capacity. In hearing aids typical capacities will be not in Ah but milliampere hours. To calculate the life of a cell in a particular hearing aid, take the capacity of the cell and divide it by the current taken by the aid as in the example below.

Current taken by aid 1.5mA. Capacity of cell 180mAh

$$\text{Expected life of battery} = \frac{180}{1.5} = 120 \text{ Hours}$$

Objective Measurement of Hearing Aid Performance

It is possible to measure the electro-acoustic performance of a hearing aid in a variety of ways. It is quite possible that each of these ways will give a different answer and therefore it becomes important to standardise the methods of measurement. The International Electrotechnical Commission (IEC) has laid down a series of standards (listed in Table 9.1) that describe the agreed method of measurement, as well as important features of hearing aids. These standards are reflected in national standards such as those produced by the British Standards Institute (BSI). It is most important to note that the measurements described in IEC hearing aid standards are objective and not subjective and therefore do not necessarily relate closely to what will happen when the aid is worn by a hearing-impaired individual.

Table 9.1: List of IEC Standards relating to Hearing Aids

IEC 118-0	Hearing aids. Measurement of electroacoustical characteristics.
IEC 118-1	Method of measurement of characteristics of hearing aids with induction pick-up coil input.
IEC 118-2	Hearing aids with automatic gain control circuits.
IEC 118-3	Hearing aid equipment not entirely worn on the listener.
IEC 118-4	Magnetic field strength in audio-frequency induction loops for hearing aid purposes.
IEC 118-5	Nipples for insert earphones.
IEC 118-6	External electrical inputs to personal hearing aids (in preparation).
IEC 118-7	Measurement of performance characteristics of hearing aids for quality inspection for delivery purposes.
IEC 118-8	Measurement of hearing aids under simulated in situ working conditions (in preparation).
IEC 118-9	Measurement of characteristics of hearing aids with bone vibrator outputs (in preparation).
IEC 118-10	Guide to hearing aid standards (in preparation).
IEC 118-11	Symbols and other markings on hearing aids and related equipment.
IEC 90	Dimensions of plugs for hearing aids.
IEC 126	IEC reference coupler for the measurement of hearing aids using earphones coupled to the ear by means of ear inserts.
IEC 303	IEC provisional coupler for the calibration of earphones used in audiometry.
IEC 318	An IEC artificial ear of the wide band type, for the calibration of earphones used in audiometry.
IEC 373	An IEC mechanical coupler for the calibration of bone vibrators having a specific contact area and being applied with a specific static force.
IEC 711	Occluded ear simulator for the measurement of earphones coupled to the ear by ear inserts.

152 *The Design and Use of Hearing Aids*

Equipment for Measuring Hearing Aid Performance

In order to measure the performance of a hearing aid it is necessary to place it in a known sound field to ensure that the input to the microphone is accurately known. Furthermore the acoustic output from the earphone must be measured in an agreed manner. The ideal situation for objective hearing aid testing is in a free field such as that produced by an anechoic chamber. In a free field the walls of the room do not influence in any way the sound falling on the hearing aid. In practice only a few specialised laboratories will have anechoic chambers and the tests have to be undertaken in test boxes or chambers. Depending upon

Figure 9.2: Difference in Output of Hearing Aid measured in 2 cc Acoustic Coupler (lower curve) and Occluder Ear Simulator (upper curve)

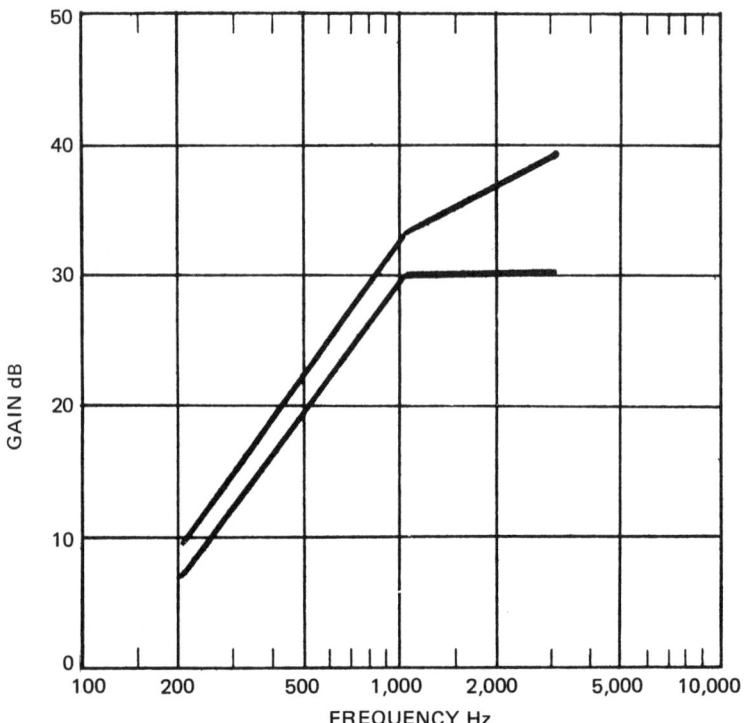

their design, these boxes will approximate to a free field condition to a greater or lesser extent. Measurement of the performance of aids with directional microphones cannot usually be made in a test box and this is an indication of their limitations.

Acoustic Couplers and Artificial Ears

The measurement of the sound from a hearing aid earphone is complicated by the fact that there are two standardised devices to perform this task. One is the 2 cc acoustic coupler (IEC 126) while the other is the IEC 711 occluded ear simulator. The difference between the two devices is that the acoustic coupler is not designed to replicate the acoustic properties of a real ear whereas the ear simulator has acoustic properties that relate to the average adult ear. The same hearing aid measured on these two devices would show a different performance (Figure 9.2). It is therefore important when looking at hearing aid measurements to know which device the aid was measured on. A further complication is that audiometer earphones are measured on two other different devices called an acoustic coupler (IEC 303) and a wide band artificial ear (IEC 318). Table 9.1 lists current devices for measuring the performance of earphones.

In situ Measurements

Most measurements on hearing aids are made without the presence of the user. When aids are worn their frequency response then changes and in order to take this effect into account measurements are made on an artificial head and torso. One widely used device of this sort is called KEMAR. (Knowles Electronic Manikin for Acoustical Research). Measurements made in this manner are referred to as in situ measurements and will differ considerably from other measurements.

Audiometric Zero and Hearing Aid Characteristics

There is a strong temptation by many people to relate audiograms to hearing aid performance by directly comparing the two sets of data. It must be remembered however that audiometric zero varies in terms of sound pressure level and has different values depending upon the earphone used with the audiometer. Figure 9.3 shows how audiometric zero varies with frequency and how a typical audiogram is modified in shape by converting it to sound pressure level. In summary the problems in trying to relate audiograms to details of hearing aid characteristics with any degree of accuracy are large, leaving aside any perceptual

Figure 9.3(a): Sound Pressure Level for Audiometric Zero as measured with a TDH 39 earphone with an MX 41/AR earcap in a 9A Acoustic Coupler. These values have to be added to audiogram levels to convert audiograms to sound pressure level

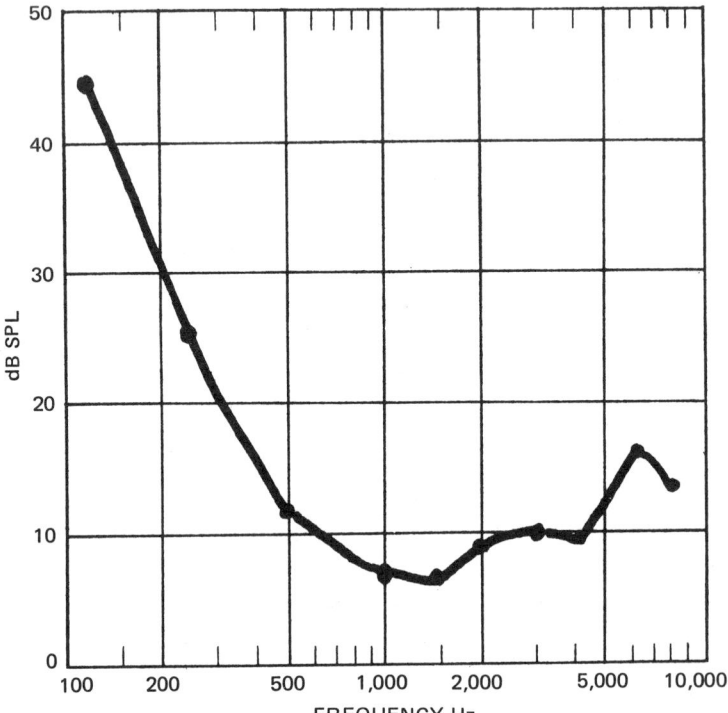

problems of the hearing-impaired person and considering acoustical factors only. The pure tone audiogram should only be used as a guide to the start of a proper hearing aid fitting procedure.

Basic Hearing Aid Characteristics

The basic characteristics of a hearing aid are best shown by a family of frequency response curves (Figure 9.4). These curves show the frequency response of the hearing aid with different input sound pressure

The Design and Use of Hearing Aids 155

Figure 9.3(b): Audiogram to be Converted to Sound Pressure Level

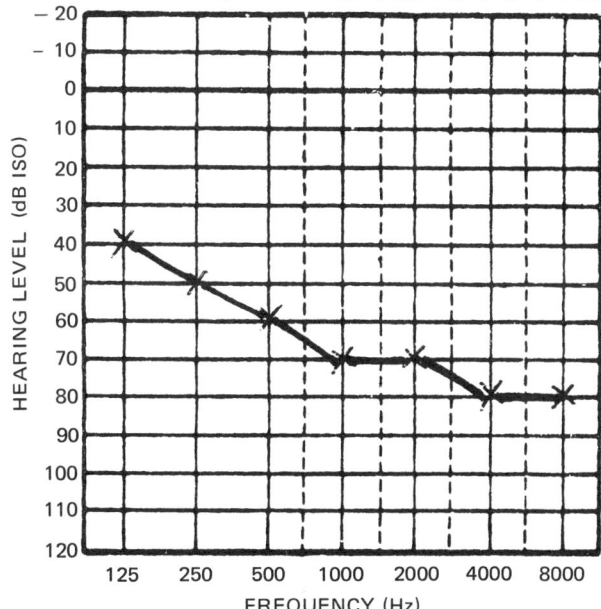

Figure 9.3(c): Audiogram Converted to Sound Pressure Level

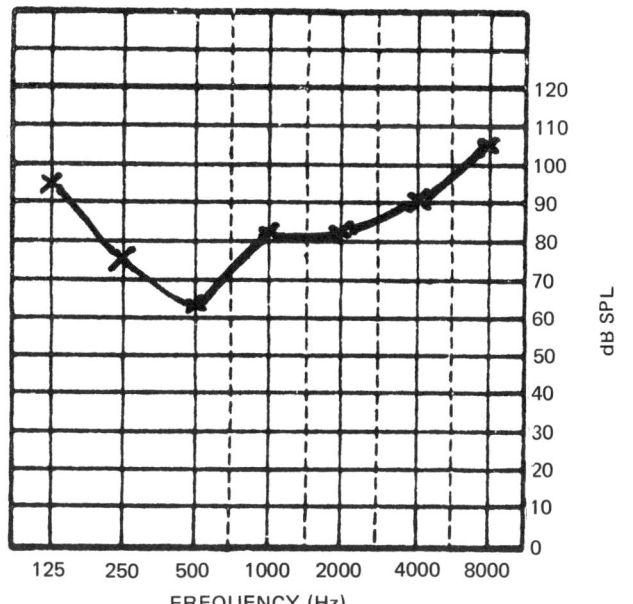

levels. The first thing to note is that the curves are parallel to each other at lower input levels and then get closer together as the input increases. Where the curves are parallel it indicates that the aid is operating in a linear manner; input and output sound pressure are directly related so that a 10 dB change in input causes a 10 dB change in output. Above the linear range the characteristic becomes non linear i.e. a 10 dB change in input does not give a 10 dB change in output, and as a consequence distortion occurs.

It is in the linear portion of the characteristic that the gain of the aid is calculated by subtracting the input from the output sound level. It is also in this linear region that what is normally called the frequency response of the aid is described. Each curve is a frequency response but at the higher input levels the response is measured in a non-linear region and therefore shows a different frequency response and gain characteristic. The highest output that the aid can give is called the maximum acoustic output and often has a nearly flat frequency response curve, particularly with body-worn aids; this is basically the response of the earphone with the amplifier and microphone responses being masked out by overloading of the output stage of the amplifier. All these characteristics, frequency response, gain and maximum acoustic output, can be changed either by selecting different aids, altering the user and preset controls, changing the earphones on body aids or by altering the earmould and/or sound outlet tubing from the aid.

The family of frequency response curves gives the fullest information but it is sometimes of value to look at the way the output changes with variation of input at one frequency (Figure 9.5). The input output graph is often used for showing the effects of volume control settings and automatic gain control (AGC) in aids.

Distortion

Distortion is often spoken about, but in order for the term to be meaningful the type of distortion has to be stated. Commonly described forms of distortion are harmonic and intermodulation distortion but also related are transient and phase distortion. In fact these distortions are all different measurements of the same phenomena, the non-linear amplification of the hearing aid.

Figure 9.4(a): Frequency Response of Post-aural Aid with inputs of 50, 60, 70, 80, 90 dB SPL maximum gain control setting

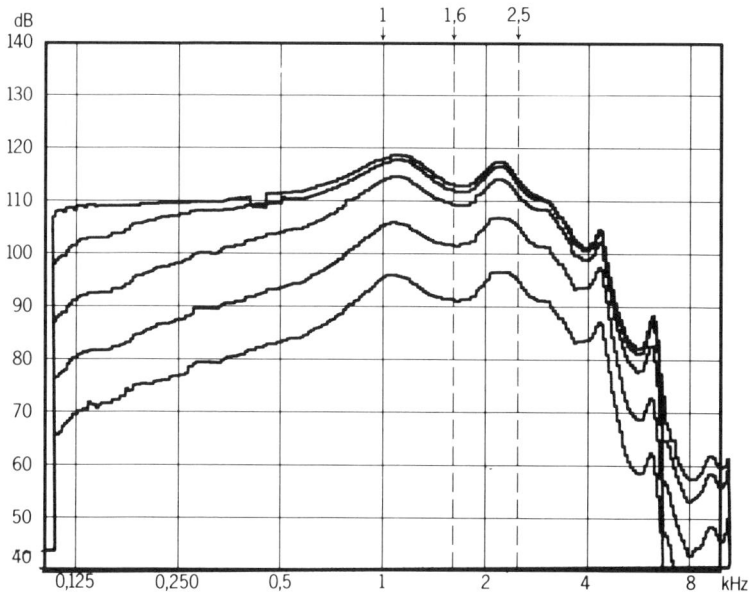

Harmonic Distortion

If a pure tone, which in theory contains energy at only one frequency, is fed into a hearing aid and the output of that aid analysed it may be found that energy exists not only at the input frequency but at other frequencies. These other frequencies may be harmonically related, that is they occur at the same interval as the test tone which is called the fundamental. A 500Hz test tone will generate harmonics at 1000, 1500, 2000, 2500, 3000 Hz and so on. In practice the first few harmonics will be the largest and they will rapidly become smaller as the frequency increases (Figure 9.6). Distortion is often expressed as total harmonic distortion (THD). This is measured by taking the level of the total signal coming out of the hearing aid and then subtracting the level of the fundamental from it. The signal that remains is then the

158 *The Design and Use of Hearing Aids*

Figure 9.4(b): As Figure 9.4(a) but with Gain Control reduced to half full setting

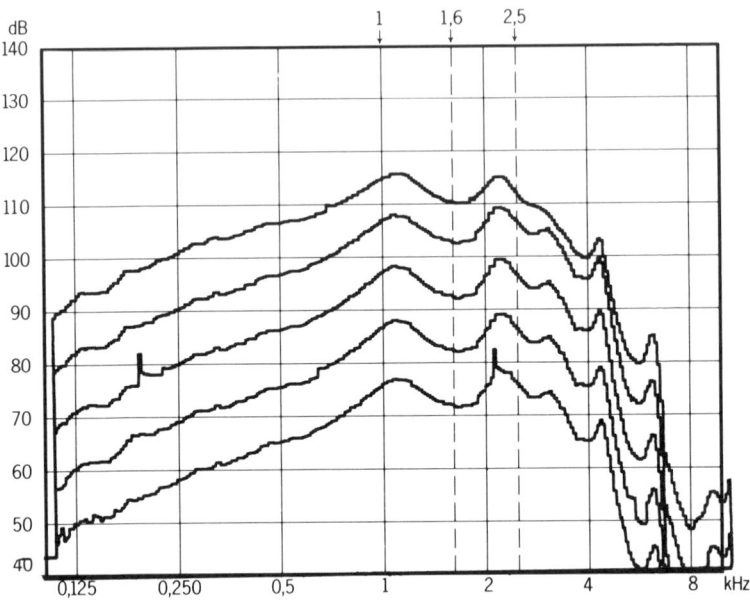

sum of all the harmonics plus whatever noise is present in either the acoustic test environment, the aid itself or the measuring apparatus. The THD figures are useful indicators of harmonic distortion but give no guide as to what the relative levels of the harmonics are. At low levels of distortion background noise will limit the accuracy of the measurements.

Intermodulation Distortion

Harmonic distortion is measured by putting a single tone into the aid and analysing the output. In real life we do not encounter many pure tones and the aid is normally handling complex signals which consist of a multiplicity of tones. Intermodulation distortion is what happens to two tones when they are fed through the hearing aid. The measurement is much more complex than that of harmonic distortion as it involves presenting two tones at a constant level to the aid and analysing the output from the earphone. If two tones are mixed in an amplifier one of the effects is to produce sums and differences of the

Figure 9.5: Input/Output Characteristics at One Frequency. Linear Mode is the same for all aids. The Non-linear Mode will vary according to the type of aid and whether or not AGC is operating. From IEC 118-2

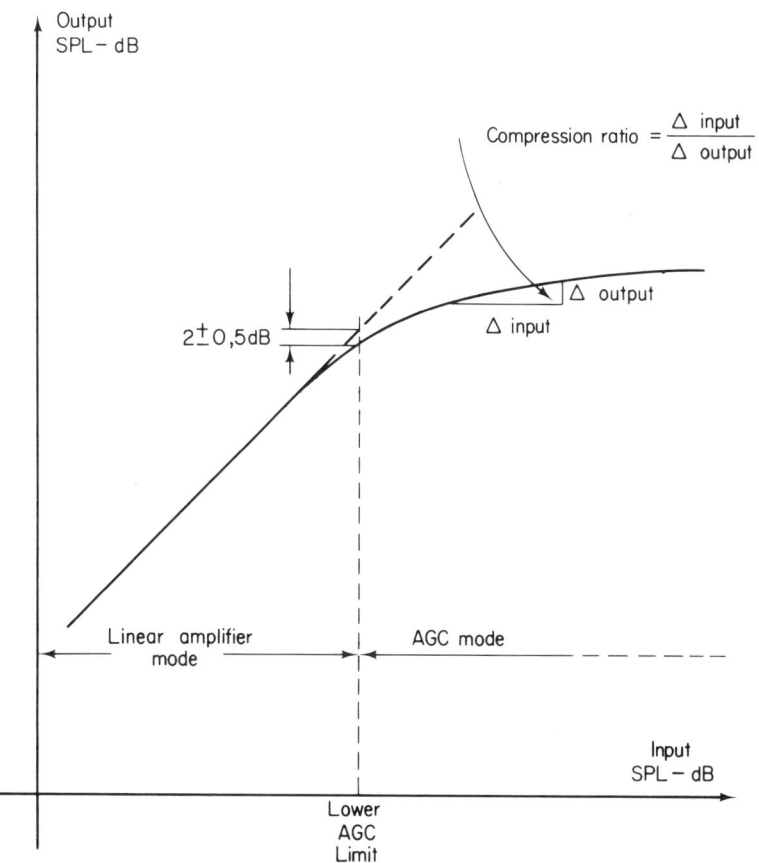

two tones in addition to the original tones. A number of different standardised methods of measurement of intermodulation are available for different purposes, but for hearing aids a method is used which uses two tones 125Hz apart, that are then swept across the frequency range. The result of such a measurement is shown in Figure 9.7.

160 *The Design and Use of Hearing Aids*

Figure 9.6: Harmonic Distortion. A 250 Hz tone is fed into an aid and the output analysed. Harmonics can be seen at varying levels at multiples of the fundamental

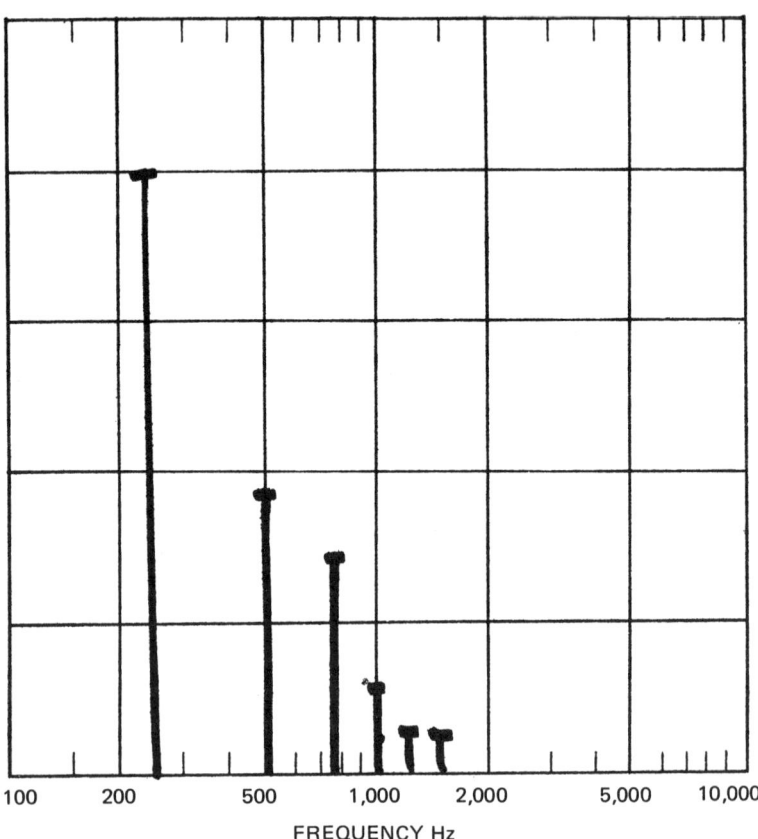

Harmonic Distortion versus Intermodulation Distortion

Harmonic and intermodulation distortion are two methods of measurement of the same phenomena, i.e. non-linearity. From Figure 9.8 it may be seen that they give different results on the same aid working under the same conditions. The question that has not been resolved is which of these measurements, if any of them, are more meaningful in terms of what hearing aid users call distortions when they use aids. For practical purposes harmonic distortion is much easier to measure.

The Design and Use of Hearing Aids 161

Figure 9.7: Distortion Produced by a Hearing Aid With An Input of 70 dB. The values of 3rd harmonic and 3rd order difference frequency intermodulation are shown

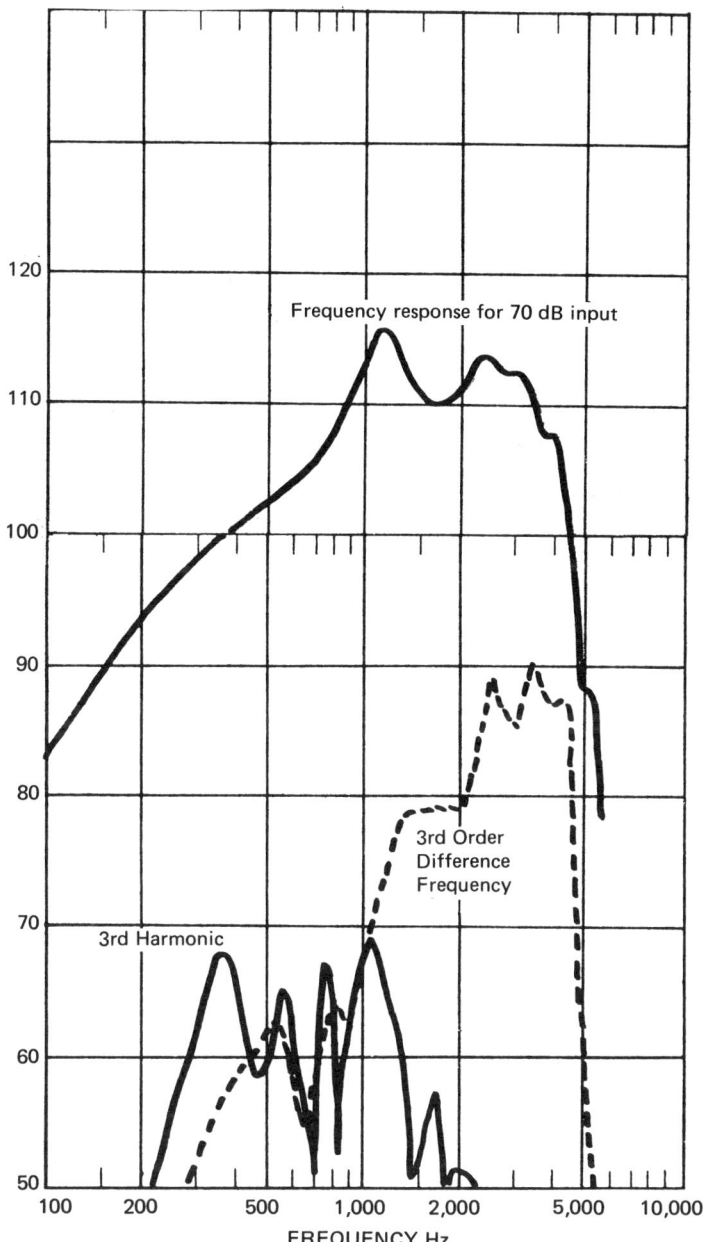

Figure 9.8: (A) Output Controlled AGC Circuit (B) Effect of Altering Gain Control (C) Input Controlled AGC Circuit (D) Effect of Altering Gain Control

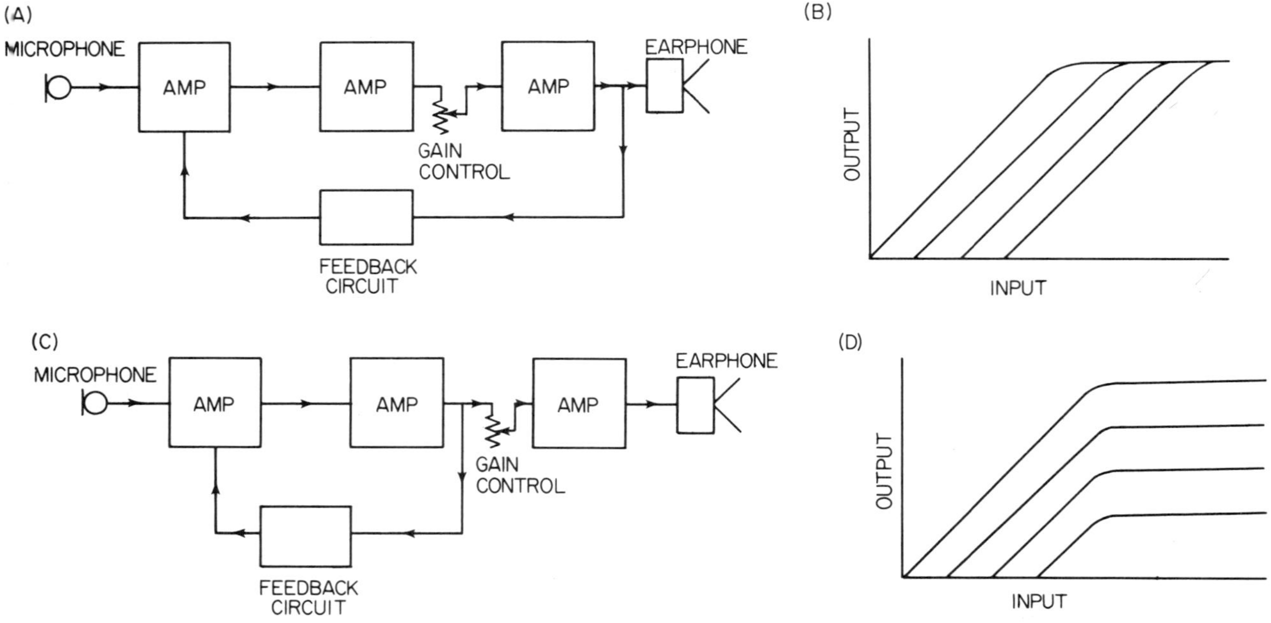

Source: *Scientific Foundations of Otolaryngology*, by permission of the publishers

The Design and Use of Hearing Aids

Transient Distortion

Transient distortion occurs when a signal is suddenly presented to an aid or suddenly turned off. The aid may take some time to respond to the signal, thus producing transient distortion.

Phase Distortion

The relationship between the timing of different components of a signal are called phase. If the aid causes the phase to change, as it will, then phase distortion occurs. It is usually accepted that phase distortion does not have any known adverse effects except on binaural listening which is very dependent upon the phase of signals.

Signal to Noise Ratio

The difference in level between a signal that is required and noise that is not can be expressed as a ratio in dB and is called a signal to noise ratio. In hearing aids the signal is the speech or other sound we want to listen to and the noise will be the ambient acoustic noise around the listener plus any noise generated by the aid itself. The noise from the aid is generated by the movement of electrons in the first stages of the amplifier causing a rushing sound. Noise from the aid is probably more important for people with smaller hearing losses because their dynamic range is larger and therefore they can hear the noise in quiet situations. As the electrical noise has more energy in the low frequencies it is also likely to be more annoying to hearing-impaired people with good low-frequency hearing.

Electrical noise is specified in terms of the acoustic signal into the hearing aid microphone that would produce the same acoustic output from the aid as the noise generated inside the aid. This is called the equivalent noise of the aid and can be calculated as below:—

(a) With the hearing aid gain control at maximum and no acoustic signal into the aid the output sound pressure is measured as 65dB and is noise.
(b) The gain of the aid is then measured as 40dB.
(c) The equivalent noise level of the aid is 65−40 = 25dB SPL.

Classification of Hearing Aids

Hearing aids may be classified in terms of manner in which they are worn and their acoustic performance. The manner of wearing a hearing aid can be divided into head worn and body worn aids. The latter can be further subdivided into air and bone conduction aids. In practice most high powered body worn aids can be used with an appropriate bone vibrator. Headworn aids may be worn behind the ear (post-aural), in the ear (the whole aid contained in the bowl of the ear and ear canal), as spectacles which may be air or bone conduction, or as a headband.

The acoustic performance of an aid may be specified in a variety of ways, gain, frequency response or maximum acoustic output. By general agreement maximum acoustic output is the parameter that allows the best overall classification of aids and the IEC working group on hearing aids has proposed the following.

Classification	Maximum Acoustic Output dB SPL
Extra Mild	<105
Mild	105-114
Moderate	115-124
Strong	125-134
Extra Strong	$\geqslant 135$

While there are hundreds of different models of hearing aids available a classification such as the above will reduce them to five groups. In each group there are a limited number of variations or facilities that can be found and the aids further subdivided into smaller groupings.

Magnetic and Electrical Inputs to Hearing Aids

Today the pick-up coil is a vital part of the hearing aid as it allows many users access to clear hearing via induction facilities over the telephone, in public places and at home for television. The important characteristics of a hearing aid with a pick-up coil are:

(a) Its sensitivity to magnetic fields.
(b) The direction of maximum sensitivity.
(c) The frequency response of the aid when using the coil.
(d) The ease of changing from microphone to pick up coil input.

(a) *Pick-up Coil Sensitivity.* Magnetic field strength is measured in amperes per metre (A/m) and for hearing aid use milliamps per metre (mA/m). A field of 1 amp per metre is produced at the centre of a loop of wire of 1 metre diameter by a current of 1 amp flowing in the wire. If 1 mA flows in the wire then the field is 1mA/m. The sensitivity of the pick up coil is expressed as the acoustic output of the hearing aid for an input of 1 or 10 mA/m for a given setting of the hearing aid, usually maximum gain.

For the sensitivity to be meaningful it is related to an acoustic input to the microphone of 70dB SPL. This is important as it relates a level of normal acoustic input to the magnetic input that would be required to enable the user to switch from pick up coil to microphone position without having to alter the volume control. The pick-up coil sensitivity must be related to the expected field strength which is now recommended as being 100mA/m for an average long-term value of speech.

(b) Pick-up coils are sensitive to the direction of magnetic field with maximum sensitivity occuring when the field cuts the maximum number of turns of wire. This will occur when the coil is at right angles to the plane of the loop producing the field. For most hearing aids the coil is mounted vertically, or near vertical, and the maximum sensitivity occurs when an aid is vertical and the person standing upright; most induction loops are laid horizontally. If the person lies down flat the signal will be considerably reduced. In some post-aural aids the pick-up coil is mounted horizontally to pick up at maximum sensitivity from a telephone earphone in which the coil is mounted vertically.

(c) The frequency response of the aid with the pick up coil input will inevitably be somewhat different from that of the microphone input. The difference with modern aids however may not be large and will usually occur at low frequencies.

(d) International agreement IEC 118-11, on markings for the input of a hearing aid are as follows:

M = Microphone
T = Pick-up Coil
E = Electrical
R = Radio
IR = Infra-red.

The M position is often joined with the T position to allow inputs to be received from the microphone on the aid and through the pick-up coil input or other inputs. For pick-up coil and microphone use, MT denotes the combined position. On many aids the sensitivity on the sensitivity on the combined setting is different from that on either the T or M positions on their own. The sensitivity of the microphone is often less in the combined position to ensure that the remote signal has the best signal to noise ratio. It is important to remember that if the signal coming in to the aid microphone is high it will mask out the remote signal. The use of the microphone on the aid in the MT position therefore requires thought as to when it will be most effective. Electrical inputs, from tape recorders, radios etc., are possible on some aids fitted with special sockets marked E or ⊖. The electrical input is often in parallel with the microphone and consequently can cause difficulties if the background noise is high in the vicinity of the listener. Aids could be modified to have the electrical input in parallel with the pick-up coil or have its own switch position.

Peak Clipping

Peak clipping (PC) is a method by which the maximum acoustic output of the aid can be reduced. Clipping will occur in all aids at some point and results in the top and bottom of the signal being cut off. Peak clipping therefore introduces distortion but has an immediate action which prevents loud sounds becoming uncomfortable to the listener.

Automatic Gain Control (AGC)

AGC is a form of electronic circuit whereby the output of the hearing aid is controlled depending upon the level of the input sound. Many terms are used to describe AGC hearing aids, such as compression, comfort control, linear dynamic control, etc. In spite of all the names used to describe AGC there are only a limited number of variables and these will be described below. The main function of AGC is to limit the output without introducing distortion which occurs with peak clipping.

The input output characteristics of an aid as shown in Figure 9.5 can be divided into two areas, namely linear and non-linear. The linear area is the same for all hearing aids but the characteristics of aids differ in the non-linear area. Peak clipping aids limit the output instantaneously to a predetermined output and because the waveform is clipped distortion occurs. With AGC the output is limited but will still increase at a reduced rate and with little distortion. The ratio of input to output is called the compression ratio. The compression ratio in many aids is predetermined but may be variable in some aids. CR designates the compression ratio control. Unlike peak clipping AGC normally takes some finite time to operate. The values of the attack and decay times may be variable but the attack time will always be shorter than the decay time. Short time constants are found in many modern aids, for example 10 msec attack and 20 msec decay times. Such short time constants will follow rapid changes in signal level and can cause unpleasant 'pumping' sounds through the aid if too short. Long decay times, however, may cause quieter sounds to be missed if these follow a loud sound, giving a blocking-off effect.

The point at which compression starts is often called the kneepoint and is probably one of the most important parameters for the user; it is also the most difficult to determine correctly in everyday life. Two types of electronic circuit are used in aids, called input and output controlled AGC designated AI or AO. The main difference from the user's point of view is how the volume control alters the signal. Figure 9.8 shows the difference in circuits and their effect.

Subjective Aspects

Objective measurements on hearing aids using pure tones can be made with a high degree of accuracy and repeatability, often within 1dB. However, when subjective measurements are made, particularly with a hearing-impaired person, the accuracy and repeatability of measurements becomes far less than objective measurements. This loss of accuracy is not specific to hearing aids and their use but is common to all measurements of human performance to a greater or lesser degree. The ability to benefit from a hearing aid depends upon a number of factors, not all audiological. It is also important to describe what is meant by benefit as this is related to the needs of the individual. A person with a small hearing loss may use their aid only in certain circumstances, for example in church, listening to TV, etc. Another person might be profoundly deaf and not be able to discriminate one word of speech from another using the aid but may wear it all their waking hours to obtain help with lipreading and in hearing environmental sounds. It is therefore important to differentiate between the types of benefit that can be obtained.

Benefit from using a Hearing Aid

Benefit can be described in terms of a wide range of factors which include psychological, social, discrimination or threshold improvements. Psychological and social benefit is a main effect that comes about by the proper use of hearing aids. These aspects of benefit are difficult to measure with any degree of accuracy although anecdotal evidence will often confirm that benefits exist. It is not the intention of the author to cover this area but to concentrate on the problems involved in obtaining the optimum benefit from an aid in terms of discrimination and threshold improvements.

Threshold Improvements

It is obviously essential that if a person is to discriminate one sound from another he must be able to hear over a sufficiently wide frequency range. By hearing we mean the ability to say that a sound is present, that is, to be able to detect the presence of sound.

Pure Tone Measurements

Threshold measurements are usually detection thresholds like those shown in pure tone audiograms. While pure tone audiograms are undertaken through earphones it is not possible to repeat this measurement when a hearing aid is being worn. Threshold measurements when an aid is worn therefore have to be made with the sound presented through a loudspeaker with the patient seated at some fixed point in front of it. Improvements that are due to the hearing aid can be measured by finding the user's threshold with and without the aid. The equipment required for this is an amplifier and loudspeaker to present the sound; if pure tones are used as the source of sound, they can be easily obtained using existing audiometers. Problems may exist in accurately controlling the level of the sound field at the test point due to standing waves in the room and defraction effects. This problem can be minimised if either warble tones or narrow bands of noise are used instead of pure tones.

Free field threshold shifts can be measured using the equipment shown in Figure 9.9 in exactly the same way as a pure tone audiogram is taken. The hearing aid, however, becomes a variable in the test and can be adjusted to give optimum benefit. Figure 9.10 shows the results of a free field test and superimposed on this is the threshold of hearing for a group of normally hearing people and the spectrum of speech at a conversational level of 70dB. These two pieces of information put the hearing-impaired person's performance in perspective; he is unlikely to achieve a normal threshold aided, but should be able to hear conversational speech. The aided threshold should therefore be above the 70dB speech level. This will not often be achieved in the case of profoundly deaf patients. Care should also be taken at higher

Figure 9.9: Equipment for Free Field Evaluations: A, Tape Recorder; B, Warble Tone Generator; C, Audiometer with Tape Input and Free Field Output; D, Audio Power Amplifier; E, Loudspeaker capable of handling High-frequency Signals at High Intensities; F, Test Point at say 1 metre from Loudspeaker

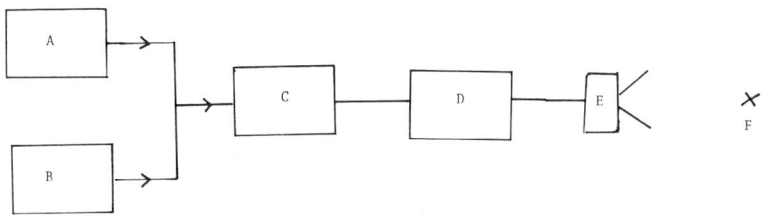

Figure 9.10: Free Field Audiogram showing aided X—X and unaided ●—● results with 70 dB spectrum level for speech o—o and a 'normal' threshold for warble tones □—□ obtained in the same test rooms

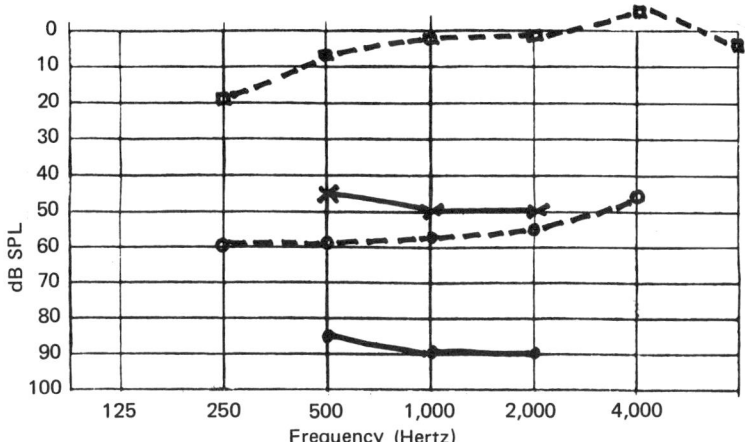

frequencies with profoundly deaf patients that they are not responding to the warble rate when using warble tones as the sound source, rather than the test frequency. At low frequencies the patient may respond to chest resonances rather than hearing the signal.

Loudness discomfort levels may also be measured free field and are particularly important when the aid is being worn. With severely deaf people it will not be possible to produce sufficient sound to elicit discomfort or even threshold unaided. Comfortable listening levels for pure tones may well be of little value and provide no useful information. Comfortable levels for speech are, however, vital.

Speech Testing

The main purpose of a hearing aid is to allow a user to hear and understand speech. To test the effectiveness of an aid on an individual, two types of measurement can be made, qualitative or quantitative. A qualitative test measures some aspects of quality such as loudness or tone but does not measure speech discrimination. Quantitative measures are those of speech discrimination and often give an answer in terms of a percentage of words scored correctly in a particular test.

Qualitative Tests

People with normal hearing will have a preference for listening to sound at a level that is comfortable. If the level of sound becomes too high or too low the listener will try and change the situation to bring the sound to the preferred listening level. The situation is no different for a hearing aid user and therefore the measurement of comfortable listening level (CLL), or most comfortable level (MCL), the term used in the USA, is important and of direct practical value to the hearing aid fitting procedure. The test material for the evaluation of CLL is recorded running speech and the CLL or range of CLL is found by a bracketing procedure as used to find the threshold for pure tone audiometry.

The loudness discomfort level (LDL) for running speech is a further important measure as it determines what level of sound into the hearing aid will cause discomfort, a factor which often leads to rejection of the aid. Adjustment of the maximum acoustic output of the aid can be made to allow the user to receive a range of everyday input sound levels without discomfort. Given the above measurements, it is possible to determine how effective an aid will be for the user. Figure 9.11 shows the results obtained from a group of hearing aid users for the three measures of LDL, CLL and detection. It is interesting to note that for sensorineural losses the CLL and LDL are not very different, for losses up to 60dB, from those of normally hearing people at higher sound levels. However, faint sounds are obviously not heard as well

Figure 9.11: The CLL and LDL for Running Speech for Subjects with Sensorineural Hearing Loss. The Threshold of Hearing at 1kHz is also plotted

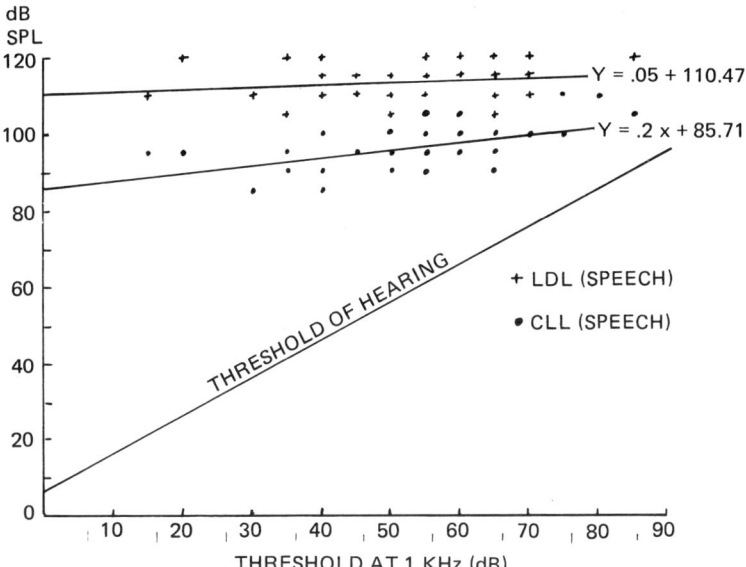

as by hearing-impaired people. Thus the hearing aid has to bring up the level of the weaker sounds while keeping the louder sounds near normal for small to moderate losses.

Quantitative Measurements

In order to establish how a hearing aid user will function with an aid it is important to know how well speech is discriminated. Speech audiometry is normally conducted in the UK using lists of monosyllabic words, each presented at a specific level, and with the number of words or phonemes correctly scored and presented in the form of a speech audiogram as in Figure 9.12. This measurement indicates the overall speech discrimination problem of the user and this information should be available for each ear. As speech audiometry is time-consuming it is often useful just to measure discrimination at the CLL. This procedure gives a good indication of the rehabilitation problem to be faced. It also allows the effectiveness of different aids to be assessed. It will be noted, however, that the use of a hearing aid does not necessarily improve the maximum discrimination score although it should reduce the sound pressure level required to obtain that score.

Figure 9.12: Speech Audiogram. The horizontal scale is increasing speech sound level while the vertical scale is the number of words repeated correctly from given lists. The left-hand curve is that of a normally hearing person while the middle curve is that of a person with a conductive hearing loss who hears like a normally hearing person providing the sound is loud enough. The right-hand curve is that of a person with a sensorineural hearing loss. Note that as the level increases this person gets more words right, but never gets more than 60% right. If the sound becomes too loud the score goes down. This clearly illustrates the problem of sensorineural deafness, i.e. a lack of clarity not compensated for by increasing volume.

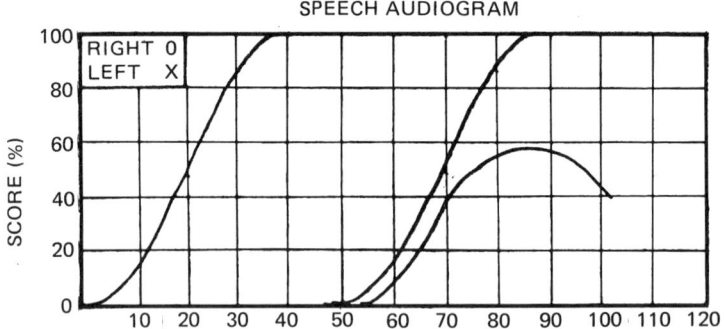

Processing Time

One aspect of speech processing that is often not taken into consideration when evaluating hearing-impaired people is the time it takes to recognise a word. When carrying out speech audiometry it is very noticeable that when the word is difficult to understand, a considerable pause occurs before the subject responds. Measurements of this delay have shown that even if the subject gets the word right, in the case of sensorineural hearing loss it will take the subject twice as long to respond as a normally hearing person. This factor leads to some misunderstanding as to why people who perform well on speech tests still complain that they have difficulty in understanding speech. In running speech the time interval between successive words, which are not separated out as in the written form, is too short for the user to understand and this time delay means that the listener is always trying to catch up.

Suggested Procedure for Initial Hearing Aid Evaluation

Below is a suggested test battery that will provide the initial relevant details for estimating the effectiveness of a hearing aid. Steps 4, 5, 6 and 7 are to be used according to the particular patient's problems.

(1) Pure tone audiogram with LDL.
(2) CLL, LDL and detection for running speech through earphones. Both ears.
(3) Speech discrimination at CLL. Both ears.
(4) Unaided free field CLL, LDL and detection for running speech. One ear at a time.
(5) Aided free field CLL, LDL and detection for running speech. One ear at a time.
(6) Aided free field detection for pure tones. One ear at a time.
(7) Unaided free field detection for pure tones. One ear at a time (providing loss is not too severe).
(8) Change aid characteristics depending upon results and patients comments.

Summary

A very comprehensive range of hearing aids exists today and these aids should cater for the majority of needs. The degree of help that a hearing aid gives will always be limited and in many circumstances aids other than hearing aids will be of greater benefit (see Chapter 11 on environmental aids). However, given that proper care is taken in the fitting of aids and that appropriate follow-up and after-care is established, most people should get some benefit from a hearing aid and it should always be tried. The adjustments in performance that can be made to present-day hearing aids and the accuracy of objective performance far outweigh our present ability to test and evaluate accurately the ability of people to hear with aids.

10 EAR IMPRESSIONS AND HEARING AID EARMOULDS

Roger Wills

Nobody who has regular contact with hearing-impaired people who use hearing aids can fail to appreciate at an early stage the true significance of the moulded earpiece. Among audiologists and audiology technicians, the ever-present need to provide effective earpieces for hearing aid users in their care is a constant source of discussion, research and experiment. The patient, whose ambition is to become progressively less aware of and preoccupied with the aid that he is obliged to use, may learn to tolerate and accept inadequacies of its performance in acoustic terms, given time; but the problems caused by a poorly made earpiece can never be ignored. An earpiece which causes feedback, whistle or pain in the ear, or which the patient cannot insert successfully, will limit the value of time and effort spent on hearing aid selection and rehabilitation guidance.

Clinical Considerations

Before explaining the specific techniques for making earmoulds, some consideration needs to be given to the qualifications and organisation of those engaged in this work. The fact that an ear impression can be carried out in a few minutes has led some people to conclude that the process is unskilled and harmless. This is not only erroneous but dangerous and professionally irresponsible. The individual disciplines and qualifications within the group of professions involved in audiology are not all given specific training in earmoulds and impression-taking to the same degree. Some professions are clearly expected to be directly involved in this work, while others are only expected to be aware of its implications. Patients do not know who is qualified and meant to carry out this work. Nor do patients know which professional person is in direct contact with the medical supervisory services and is appraised of all the clinical considerations arising directly from a medical examination of the ear. It is of considerable importance that ears should be examined thoroughly, before an impression is taken, by a competent person qualified to recognise significant abnormalities which may be a contra-indication for this procedure. For example, if examination of the ear reveals any of the following conditions, the patient should receive medical advice before an impression is made.

(1) Significant accumulation of wax
(2) Perforated eardrum
(3) Skin infections of the ear canal or pinna
(4) Congenital abnormality of the ear canal or pinna
(5) Discharge from the ear
(6) Any swelling or bleeding affecting the ear canal or pinna
(7) Ears which have been modified by surgery: mastoid, fenestration, reconstructive plastic surgery, grommets and so on.

Only when an examination has shown no such problem, or when medical advice has been sought in a case of doubt, should there be any question of proceeding to make an impression of the ear.

Impression Techniques

Materials

In the past, many different materials have been used to take impressions of the ear. Most of these materials have been borrowed from the dental profession, where the requirement for a non-toxic, fairly rapid setting material giving good definition is identical to that needed in ear impressions. Some early materials were not straightforward to use in the ear since they were only usable when made warm. Other materials were of a very liquid consistency when first mixed, making it necessary to arrange for the patient to lie on one side during the making of the impression. It was also necessary to cast the resultant impression in plaster of Paris within a few minutes of completion, if the very marked shrinkage which occurred rapidly was not to invalidate its accuracy. In recent years, however, there has been a quiet revolution in ear impression techniques, with the introduction of the silicone rubber materials produced by many manufacturers and widely available at modest cost. This substance is made in a putty form, usually white, to which a coloured catalyst or hardener is added from a tube. Setting time is three-and-a-half to five minutes and shrinkage would appear to be nil for all practical purposes. The processing laboratories will accept the finished impression without the need for any further preparatory work, provided that adequate instructions are included as to the type of finished mould required. This system has been so successful that it is currently used for the great majority of impressions made anywhere in the world.

Preparation

Following the examination of the ear and exclusion of any contraindications for impression, the patient should be seated in a well-lit position. Whenever possible the patient should be told how the impression will be taken. This is a surprising omission from the procedure of some centres. The feeling of pressure in the ear canal, the odd sensation as the material sets and even the setting time are all reassuring pieces of information for the apprehensive patient. It may be necessary to pin back any overhanging hair to ensure unimpeded access to the ear and for the same reason it may be better to ask the patient to remove any earrings. Patients who wear a wig or hairpiece also need careful consideration, since afterwards there will be some change in the shape of the pinna when the wig is in place. This effect also applies to spectacle frames and post-aural hearing aids which may move the pinna from its 'at rest' position. It must be decided whether the impression as it sets will be better with these other devices in position or without them.

There are two main techniques for the application of the silicone rubber materials to the ear, the manual or hand technique and the syringe technique. In either case it is necessary for the ear canal to be packed in some way, both to control the depth of the impression and to ensure that the materials, in flowing into the canal and meeting this obstruction, will flow out and fully contact the canal wall. A suitable canal block can be made simply by tying a piece of sewing thread to a small piece of cotton wool. This cotton wool should be inserted into the ear canal using an earlight probe or a head mirror and suitable forceps, since this operation clearly demands an adequate view of the position the cotton block will occupy. As an alternative to making up these cotton blocks, most audiology suppliers will have available in a variety of sizes suitable blocks made of foam rubber. The cotton thread attached to the canal block can be positioned over the top of the ear so as not to impede the actual impression. After the impression material has set, the cotton block and thread will have been set into it, and the whole can be removed together from the ear. The cotton wool or foam block can be cut from the impression, but the thread need not be disturbed since it will not impede the making of the earmould.

The manufacturer of the impression material will have given instructions as to the proportions of putty to hardener to obtain the best consistency of material mix. Materials using a hardener of a contrasting colour are most helpful since the thoroughness of the initial kneading to mix the material and hardener can be easily judged by an even colour throughout the mixed material. Usually a 'walnut-sized' amount of material is adequate for most ears; with experience one can soon select the appropriate amount for each individual ear. The aim should be always to have a little too much, since the material is not expensive in relation to the value of the end-result, and there is nothing more frustrating than not having enough. Furthermore, with certain types of patient one may not easily get a second chance to take an impression. A mental note, even perhaps a stop-watch for the less experienced, should be kept to ensure that the impression material is used before it begins to set, and as a guide to when the impression is ready for removal from the ear. The many brands of material available will vary a little in application and a typical example would be as follows:

Add hardener   0 to 30 seconds — mix thoroughly
30 secs to 1½ minutes — take impression
1½ minutes to 5 minutes — leave material to set
5 minutes — remove impression from ear

Inadequate mixing of the hardener will lead to a weak impression which will not retain its shape. Too much delay after adding the hardener will cause the impression to have obvious 'folds' in the material, since setting has begun and the material will no longer amalgamate successfully in the ear.

The manual method for taking an impression involves forming the mixed material into a cone and feeding it into the ear canal and progressively back into the concha and helix area. This is accomplished using a finger or thumb or a small spatula. The fact that the concha narrows considerably into the ear canal means that significant pressure is necessary to ensure that the material flows to the required depth. This can be very disagreeable to some patients, since the trapped volume of air in the canal is being pressurised as the material is being inserted. It should be borne in mind that this effect can occasionally give rise to vertigo or pain. In addition many patients will need their heads supported on the opposite side, since they may be unable to counteract the pressure applied to the impression material. One further consideration during the impression procedure is that ears which are soft in texture may well deform considerably in comparison with the 'at rest' position. Because of these various problems the manual method, once the main one in use, is now somewhat discredited in favour of the syringe technique, which is widely regarded as more acceptable and accurate.

178 *Ear Impressions and Hearing Aid Earmoulds*

Figure 10.1: Ear Impression Syringe (Courtesy Anatomical Plastics (London) Ltd)

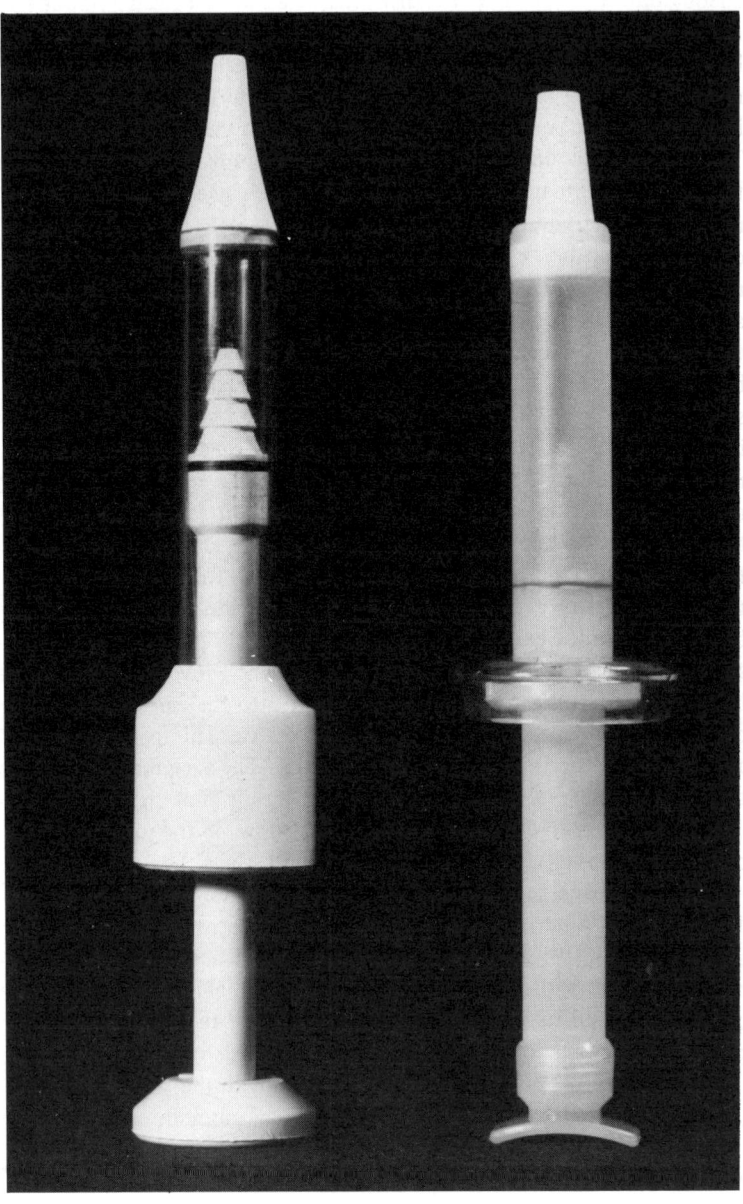

Audiology suppliers can offer a variety of syringes designed or adapted for use with silicone rubber impression material. Those most widely used have a capacity of about 20 cc which is more than adequate for the majority of ears (Figure 10.1). The procedure for the use of a syringe begins with insertion of the mixed material into the barrel of the syringe and re-fitting of the plunger to compress the material and expel any air. Next, position the nozzle of the syringe into the ear canal very near to, if not in contact with, the canal block. Then, begin to expel the impression material while slowly withdrawing the syringe, but ensuring that the nozzle remains submerged in the material. When the nozzle has reached back to the concha the material can be expelled at a faster rate to fill this area, and by moving the nozzle upwards as the concha fills the material can be fed into the helix area. Any remaining material can either be left in the syringe to set or expelled onto the concha area. The material can now be gently pressed home into the outer ear and given a flat outer surface. At no time should the nozzle of the syringe be withdrawn from the developing impression, so that the material can be expelled in one continuous movement until sufficient has been used. This technique ensures that no pressure is applied to the trapped air volume in the ear canal and that there is no significant sideways pressure on the patient's neck. Furthermore, since the material is applied first to the deepest part of the ear canal, and flows outwards thereafter, the likelihood of the ear being deformed from its 'at rest' position by the very process of impression is considerably reduced. It is well known that during audiometry in some ears the pressure of the headphones on the pinna and concha can cause the collapse of the ear canal. With the use of a canal block and avoiding the use of pressure on the outer ear during the impression, the result is much more likely to be successful.

When the material has set the impression can be eased out of the ear by first loosening the contact around the concha rim, and then lifting it so as to remove the lower area between tragus and anti-tragus first. The canal block should be seen to be attached to the extreme end of the meatal section as evidence that the intended depth of impression had been achieved. Finally the ear should be examined thoroughly once again to ensure that no material has been left behind, and no harm done to the ear during the impression-making process.

Earmould Processing

Today there are a growing number of laboratory processes for manufacturing the moulded earpiece. Most laboratories employ qualified and highly skilled dental technicians at least in supervisory roles if not throughout the workforce. This is understandable since the materials and techniques have so much in common with dental work. There are fortunate audiology departments who have their own earmould laboratories but they are the exceptions rather than the rule. The very fact that processing techniques are continually changing makes it hard even for commercial laboratories to keep up with the changes in equipment and the staff training necessary to remain up to date. This problem is even more acute for small departmental laboratories. It is natural, therefore, that most of us turn to outside commercial earmould manufacturers for most, if not all, of our reqiuirements.

Individual laboratories usually devise their own coding system to describe the many types of earmould and materials, or combinations of materials, which can be obtained. Unfortunately there is a lack of agreement as to names for the various types of earmoulds. An example of earmould types and codes is provided in Figure 10.2. It might well be felt that some guidance could be given about which types of earmould should be ordered for a particular type of hearing aid or ear. Such a comment would, however, betray a lack of experience in audiology, which is not a discipline that lends itself to stereotyped rules. Some basic suggestions which could be considered and adapted for each individual case would be more helpful.

The earmould as an integral part of the hearing aid system can be usefully regarded as having three main functions: to ensure the security of the aid at the ear; to provide a comfortable connection between patient and aid; and to contribute to the actual acoustic performance of the aid system. It is clear from these points that the choice of earmould type will be influenced by all these factors, together with a fourth, which is the capability of the patient to handle the earmould successfully. Patients with impaired manual dexterity may well need an earmould which is a compromise from the security point of view, in order to be able to insert it successfully. Some patients will need an earmould which is physically robust, rather than refined in cosmetic terms, for example a shell mould rather than a skeleton to minimise breakages. When a tight-fitting earmould is needed, a softer material will be more easily tolerated in the ear than hard acrylic plastic. Experience will lead to the most appropriate choices of earmould type and material.

Figure 10.2: Earmould Types and Codes (Courtesy Anatomical Plastics (London) Ltd)

A: IA (SOLID)

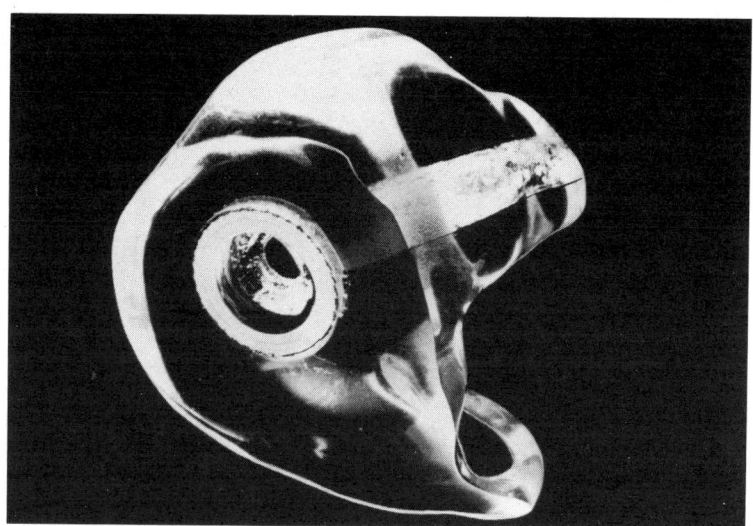

B: IS/F (SHELL)

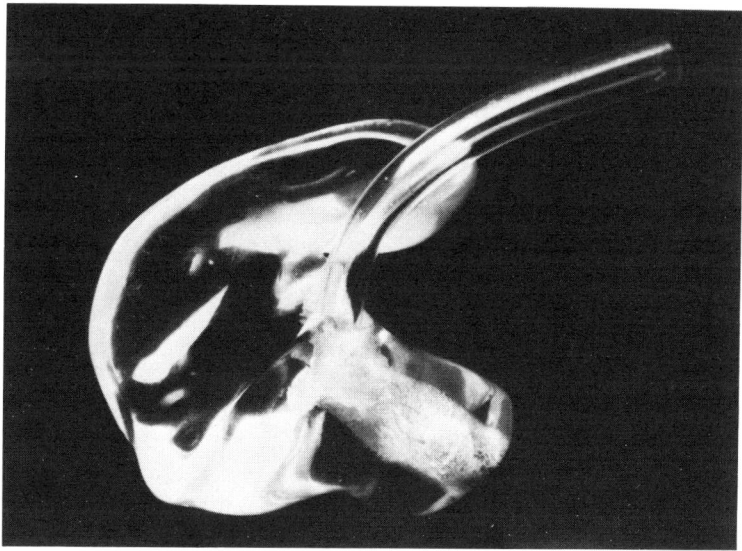

182 *Ear Impressions and Hearing Aid Earmoulds*

C: IP/F

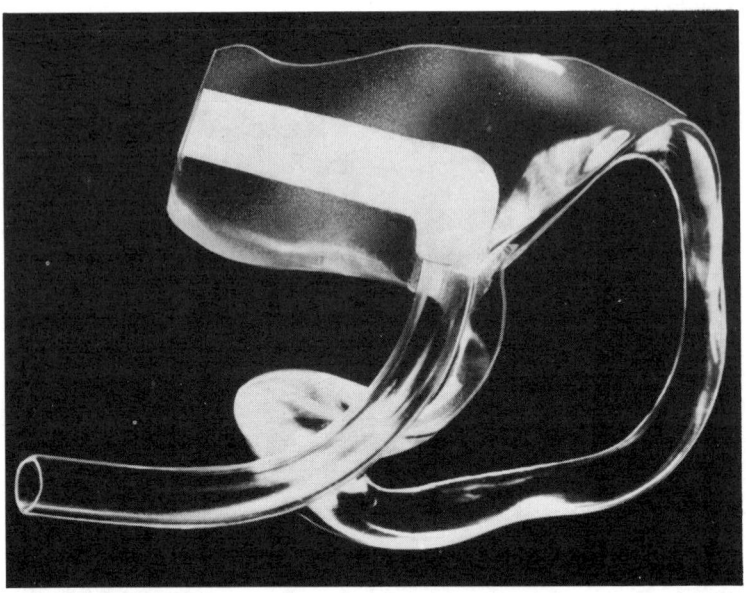

D: IP/F/CROS

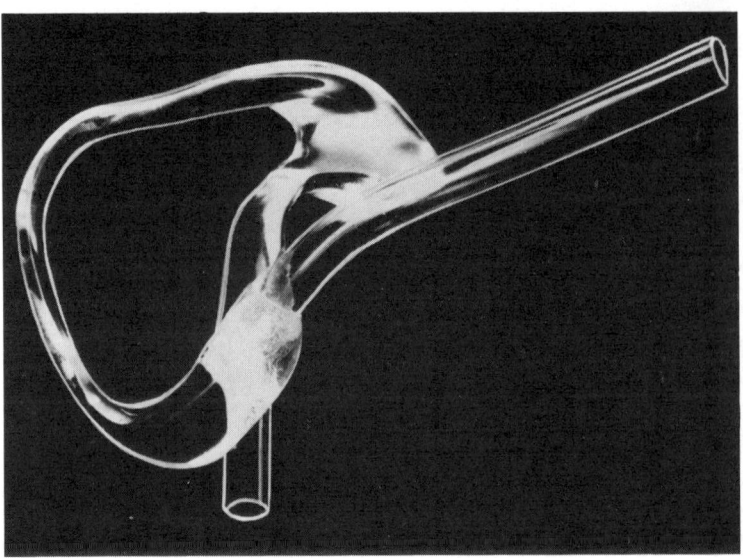

E: IP/EM (Edinburgh Masker)

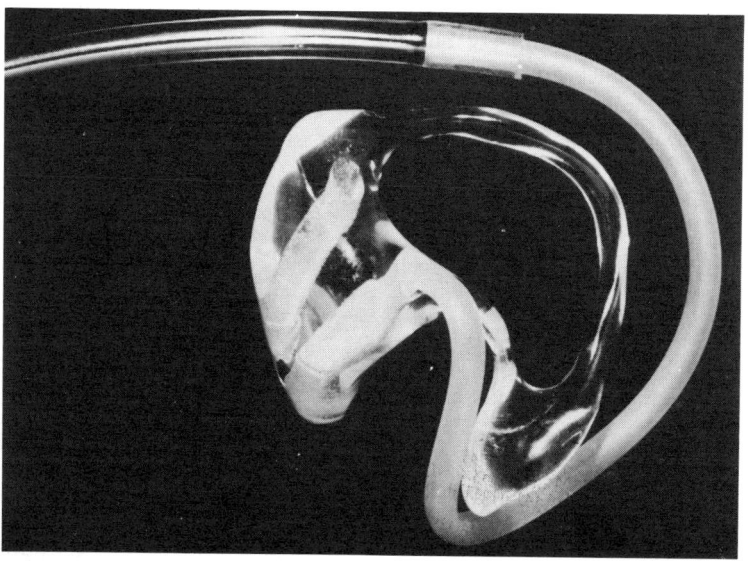

F: IH/F

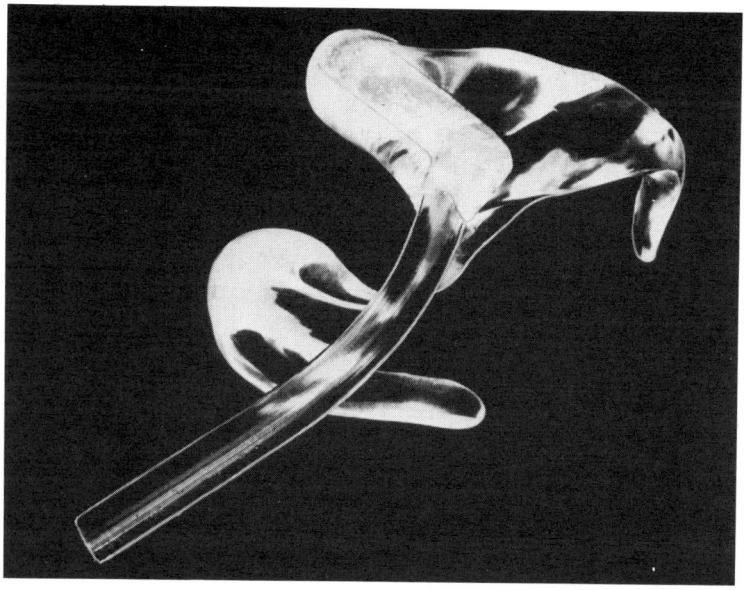

It is worth mentioning that even those hospital departments which do not have their own processing laboratory will occasionally need an earmould made extremely quickly, and that the cold cure materials are most valuable in this respect. These materials differ from conventional impression material in that the impression itself actually becomes the moulded earpiece. This is possible since the material when set or cured, no heat being necessary to cause curing, is sufficiently robust to be coated with lacquer and used as an earpiece. Setting time is similar or slightly longer than that of silicone rubber and a choice is available between materials which will set hard or soft. When using this technique considerable heat is produced in the impression by the chemical action as it sets. It is usually necessary, therefore, to remove the impression from the ear once it has set enough to prevent distortion, even if it is not fully hardened. Failure to do this may subject the patient to extreme discomfort. Much skill and practice are needed to fashion an earmould from the impression because the material is opaque and therefore the drilling for the sound tube has to be accomplished 'blind'. Nevertheless, it is possible to make a workable if not cosmetically beautiful earmould in less than an hour from start to finish, and in even less time with practice. Cold cure earmoulds tend not to be very strong and to discolour in use, so these are not a good long-term alternative to a conventionally processed earmould. One further limitation is that the mixed material will not syringe satisfactorily, so a manual method must be used when making the impression.

Problems with Impressions

There are some less familiar problems associated with the taking of impressions on which the following comments may be helpful.

Minor abnormalities such as the collapsed meatus often found in elderly patients are usually adequately dealt with by the meatal block inserted prior to impression. This tends to distend the meatus somewhat, in order to permit an impression of adequate depth. It should be borne in mind that the laboratory will require a minimum thickness in the meatus to allow for drilling the sound tube, and that too thin a meatus portion would be impossible to drill, or too fragile if left with a very thin section. This is why it is sometimes necessary to reduce the length of the meatal portion to that area where sufficient width is found. Techniques such as building up the thickness during laboratory processing may lead to discomfort from the mould in use.

The hair in unusually hairy ears will have to be cut short or coated with Vaseline to ensure that the impression will be satisfactory and also that it can be removed easily and painlessly from the ear when set.

Other, more significant abnormalities in the structure of the ear, whether congenital, acquired, or the result of surgery, need careful consideration. It is particularly necessary to seek clinical guidance before taking impressions of these ears. Arranging the placement of a canal block prior to impression may well be more difficult and removal of the impression may also be less straightforward than usual.

Earmould Fitting

Once the new earmould has been completed, it should be inspected for any surface imperfections which could cause discomfort in use, and then offered up to the ear to confirm both that the fit is satisfactory and that insertion is straightforward. In the case of solid moulds for body-worn aids, the position of the hearing aid receiver-retaining ring should be checked to ensure that the outer rim of the receiver will not cause pressure and discomfort. With moulds for post-aural aids the tubing coming from the mould should fall naturally in line with the acoustic elbow of the aid, and show no signs of kinking or of tending to pull the aid away from its resting position behind the ear.

It is essential that the patient, or the person responsible for the patient, should demonstrate the ability to insert and remove the earmould satisfactorily. Experience has shown that it is impossible to predict exactly who will have the necessary manual dexterity and who will need additional tuition, sometimes a considerable amount. Some otherwise able and intelligent people are amazingly unco-ordinated when they have to perform this task, removed as it is for the most part from visual reinforcement. This ineptitude can be a considerable embarrassment to the patient, and it may be necessary to modify the mould, within the constraints of security and acoustic performance, to overcome the problem. The removal of the upper helix area of the mould will often help. Alterations to the mould for these or other reasons are best carried out on site. The need to have the ear and the earmould together for this purpose make this an impossible task for the manufacturing laboratory. A small electric grinding machine and polishing wheel, and a dental-type drill with a collection of drills and burrs, are all that is necessary. The mould surface must be smoothed and re-polished whenever such modifications have been made. Most patients soon learn to cope with the earmould but for those who do not there are various helpful teaching aids. The simplest way is to have earmoulds made to fit your own ears, a necessary experience in any case for someone intending to work in this field, and use them to demonstrate the technique. Another useful idea are the dummy rubber ears available from audiology equipment suppliers. These can be used to practise impression procedures and if earmoulds are made up they can be used to demonstrate to the patient the best way to insert and remove the earmould.

Problems with Earmoulds

Discomfort

With a large proportion of earmould fittings, the objective must be to achieve the tightest wearable fit in order to allow the hearing aid system to function acoustically as intended. This may result in an earmould which, while tight, is also less than straightforward to insert in the ear. Audiologists are naturally inclined to seek the best possible fit so as to promote better hearing, but there is sometimes a risk of causing soreness in the ear due to incorrect insertion. Often the patient believes the earmould has been well fitted but then notices discomfort after a few hours of use. There may be a report of undue acoustic feedback when the patient fits the earmould, but not when the professional fits it. Occasionally it can be seen that the reddening and soreness on the ear is in a place which a properly inserted earmould would not touch. The patient should be asked to insert the earmould so that the technique he uses can be observed, but it should be remembered that the patient may not always insert it incorrectly. It may be that the discomfort arises not because of insertion problems but from the fact that the earmould has been made too tight to be wearable. This can sometimes be corrected by the careful use of the grinding machines or the dental drill to reduce the size of the earmould, if it is clear which part is at fault. The ear should be examined carefully to see whether the meatal portion of the earmould is too long, because soreness deep in the ear canal can result from the deformation of the ear canal shape during normal jaw movement. Discomfort when the patient smiles or eats can also be caused when the meatal portion of the earmould is too long.

Skin Reactions

It may be that neither earmould insertion difficulties nor possible over-tightness can account for the soreness of the ear. This should raise the question whether ear canal occlusion or possibly allergic skin reaction is responsible. These two possibilities are separate in cause and effect. Skin infections in the ear canal or pinna, such as otitis externa, can and often do occur in patients whether they use a hearing aid or not. However, the hearing aid user is far more susceptible to these conditions. An ear canal which is occluded by an earmould provides an ideal environment for bacterial growth with almost continuous warmth and humidity. The patient's management of earmould hygiene may be suspect, increasing further the possibility of skin infection. These skin reactions often recur despite local antiobiotic treatments, once the hearing aid is back in use. Patients may need regular aural toilet and may never be completely free of re-infection. If the audiological considerations permit, it may be possible for the patient to have left and right earmoulds, in order to alternate the use of the aid between the ears every few days. This will often considerably reduce the incidence of re-infection.

Skin troubles are often wrongly attributed to an allergy to the plastic from which the earmould is made. Certainly genuine allergic reactions do occur, but they are extremely rare. A patient with a supposed allergy to the earmould may well be wearing a dental plate made of the same material. A simple way to confirm an allergic reaction is to carry out a 'patch test'. A piece of earmould, or more conveniently a coin-shaped piece of earmould material, should be fixed to the inside forearm of the patient, using non-allergic adhesive tape. After three days, the site of the patch test application should be 'read' some 20 minutes after removing material and tape. In a case of genuine allergy, considerable reddening, swelling and itchiness will be apparent. In many cases, however, no such reaction has been found. It should be remembered that the dental profession has gone to enormous lengths to ensure that commonly used materials do not produce toxic reactions, and that in the making of earmoulds the same materials are being used. In the comparatively few cases where allergy is confirmed, it can usually be overcome by specifying an earmould made of a different material, such as synthetic rubber, Vulcanite or PVC.

Acoustic Feedback

The irritating whistling noises that hearing aids sometimes make when in use can be due to a variety of causes. A loose earmould which allows leakage of amplified sound back to the microphone of the aid is a common cause. If the earmould is old or damaged it will be obvious that the time has come to replace it. If the earmould is of recent manufacture then a number of other possibilities should be investigated. An accumulation of wax can result in feedback because the patient uses a far higher volume setting to overcome the additional hearing loss caused by the wax. A faulty hearing aid can also be responsible. Post-aural hearing aids sometimes feedback within the casing of the aid after accidental damage or when overdue for servicing. The receiver of a body-worn aid may be cracked or faulty and the absence of the small polythene sealing washer fitted to the receiver may allow sound to escape in a similar way. In the case of head-worn aids, when the hearing loss is severe and the patient has been found unable to tolerate the necessary tightness of earmould fit to eliminate feedback, it may be necessary to consider a change of hearing aid, to either body-worn or power CROS. This physical separation of the microphone and earpiece may solve the feedback problem and with proper counselling the patient will usually accept the change in view of the real advantage it offers.

Conclusion

Anyone wishing to pursue a career in or related to audiology cannot fail to appreciate the ideas which have been described concerning ear impressions and hearing aid earmoulds. It is hoped that the practical ideas set down here concerning the various clinical considerations, impression techniques, processing and its problems, earmould fitting and its difficulties, may have reinforced the importance of successful earmould fitting in the wider context of aural rehabilitation. No attempt has been made to discuss the ways in which the amplification characteristics of a hearing aid system can be influenced by earmould modifications; this is very much a subject in its own right and is somewhat outside the remit of this chapter.

11 ENVIRONMENTAL AIDS

John D. Pym

In addition to the assistance provided by the individual hearing aid, there are a variety of aids designed to help people with acquired deafness to cope with their difficulties. These aids may use a form of amplification or draw upon the senses of sight and touch; the environmental circumstances may also be modified to enable the individual to function more effectively. The selection of aids will be based on the needs of the user, the nature of the hearing loss, and the availability and cost of the aids. Environmental aids do not necessarily exist in isolation and the co-operation of others may be required to provide the necessary sensory compensation — these co-operators might be described as environmental *aides*.

The individual hearing aid has increasingly become more unobtrusive and an environmental aid or adaptation may well be the only visible evidence of a person's hearing loss. Any explanation of their use could include a more general description of the individual's particular hearing loss, that is, which sounds, especially speech, they do not hear. This gives a further opportunity to explain that success in communication depends on an understanding environment in addition to lipreading and amplification. The extent to which individuals cope will depend on personality factors and other circumstances as well as the degree of hearing loss. Lysons (1978), writing of the stigma of deafness, points out that 'The stigma is accentuated by the general tendency to label everyone with a hearing loss as "deaf" irrespective of its extent or time of onset.' In addition to this clumsy designation he identifies some of the variables that may be relevant. 'Your adjustment or your friends' or relatives' adjustment to loss of hearing depends not only on the cause, severity and expected progress of the disability, but also on such variables as age, intelligence, personality, education and support received from family, friends and employers.'

The Sympathetic Hearing Scheme launched in Britain in 1982 by the four leading organisations for the deaf and hard of hearing issued a card to its membership with these succinct statements printed on the back:

Please speak clearly and not too quickly
Turn towards the light and face me
Cut out as much background noise as possible
Don't be afraid to write things down

Public knowledge of the problems of hearing loss varies with personal experience. With the aim of securing a more understanding environment, the recent survey of public attitudes (Bunting 1981) is encouraging. A total of 537 subjects took part in this survey carried out for the Department of Health and Social Security in Britain. Thirty-two per cent thought all deaf people could be helped by a hearing aid, 62 per cent did not think this was so, and six per cent did not know. Seventeen per cent thought a hearing aid restored a person's hearing to normal, while the majority, 71 per cent, recognised that hearing could not be restored to normal. Two-fifths of the public were aware that the usefulness of hearing aids was restricted in some situations because of factors such as competing sounds or background noise.

The education of the public is a long-term and continuing need. However, the possibility of educating family and friends can be seen as a more immediate aim. Both long- and short-term aims need to be encouraged to secure an understanding environment.

Environmental Acoustics and Listening Areas

Intelligibility of speech, especially when amplified, will be affected in two broad areas: (1) sound quality within the area used and (2) prevention or lessening of sound from outside. In seeking the most favourable listening conditions, the acoustic quality of the room or area is significant. As Sanders (1971) states, 'Acoustic noise will serve both to distract attention from the stimulus sound and also to mask it'. This practical aspect of listening in noisy places is emphasised in the booklet *General Guidance for Hearing Aid Users* issued by the Department of Health and Social Security. This points out that 'It is much harder for anyone with a hearing aid to hear speech properly if there is a high level of background noise; even the noise itself can be distressing.' The sound quality of rooms will depend on size, construction, furnishing and decoration. The following items contribute to the overall acoustic quality of an area by reducing reverberation.

Floors

Carpeting with an underlay will affect the sound quality and eliminate the scraping noise of chair legs and other moveable objects on the floor.

Environmental Aids

Ceilings

If ceilings are absorbent this will reduce echo. Acoustic tiles are an ideal solution together with a lowered ceiling in an excessively high room.

Walls

Again, acoustic tiles would provide a complete answer; however, walls are often helpfully masked by furniture and fitments. In an office, screens covered with material can be used for their acoustic properties as well as for pinning up notices.

Windows

Excessive window glass tends to reflect most sound frequencies. Aluminium slatted sun blinds resonate in a way that hessian-covered blinds do not. Curtains have a softening effect but the darkening caused will need to be balanced against the necessity for a good light for lip-reading.

Furniture

Wooden finish has advantages over metal. Working areas and storage places will be sources of noise, so treatment such as felt-lined drawers would be beneficial, as would the use of a cloth on a plastic-topped table. Metal waste bins are potentially noisy, as are kitchen utensils. Rubber or felt pads would reduce the sound of appliances. Care in the choice of kitchen aids such as mixers would enable quieter models to be selected.

The thoughtful and effective improvement of the sound quality of a room need not be carried out at the expense of an attractive appearance.

Suppression of Sound from Outside

Just as care can be exercised in the choice of potentially noisy appliances and where they are located, so thought can also be directed to sources of sound from outside. Traffic and aircraft noise are common, and apart from double glazing little can be done except by public protest. More common, however, is the noise through walls from adjoining property or flats. The sounds of plumbing, television, radio and conversation can be heard through inadequately sound-proofed walls. Additional noise is also transmitted through adjoining floors and ceilings. Ideally, noise-making appliances and equipment should be sited away from adjoining walls. The techniques which have already been described for improving the sound quality in a room will not eliminate the intrusive sounds from outside. For this, dense materials like brick and sand are needed. Double glazing with wide spacing between will reduce noise coming through windows. To resolve the problems of background noise, the co-operation of people in the household or the neighbourhood may be required, and may well be obtained if the particular problems involved are explained to them, especially where there is recruitment associated with their hearing loss. People are often baffled by the hearing-impaired complaining of noise. The analogous example of the tape-recorder may illustrate this point, as we are all familiar with the need for quiet when a recording is being made. Background noises sometimes appear disproportionately loud on playback of such recordings and in the same way the hearing aid user has to contend with increased background noise of a similar nature. The benefits of a much quieter neighbourhood and society go well beyond the needs of the hearing-impaired. Normal everyday stress could be reduced, and in extreme cases noise-induced deafness itself within the population at large.

Household Environmental Aids

Audible Door Bells and Chimes

An early symptom of hearing loss may be the inability to hear an existing doorbell and the tell-tale note on the doormat: 'I rang several times, you must be out. I'll call again later. Sorry to miss you.' This difficulty has to be seen in context; if a hearing aid has been prescribed existing arrangements might suffice if the aid was worn continuously. This may well be inappropriate and a change made on the basis of unaided hearing. In choosing warning systems such as door bells, the hearing-impaired householder can be helped by appreciating the nature of his hearing loss, for example interaction of volume and frequency. This could indicate that increased volume may not be necessary rather than the substitution of a bell, or chime of a frequency within their hearing range. The word tone could probably be substituted for frequency using the terminology that is more familiar; tone has association with bass and treble tones on familiar household equipment. The simplest solution is to replace the existing doorbell/chime with a proven substitute and retain the rest of the system. A particular choice can be made by visiting a local stockist or environmental aids centre and simulating the home conditions of distance and background noise. A comparable exercise would be made in choosing a telephone bell of suitable tone and volume. If a chime or bell cannot be heard from a conventional range there are specialist suppliers of extra loud doorbells. The extra resonance of a door knocker should not be overlooked. An example of resourcefulness was the social worker who, when calling on a deaf-blind client, exhaled cigarette smoke through the letter box to draw attention to his call: this was in the absence of any tactile system.

Visual Door Bells and Alarm Lights

There are several possible choices in substituting a visual system for the conventional one.

(1) *Continuous portable system.* Battery-powered units activated through the bell-push flash continuously until stopped by the person inside. A bell can be incorporated in this small-scale system for one or two rooms.

(2) *Small mains unit.* A bright light remains on for about 30 seconds when the bell-push is used. A small scale unit for two or three rooms with which a bell can be connected.

(3) *Whole house system.* Using an existing house light system which is professionally fitted with a day and night switch. In the day position the lights come on and at night the lights flash off. In the absence of any natural lighting, special arrangements can be made. The system can also be connected by telephone engineers to allow the house lights to indicate an incoming telephone call.

(4) *Multiple mains unit with light and microphone.* In addition to a conventional light and bell system a microphone with a long lead can be connected to a sensitivity centre so that the lamp will light in time with whatever sounds are close to the microphone, for example, telephone bell, entry buzzer in high-rise flats or apartment blocks, or the cries of a baby or young child.

(5) *Baby alarm.* Non-specialist equipment can be obtained to light up lamps in several rooms to monitor a baby sleeping elsewhere.

(6) *Warning doormat.* When callers stand on the doormat two contacts underneath close and a light goes on inside the house. This has a further application for the hard of hearing at work to prevent them being startled by the sudden appearance of a colleague by their desk.

This section would not be complete without a reference to the household dog. Trained, he can draw attention to the sounds of the telephone or the front door. Furthermore, he can travel to the bottom of the garden to deliver his message.

Clocks

Alarm Clocks

Waking from sleep presents particular problems. Before special solutions are sought there are a variety of alarm clock and clock radios to choose from and it is possible to match these up with particular hearing characteristics. Some clock radios have a tape cassette that could play a tape of known effectiveness at the required time. Conventional alarms placed on tin plates have been known to have sufficient added resonance to wake people.

Flashing Light Clock

This incorporates a flashing light in addition to its conventional buzzer but it is less effective during broad daylight.

Vibrator Clock

The vibrating element is connected to the clock and placed under the pillow or mattress. An experimental model is known that uses a hot air-blower (hairdryer) in conjunction with an alarm clock.

Telephone Attachments

Portable

Small portable battery-powered devices are available that slip on to existing telephone handsets and operate in conjunction with the user's hearing aid, where this is provided with an induction coil (Figure 11.1). When attached to the handset the small internal microphone gathers the signal from the earpiece of the headgear. The signal is fed to an amplifier and on to a coil creating the necessary magnetic field which the hearing aid can pick up. The aid and the handset are inductively coupled and thus the risk of feedback is reduced and greater intelligibility is obtained.

Extension Bells

If a person has difficulty in hearing the standard equipment a choice of bells can be made of greater power and different frequency characteristics. They can be so arranged that extension bells ring intermittently, or in time with the ringing tone or continuously. As has

Environmental Aids 195

Figure 11.1: Induction Coil Used With The Telephone

Source: Courtesy of P.C. Werth Ltd, Audiology House, 45 Nightingale Lane, London SW12 8SU.

already been described, extension bells may be wired into the house light system and a visual signal. This signal can be incorporated with individual handsets.

Amplified Handset

A handset which contains a transistorised amplifier that replaces the normal telephone. The volume can be increased by using the control in the side of the earpiece.

Inductive Coupler

The portable coupler described earlier can be permanently fitted inside the handset and will function with the inductive coil switch of the aid.

Loudspeaker Telephones

These devices remove the need to hold the telephone handset. Speech heard from this type of unit may be more easily heard by some hearing aid users.

Extra Earphone

An extra earpiece helps a person who is hard of hearing to listen to the incoming speech with both ears and so reduce interference from the other noises. The earpiece can also be a help against the microphone of certain types of hearing aid. The user listens through his hearing aid earpiece, but speaks into the telephone in the usual way. For the profoundly deaf, it enables another person to listen to the incoming speech and repeat the message so that it can be understood by lip-reading.

Visual Telephone or Deaf Communicating Terminal (DCT)

These units used in conjunction with the existing telephone system incorporate an illuminated display panel and keyboard. The telephone handset is placed in the coupler at the back of the unit. As the message is typed the words travel along the display panel and are transmitted at the same time to re-appear on the DCT at the other end of the line. When the other person responds the message will move across the receiver display unit. These DCTs can be portable in form and thus used in 'payphone' booths in addition to domestic use. There are add-on units that allow cassette recorders or a printer to be added. Models vary in versatility and some may incorporate message storage and permanent memory store for answer-back codes and emergency messages. To save time, another telephone handset can be incorporated for those who hear or use voice instead of the keyboard.

Visual Environmental Aids

The prime visual element will be through speechreading but, as Hazard (1971) points out, 'Explain to your student that only something like 25 per cent can be seen of what is said and therefore it is necessary to synthesize'. Away from this more specialised aspect of our visual environment, there are many other commonplace visual aspects that are taken for granted, for example arrival notices at airports and the everyday cash register. As well as these general examples, more specialised forms of visual presentation are available.

Badges may show an affiliation or make a simple statement: 'I lipread, please speak clearly'. *Queueing systems* where often the place in the queue is shown by a visual number. *Pen, pencil and paper* when communication falters, especially when proper names are introduced. Re-usable carbon paper pads are compact and unobtrusive. *Flashing lights* are used by the police, fire brigades, and ambulances. A flashing red light may be used as a fire warning in public places and residential homes where the hard of hearing may gather. *Visual indicators* can change an audible signal into a visual one, using an indicator lamp. *Finger-spelling and gesture* may be used as a substitute for pen and paper to spell out words on the fingers using a conventional one-handed or two-handed system. Gesture, a single movement for a whole word, may well provide a method of communication in familiar situations. This presupposes that both communicators are familiar with the method chosen. There are a choice of systems using visual signals, including one that combines speech with manual clues. In addition to a systematised approach natural gesture can be used in varying amounts depending on personality and need but an excess of such natural gesture can distract from lipreading.

Electronic Devices

Printout information. The advent of word processing and computer printouts are providing new visual dimensions in information transfer with the obvious benefit of eliminating the spoken word.

Teletext

Modified TV sets that show prepared visual information from a central source. Pages to be screened are selected using an index and a hand-held remote control. In Britain both the BBC and ITV carry specific news in a magazine format for hard of hearing and deaf viewers.

Subtitles

These have advanced from their purely foreign film setting: some feature films have been subtitled in the same language as the sound track to assist those with a hearing problem. Subtitling on TV is available where viewers have the Teletext facility. This is not without problems Baker (1981) points out 'It is important to remember that there are significant differences between written and spoken language, by intonation and timing'. The speed of normal language presents a predictable situation, and 'The rate of speech on most TV programmes is so fast that if every word is subtitled it can be very difficult to keep up with all the reading let alone have the time left to watch the picture.' Live coverage on TV using subtitles presents problems of editing out redundant language to enable the operator to keep pace with fast moving events. A phonetic approach to this problem uses the following methods in Britain.

Palantype. This is a coded phonetic approach in which a trained operator works a special keyboard. This coded output is fed into a process unit that translates the code with phonetic English and then on to the TV screen. This method has been used in the House of Commons and by hearing-impaired executives who require an accurate account of meetings.

Prestel. The presentation is similar to that of Teletext; however, the information is screened via a keyboard connected to a British Telecom computer with access to more than 100,000 pages of information.

Vibrating and Amplified Environmental Aids

The vibrating alarm already described under alarm clocks is a prime example of how the sense of touch can be used as a substitute for hearing. Wooden floors will often vibrate to the movement of feet and they provide advance warning of someone coming. This awareness can be helped by anticipating the shock of a sudden appearance. A sudden touch without warning can be dramatic and upsetting. Vibration may be seen as a distant early warning system. A specialist use of the tactile sense is by providing a portable device that vibrates at a prescribed volume thus indicating when unheard speech has become unacceptably loud. The following aids may provide greater or more selective application than individual hearing aids, or allow private listening at a level that does not disturb others.

Portable Communicator

An example of a portable battery-powered amplifier is the 'A and M Communicator' (Figure 11.2). It is easy to operate and consists of a hand-held microphone linked to a lorgnette-type amplifier. The lorgnette is held to the ear and adjusted for volume while the speaker uses the microphone in a normal voice. It is useful in observing confidentiality

Figure 11.2: The Communicator — Personal Amplifier and Listening Device

Source: Courtesy of A & M Hearing Aids Ltd, 7 Kelvin Way, Crawley, Sussex.

in public places like hospital wards for hearing-impaired people who do not have an aid or are unable to use one. The hand-held microphone eliminates most background noises. This type of aid is a useful introduction to the potential benefits of amplification.

Speech Trainers

These portable amplifiers with headsets and microphones had their origins in providing amplification for deaf children to provide more aural clues than the lower-powered individual hearing aid. Speech trainers can provide greater amplification and wider frequency response through a headset with separate controls for each ear, and a tone control to match individual hearing losses.

Domestic High-fidelity Equipment

Many households have sophisticated radio and tape recording equipment which incorporates headsets and microphones. These would normally include tone controls, allowing for experiments in seeking the most intelligible response to speech and music.

Portable Cassettes and Radios

Small units often incorporate lightweight headsets with high quality sound reproduction. Some include a talk-through facility that overrides the pre-recorded tape or radio station.

Headset Radio

There are headsets available that incorporate a transistor radio.

Separate Ear-piece

Radios, cassettes and TV sets sometimes incorporate a private listening capacity with an ear-plug.

Amplified Stethoscopes

These can transmit selectively sounds from the heart and lungs, and are useful to doctors as well as those with a hearing loss.

Reflectors

Most television sets have forward-facing loudspeakers but if there is a side-mounted speaker, then the sound quality is affected. Fitting a reflector may improve listening; this could be a plywood or plastic panel angled to the front.

Tone Controls

Where bass and treble controls are fitted to sound equipment these enable the listener to experiment; for example, reducing the low-frequency content (bass) may enhance the intelligibility.

Extra Loudspeakers

These may be connected to television and radio sets. They can be placed with advantage closer to the ear, and could be of a higher acoustic quality than the original specification.

Radio Microphones

These portable microphones eliminate the need for trailing microphone leads and can be used with an inductive loop or with a conventional loudspeaker system.

Specific Television Aids

Headphones

Some television sets have a plug facility or a private listening device as already described. In the absence of a socket a headphone can be fitted by a competent electrician, incorporating mains-isolation, but the headset chosen needs to be compatible with the particular characteristics of the television set. Headsets vary considerably in quality and some have individual controls for each ear.

Adaptors

These are compact units that work on the same principle as headsets. They have a control box fitted to a lead from the set, which must be suitably isolated. These units can be designed to rest on a chair and are provided with a cord and earphone, or the earmould from a body-worn aid. The volume controls allow for private listening at greater amplification than that used for listening by other people through the conventional loudspeaker. The limitation of both headsets and adaptors is the fact that the user is attached to the television set.

Microphone Aids

The sounds from the TV can be picked up by a microphone placed near or attached to the loudspeaker grille (Figure 11.3). The sound picked up can be brought to the ear by way of an amplifier and earpiece. These are portable and require no special modification of the TV set. Microphone aids can be used in the same way as portable communicators with the microphone handheld.

Inductive Loop System (Figure 11.4)

Used in conjunction with the inductive position on hearing aids. There is no direct connection between the listener and the source of sound. The system permeates an area with a magnetic field produced by a flow of electric current in a loop of insulated wire and this is picked up by the pick-up coil in the aid or specialist listening device. If a loop is fitted to a TV set or mains-operated radio a suitable main transformer is needed, unless it is the type of loop system that employs a free-standing or stick-type microphone. In some hearing aids it is possible to have a combined microphone and inductive control which enables the listener to use the aid conventionally. This would allow conversation and the hearing of domestic signals like doorbells or telephones.

Figure 11.3: Television Listening Aid in Use

Source: Courtesy of P.C. Werth Ltd, 45 Nightingale Lane, London SW12 8SU.

As well as the specific use of the inductive loop with the television, it can be used in other situations to provide added intelligibility.

This system has for some time been used in schools where the hearing-impaired are educated individually or in groups, and its usefulness has been recognised by the adaptation of public buildings and places of entertainment to provide the system. Churches, chapels, synagogues and other places of worship have also been 'looped' for their congregations, and theatres, cinemas and concert halls are now installing loop systems as part of a growing access programme. An infra-red system similar in principle to the loop has been introduced; this uses a specialised listening unit.

Other Forms of Amplification in Public Places

Acoustic conditions are not necessarily very good in some places, especially churches with high ceilings. Reverberation can result, and this makes for difficulties with hearing aid users. Low-level amplification over a wide area is one solution; this would use a number of

Environmental Aids 203

Figure 11.4: Inductive Loop Unit for Television

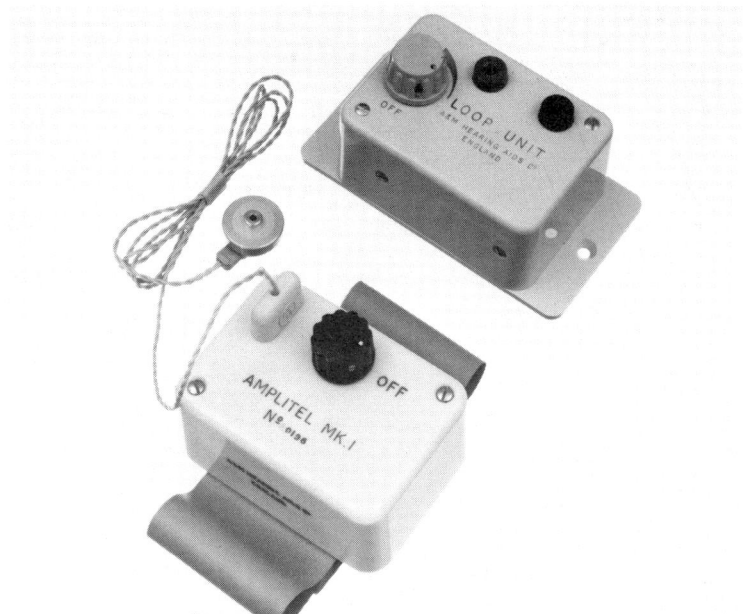

Source: Courtesy of A & M Hearing Aids Ltd, 7 Kelvin Way, Crawley, Sussex.

compact speakers to give an even distribution of sound. Care must be taken to direct sound horizontally rather than upwards. Specific listening places can be located for the use of hearing-impaired people. These would be a number of control boxes linked to a central system and allowing earphones or headsets to be plugged in. International conferences have a similar facility to allow for simultaneous translation.

Conclusion

The environment is the test-bed for all the skills which those who suffer from acquired deafness need to master. Speechreading and the use of amplification are the techniques for survival that are used in an often unstructured and seemingly bewildering world. In addition to these basic techniques, the use of environmental aids can be seen as part of the philosophy necessary for a co-operative mastery of the human and physical environment by those who are deaf.

References

Baker, R.G. (1981) *Guidelines for the Subtitling of Television Programmes*, Research report from Southampton University for Independent Television (UK)

Bunting, C. (1981) *Public attitudes to deafness*, Office of Population Censuses and Surveys, Social Survey Division, a Survey carried out on behalf of the Department of Health and Social Security, London

Department of Health and Social Security *General Guidance for Hearing Aid Users* (HA1 (Rev)).

Hazard, E. (1971) *Lipreading for the Deaf and Hard-of-hearing Person*, Thomas, Springfield, Illinois

Lysons, K. (1978) *How to cope with hearing loss*, Granada, St. Albans (RNID Handbook London)

Sanders, D.A. (1971) *Aural Rehabilitation*, Prentice-Hall, Englewood Cliffs

12 SPEECHREADING IN PRACTICE
Winifred S. Brinson

Visual perception occurs when our eyes receive visual stimuli that are interpreted within the brain centres providing us with visual information. In speechreading the hard of hearing person sees the movement of the lips which he knows to be speech, and the accuracy of his response is based on how well his visual processes enable him to discriminate in a meaningful way the articulatory movements he sees.

The development of speechreading as a receptive skill was at first inextricably bound up with the education of deaf children. Many of the early teachers of the deaf from the nineteenth century were oralists who taught language and speech to their children. Emphasis on training was usually placed on the development of speech and speechreading was not taught directly. Learning to understand through speechreading was simply believed to occur as a by-product of the development of articulatory skills. Certainly in the process of learning to speak many children also learned to speechread as they observed their teachers. So for most of the nineteenth century methods of teaching language and speech, but not of speechreading as such, emerged and were recorded in the literature. By the last decades of the nineteenth century speechreading was beginning to be thought of as a separate skill, to be taught apart from the teaching of articulation to deaf children. Speechreading was at last being thought of as an aid to the many hard of hearing adults with communication difficulties.

In various parts of the world hard of hearing adults with naturally acquired speech and language had become aware of the benefits of learning to speechread and were asking for classes to be started to help them. Many of the early teachers of speechreading to the hard of hearing were at this time dominated in their thinking by ideas of teaching articulation skills, so they used a similar approach working from the part to the whole, namely from the element to the syllable, to the word, to the phrase and then to the sentence. These confusions between speech teaching and speechreading were to continue for a number of years. The development of a philosophy and methodology of teaching speechreading as a receptive skill took time because there were three major errors in the then current thinking. The first was the assumption that the speechreader must know how all the sounds of the language were formed. The second and perhaps major error was the implicit assumption that the skill could best be developed through a cumulative knowledge of lip movements in articulatory positions. In the third place it was also assumed that all speech sounds were visible at least to some degree and sounds that were not normally visible should be made visible. It took a number of years then for the insight that there was something wrong with the part-whole method of teaching speechreading.

Everyday Consequences of Acquired Deafness and the Speechreader

The psychological and social consequences of deafness show considerable variation, being dependent on many factors such as age of onset and the degree and type of impairment. We are concerned here with some of the practical problems which arise very much as a consequence of deafness beginning in adult life. It would seem that there are no easy solutions to such problems, but certainly knowledge and awareness of the difficulties involved can be of great help to those who are deafened, to their families and everyone who comes into contact with them. One of the main reasons for the apparent lack of empathy for the hard of hearing may be the very real inability of people to understand conceptually the complex effects of deafness as a handicap.

It seems that the consequences of acquired deafness are characterised in three ways: there are problems arising from the difficulties of following speech in normal everyday situations; problems of disorientation due to the inability to hear and decode the sounds of the environment; and also the inability to listen and think beyond the immediate communication taking place because of the extra demands caused by the deafness. The communication problem should be regarded as crucial to any remediation when dealing with those who suffer from acquired deafness. Spontaneous speech between normally hearing people is by far the quickest and least laborious method of human communication. Language and speech are unique to man, and this method of conveying thoughts, ideas and factual information has influenced the development of civilisation as we know it. Certainly some forms of urban civilisation appear to have existed many thousands of years before the first known writing. So the written form of language appears to be a much later development than speech in human evolution. Writing has become widely used in Western society only with the rise of industrialisation and the need for literacy. It is interesting that in modern times the written form of language has in some cases been, as it were, superseded by speech. This has come about especially since technology and telecommunications have made possible instant communication to large audiences over vast distances.

Having emphasised the fundamental importance of understanding speech in human communication we can more readily understand the problems facing the hearing aid user. The main effects are that the reception of speech may still be difficult, demanding and inaccurate. The majority of hearing aid users are, as it were, forced to speechread whether they realise it or not, and this is particularly true in conditions of considerable background noise. It may sound self-evident, but in order to be able to speechread, it is essential that lip movements shown can be seen easily and clearly. This means that there must be good lighting, an unobstructed view, full face or at least three-quarter face over a distance of the order of 3 feet and usually not more than 20 feet and that the speech used should be uttered at a reasonable rate. It is also perhaps necessary to remind ourselves that no two people speak alike and that different accents lead to variations in lip movements. Even with normal rates of utterance the speechreader has to make decisions as to the probable meaning on the basis of a limited number of visible lip patterns presented at some considerable speed. Decisions as to the many alternatives possible have to be made in a short space of time. It is no wonder that speechreading is difficult to learn and that considerable practice and concentration are required. Even the so-called normal conditions of everyday life involve background noise which may well limit the usefulness of hearing aids much more than is generally realised, so that speechreading becomes an even more necessary part of aural rehabilitation. Sometimes it seems that the limitations of speechreading could be proportional to the effort involved, particularly in difficult situations and when there is fatigue. The discrepancy in degrees of understanding in different situations may be responsible for many of the problems at home and at work, and for the notion that many people seem to hold, that the hard of hearing are sometimes difficult. Such a view takes no account of the differences to the hearing aid user in a quiet carpeted room when compared with a tiled kitchen with the kettle boiling; or by speechreading over a short distance with good lighting as opposed to walking down the street in the rush hour and having to view the speaker side face. The importance of such environmental differences, and of the differences created by fatigue, need to be explained over and over again to those in contact with the hard of hearing. Only then will the puzzling discrepancies in comprehension which are due to real physical difficulties be more readily appreciated.

Some commonly occurring situations in which speechreading can be almost impossible include conference halls where even sitting in the front, the speaker's face may well be hidden by the desk light or microphone. Even worse, the speaker may pace to and fro, or rock backwards and forwards. Then there are the mannerisms which people use as they talk which can so often distract. People who talk with cigarettes or a pipe in their mouths, or have long hair, bushy beards or moustaches which obscure the face all prove obstacles to speech-reading. At railway stations, post offices and banks people are hidden behind grilles or reflecting glass which causes difficulty. Lighting, particularly at night in a dimly lit road, makes for difficulty, and even the relaxing atmosphere of a candlelit restaurant presents additional problems for the speechreader. So however good the speechreader may become it must always be remembered that the communication problem is not fully solved either with the use of hearing aids or with speechreading, except in a somewhat limited set of favourable environmental circumstances. The dividing line between encouraging hard of hearing adults to cope with difficulties within specific limits, and pushing them into participating in activities which are not possible by the very nature of their handicap, can so easily be crossed. To be effective counselling must therefore be realistically positive but not overtly outside the realms of possibility.

A considerable amount of disorientation can arise from the absence of everyday environmental noise. This difficulty is often related both to the degree of hearing loss and the rapidity of its onset. The inability to decipher the cacophony of sounds in crowded places, such as a shopping centre or crowded bar, leads to an odd sense of unreality and of not belonging. This unreality becomes heightened if there is the suggestion of an unusual event such as an accident or fire, because the deafness makes it difficult to locate activities at a distance or to sense the mood of the people involved. It is revealing to discover how much information environmental hearing provides in everyday life. The wash basin filling, the kettle boiling, the bacon frying, the doorbell are obvious examples which come easily to mind. Some problems can be overcome by technical devices such as kettles and percolators which switch themselves off and bells and alarm clocks connected to a flashing light. Vision must largely take the place of hearing and this so often leads to mistakes. Although it may be easy to see whether it is windy or raining, to a large extent the qualitative aspects are appreciated aurally and not visually, for sometimes a breeze and a gale look very much the same but they do not sound the same.

The sense of hearing is directional and allows us to identify with remarkable accuracy the position of the coin that has been dropped; it also locates the lost keys at the bottom of the bag, and allows the identification of people behind, children playing on the floor and pets under your feet. So that it is not surprising that the absence of environmental hearing can lead the hard of hearing to take inappropriate actions such as looking for people in the wrong part of the house. Unlike hearing, the sense of vision does not allow us to monitor events in all directions at one and the same time. Lack of directional hearing can, for instance, add stress to driving a car. It is not so easy to gauge the need for a gear change by engine vibration, and constant glances at a speedometer pose additional hazards with overtaking traffic and busy road conditions. There are many other examples which illustrate the fact that the speechreader has to face environmental difficulties, and that it is not just the understanding of speech that he has to contend with.

The speechreader has difficulty with many of the activities we take so much for granted. We eat and talk, we walk and talk, we drive and talk, we can listen and make notes, we can listen to the radio and do the washing up or other household chores, and we can even listen to two people at once. These dual activities are really impossible for the speechreader, who has to concentrate his full attention on looking at one face. All these interconnected problems of communication by speech, unawareness of the total environment, the inability to do two things at once can lead to a falling off in social competence. Each one of us would do well to ponder the very real difficulties that acquired deafness poses, and in particular our role should be concerned with the provision of information and knowledge concerning the effects of not being able to hear.

The Speechreader

Speechreading is a receptive skill. How can it be taught, one is often asked? How long will it take? Is it difficult? This is rather like asking 'How long will it take to learn the piano?' The answer to this is 'How well do you want to play?' Obviously, to play well, constant practice is required. You need to know what you are doing and you need somebody to tell you whether you are doing it properly. We do not fully know what makes for speechreading success. It certainly does not seem to be positively correlated with intelligence, social background or education. There are people who come to speechreading classes who, within weeks, have enough skill to carry on and read a reasonable conversation. There are others who come perhaps for years who, although they may gain quite a lot from the class, if only on a social level, do not progress very much. Speechreading would not be so difficult if we could educate people in a few simple rules which should be used when speaking to hard of hearing adults. But deafness can still be an embarrassment for the hearing person, and it is so much easier not to bother or to go away perplexed rather than stand firm and try to make ourselves understood. It might be thought that a hard of hearing person's family should be able to help him most. This is not always the case, possibly because members of the family are often not quite sure of anything practical they can do to help. The underlying sympathy is there but lack of knowledge leads to irritation that can quite quickly disrupt the person's own family circle. Yet this need not be so. For there are many simple ways in which various members of the family can help the hard of hearing person in the home. A few minutes spent over the breakfast table, a few minutes spent perhaps after a television programme, a few minutes spent at weekends, are all useful and practical encouragements to a person trying to learn a very difficult skill.

Let us try to understand what the deafened adult is having to do. Even hearing people at times find difficulty in communication; it may be because they are listening to people with strange accents; it may be that they are trying to hear somebody over the noise of an underground train; it may be that they are only half-listening and therefore guessing a great deal. We have to understand that the deafened adult is really having to re-learn many of the processes of a language-based communication system. What was formerly easily assimilated through the ear and turned into meaning has now changed into a mixed jumble of sound shapes: shapes which he has to learn, which he has to see many, many times before he can associate them quickly enough and translate them into letters and words. It is a truly difficult task with shapes which are so very fleeting on the lips of the speaker. Take the more simple things first, the things which are often overlooked but can really be the most helpful. First the person speechreading needs to see the speaker's face in a good light. As we have already mentioned, light needs to fall on the face, on the lips if possible; even the most proficient lipreader cannot lipread in dim, dark conditions. The speaker needs to be using a clear well-modulated voice, perhaps speaking a little more slowly and deliberately than usual. While not advocating a raised voice, adequate power should be used and it should be remembered that something like four people out of ten do not do this and use less than the average power in some degree or another, but certainly not exaggerating the lip patterns. Exaggeration merely changes the whole shape and pattern on the lips. If a sentence is not speechread the first time, it is helpful after trying the same pattern a second time for the speaker to change either the words or the position of those words in the sentence. If a sentence is not speechread after two attempts there is little use in continuing to speak it. Such repetition ends only in frustration on both sides. A pattern not speechread the second time may not be speechread the twentieth time. Far better to change a few words or put the whole meaning in a different way. This is especially important when speaking to the elderly deaf, who do get rather upset if somebody stands in front of them mouthing the same thing over and over again. Something put in another way and said with a kindly expression can be a great help to understanding.

The deafened adult understands words because he has all his language behind him to call upon, all his experience to help him to guess. Because here we must make it clear — lipreading is, perhaps, mainly organised guesswork. Such guesswork must first of all be approached in simple terms and using simple methods to examine the processes. What is this? Well, you try to say something to yourself in front of a mirror. Do you see every single sound you make? Try not using your voice. What will appear on your lips through the mirror? Perhaps most consonants will be seen, vowels, perhaps not all of them, but most vowel shapes will be there for you to learn to remember. But try saying some of the small words — an, is, on, get, it, is, at, did, she can — there is very little visual shape there for you to pick out and remember. This means that the deafened adult is speechreading what he can and guessing what he cannot see on the lips. How much easier for him to guess if you can give him a clue. Instead of something just like a bolt from the blue it is most helpful to be able to say to a deafened person — 'Now, I'm just going to tell you something I did this morning'; or, 'I've just had a lovely holiday — let me tell you about it'. With clues like this the lipreader can limit the variety of words he can expect to be speechreading in the next few minutes.

Some people are very much more difficult to lipread than others. We have already mentioned how distracting a prominent beard or moustache can be on the face of a speaker. We know that thin-lipped people with an immobile mouth appear to speak with hardly any lip movement whatsoever. We know there are some people with perhaps some facial characteristic which distracts our attention from their lips; that a woman wearing a vividly patterned blouse or a distracting brooch can make us lose our concentration upon the lips. We know that a nodding head or hand movements or somebody keeping their eyes down and looking at their feet while talking, all make extra difficulties for the speechreader. But we know that we are going to meet people in the street who have similar gestures and characteristics. We must either do our best to speechread them as they are, or accept that there are going to be a good many people whom we can never learn to speechread satisfactorily. But this is not our fault, as deafened adults. This does not mean that we shouldn't take the initiative and say — perhaps to a person looking downwards at their feet — 'Would you mind looking at me when you speak, I find it so much easier then to see your lips'; or 'Do you think you could take your cigarette out when you're speaking, it's distracting me from trying to speechread'. It is difficult enough for the deafened adult to concentrate on the mouth when he has formerly been used to looking at eyes or anywhere but the face of the speaker.

Speechreading Lessons

Speechreading is a skill, and just as we would never expect to learn to play a musical instrument adequately if we devoted only two hours weekly to practice, so with speechreading one or two lessons each week are not going to result in tremendous progress. With the help of ideas to be used in spare time, or in made time, both teacher and student will succeeed. A wife or husband, son or daughter, friend or companion, can take a lesson page and, sitting in a good light, read out in a clear, well-modulated voice, stopping when the hard of hearing person seems in difficulties, and patiently repeating, in a speed slightly slower than conversational speech but without any exaggeration or change in rhythm. So many of us 'dry up' when asked to speak on a topic for more than a few minutes or when we are asked to make up something from our own head. Some lessons can be done without preparation or by simply using common objects to hand in most homes.

To avoid repetition, let us assume that it is the husband who is hard of hearing, but the roles can equally well be reversed. Breakfast times may be a rushed affair in some homes but there must be times, perhaps at weekends, when a leisurely breakfast is possible. Here there is opportunity for much valuable simple speechreading practice. The wife could well say to her husband: 'I'm going to say, "Pass me something on the table".' Here it can be shown that the sound 'p' will look like the sounds 'm' and 'b' on the lips.

> Pass me the marmalade — pass me the bread — pass me the butter — pass me the salt — pass me your cup — pass me your plate — pass me your knife and fork.

Would you like . . . . ?

> Would you like another cup of coffee? Piece of bread? Piece of toast? Piece of bacon? Helping of cornflakes? Helping of porridge? Egg? Sausage? Tomato? Kipper? Glass of fruit juice? Glass of milk? Some more prunes? To read the paper? To open your letters? To read my letter?

She is not doing all these things as she speaks but is running her eye round the table using all the things to hand or simply reading through these lists.

Shall we go . . . . ?

> Shall we go to the library? The bank? The shops? The market? Take your shoes to the menders? Take your suit to the cleaners? Take the books to the library?

Numbers are a useful exercise, as confusion arises between eight, nine, ten and six which do not have a very clear shape. Go through 1 to 12, saying each one clearly: one two (to, too — now you've learnt three words at once); three four (fore, for); five six seven eight nine ten eleven twelve. Mix them up or say them backwards and let the speechreader repeat what he thinks you say. Now show —

> half past — a quarter past — a quarter to — . . . o'clock (here you must be quick as the numbers come in front).

Go through this list of times

> half past three − a quarter past two − a quarter to two − four o'clock − twelve o'clock − half past seven − a quarter to one − half past eight − a quarter past ten − half past five − six o'clock − half past nine − eleven o'clock.

Find a pack of cards for more number work but first see what the picture cards look like.

> This is a King (nothing visible) − This is a Queen − This is a Jack − This is an Ace (like 8) − These are hearts − These are spades − These are clubs − These are diamonds (confusion arises with these two as the 'm' and 'b' look alike and diamonds look a shorter word because 'dia' is difficult).

Shuffle the pack, look at the top card in your hand and say, 'This is the three of hearts'. Ask him to repeat what you say and then show the card for confirmation. Go through the pack. Later this can be quickened up for faster speechreading.

For speed and repetition:

I'll see you at . . .	four-thirty
	eleven o'clock
	half-past two
	quarter to two
I'll meet you at . . .	twelve
	six-thirty
	eight
	quarter-past seven
I'll be with you by . . .	four
	eleven
	seven-thirty
	eight

Short sentences with repetition give practice in a flow of language. Once the speechreader has mastered the format then each part can be repeated for further practice.

> I was walking in the street one day. I came to a house. What was in the house? A room. What was in the room? A table. What was in the table? A drawer. What was in the drawer? A large bundle of papers.

I was walking in town one day. I saw a museum. What was in the museum? A gallery. What was in the gallery? A glass case. What was in the glass case? A coffin. What was in the coffin? A mummy (or Tutankhamen). I was looking round the room one day. I saw a cupboard. What was in the cupboard? A box. What was in the box?

A speechreading class is very much an extension of the family situation we have just described. In a speechreading class we have to continually ask ourselves, has the class understood? That is, has each one understood? Ideally classes should be graded into beginners, intermediate and advanced groups. With beginners one is always asking have you, as the teacher, repeated the difficulties often enough? Can you repeat these in another lesson soon? Did you give them some sense of satisfaction with some easy material? Did you help all members, old and young, slow and quick? As we leave the beginners' stage behind, our choice of suitable material can be expanded and made more difficult.

As class members feel more assurance and are able to turn a mixed jumble of shapes into meaning, then they should be encouraged to attempt more difficult material. There is great benefit from using material based on one's own experience or from daily routine which provides a natural flow of information.

Principles of Speechreading

From our own observations and those of other experienced teachers of speechreading we have known, and from the hard of hearing themselves, have come suggestions and ideas which have developed into principles to be accommodated into the teaching situation. Teachers of speechreading need to prepare their lesson material with the following objectives in mind. Although it may not be possible for all the principles contained within these objectives to be accommodated in every lesson, they do provide a framework that will give both visual and auditory practice in an intellectually stimulating selection which will encourage the speechreader.

Drill

Either with single words to show changes in phonemes or with colloquial phrases for quick recognition. Use initial, medial and final changes of consonants and vowels. These may also be used to develop speed. They may be used both visually and aurally.

Aim — to teach shape recognition and develop instant recall.

Practical

Relaxes concentration and enables class participation, as for example the teacher emptying pockets, rummaging in a bag, discussing an antique or curious object, describing a well-known picture.

Involvement

Learning by 'doing' with each member participating. This can be done by useful speechreading games, composing a map, a view or a picture, designing a plate, cloth or cigarette packet, or simply being asked to give things used to put up a shelf, mow the lawn, make a dress and so on. For a slow or beginners' group, a one-answer reply can be used. 'Tell us something sweet/that grows on a bush/flies in the sky/runs on wheels'.

Intellectual Aspect

Aim — to encourage good listening habits and maintain the memory of sound. Because of the problems of language that face the speechreader and the fact that not all speech sounds present a readable shape, intelligent guesswork is essential. Lessons requiring imaginative thought and a quick response to a clue are not easy to prepare but it is essential that the speechreader be encouraged to 'make a guess' and learns to anticipate meaning from the clues that are provided.

Simple sentences, where one word will give a clue to another, can be used and the speechreader encouraged to complete the whole sentence or thought process, the vital clue perhaps being at the end.

I'm searching in   my drawer for a handkerchief
                      my bag for my keys
                      my laundry basket for an odd sock
                      the desk for an envelope

Later a story or topic can be developed and the speechreader encouraged to think what could fill the gap from the contextual clues. If the teacher concentrates on everyday phrases perhaps based on subjects like the weather, health, family, jobs, holidays, visits, weekend pursuits, then useful participation can be devloped.

This kind of individually based exercise is so important to the skill of the speechreader, who must depend on his ability to decode the often distorted visual and auditory patterns he receives.

Listening

Practice to conserve memory of sound, of everyday noises, and to encourage listening concentration. This needs careful preparation if a class includes a profoundly deaf member since for him it has to be a speechreading lesson. Tapes can be made of well-known sounds and the class asked if they recognise these: a telephone ringing, a siren, a door slamming, money dropping, an alarm, a vacuum cleaner. Sounds of musical instruments, different voices, vehicles, animals and birds are useful. These sounds can be developed into a story to encourage imaginative thinking. If tapes are not available it is possible to make many sounds in a classroom related to normal movement and happenings.

Postscript

Although speechreading has been taught for many years there has been relatively little research in this area. Teachers seem always to have been more concerned with teaching than with research, and with results rather than theory. The 'why' and 'what' and the content of what is taught is of course better underpinned by sound theory and research. Even today some of the most skilled teachers of speechreading find difficulty in analysing exactly what they are doing in the intuitive approaches they use. Even so, it is surprising that in Britain there appears to have been little well-documented research information concerning speechreading until very recent years with the work of Markides (1977), Watts and Pegg (1977) and Watts, Ballantyne and Pegg (1980). However, the American work has been considerable over the years, and marked by a consistent qualitative standard. It would be impossible to do justice to all those who have contributed in some degree to our understanding of the speechreading process although some names spring readily to mind (O'Neill and Oyer 1961; Jeffers and Barley 1971; Sanders 1971; Berger 1972; Alpiner 1978; Hipskind 1980).

The approaches to speechreading instruction today do not seem to be substantially different from what they were 50 years ago and some would go as far as to say that they may not have changed significantly since the early years of this century. Theoretical constructs and description of approaches to speechreading training offer possible help with the understanding of the speechreading processes. But until the complicated processes involved in speechreading are better understood, we can expect little change in the methodology of teaching. Even so, it is hoped that the ideas and materials described in this discussion on speechreading, especially with its emphasis on the conceptual level, may be of positive help to those providing speechreading instruction as part of aural rehabilitation. The principles and models suggested reflect everyday practices, concerns, familiar things and places and have immediate value for interest as well as familiarity, which acts as a part of self-actualisation for the speechreader.

References

Alpiner, J.G. (ed) (1978) *Handbook of Adult Rehabilative Audiology*, Williams and Wilkins, Baltimore

Berger, K.W. (1972) *Speechreading: Principles and Methods*, National Educational Press, Baltimore

Hipskind, N.M. (1980) 'Visual Stimuli in Communication', in Schow, R.L. and Nerbonne, M.A. (eds), *Introduction to Aural Rehabilitation*, University Park Press, Baltimore

Jeffers, J., and Barley, M. (1971) *Speechreading (Lipreading)*, Thomas, Springfield

Markides, A. (1977) 'Rehabilitation of People with Acquired Deafness in Adulthood', *Br J Audiol, Suppl 1*

O'Neill, J.J., and Oyer, H.J. (1961) *Visual Communication for the Hard of Hearing*, Prentice Hall, Englewood Cliffs

Sanders, D.A. (1971) *Aural Rehabilitation*, Prentice Hall, Englewood Cliffs

Watts, W.J. and Pegg, K.S. (1977) 'The rehabilitation of adults with acquired hearing loss', *Br.J.Audiol.*, *11*, 103-10

Watts, W.J., Ballantyne, J. and Pegg, K.S. (1980) *Aural Rehabilitation. Further Investigation into the Rehabilitation of Adults with Acquired Hearing Loss*. Phillips Research Unit, University of Sussex. Report to the Department of Health and Social Security, London

13 THE BASIS OF PRACTICAL AUDITORY TRAINING

Gaynor M. Freestone

Auditory training involves a number of steps whereby the aurally handicapped person learns to take advantage of all the acoustic clues still available to him. There must first be a development of awareness of sound, then experience and training in differentiating gross sounds from each other, making broad discrimination among speech sounds, and finally close discrimination among speech sounds with highly similar acoustic characteristics. We need to provide more definite structure in the area of aural rehabilitation than is usually given. Auditory training is a part of the entire process of aural rehabilitation which must be open to those adults with acquired hearing loss, so that in practice auditory training is combined with speechreading, speech rehabilitation and conservation, and the use of hearing aids.

Development

Ideas of using auditory stimuli as a means of helping the deaf stretch back far into time; however, the first really significant use of auditory training did not take place until the beginning of the nineteenth century. Jean Itard, a prominent Paris otologist in 1802, can be regarded as the pioneer accomplishing systematic auditory training with severely deaf children. These ideas were tentatively tried in others parts of the world. The next significant contribution came from Vienna, where in 1892 Urbantschitisch carried out a series of experiments with deaf children. The stimulation he used was by means of a loud voice close to the ear, by conversation tubes and harmonic work with reeds of differing pitch. In 1900 Alt, an assistant at the Poletzer Clinic in Vienna, produced what was probably the first electrical amplifying device. It was a most significant advance on large hearing trumpets and the other acoustic devices of that time. With the rapid development of electronics in our time arising from radio, sound cinematography and sound recording, the technological basis was laid of modern electronic hearing aid construction. Ewing and Littler (1935) were the pioneers in England and they considered the effects of stimulating the ears of normal and partially deaf subjects by large intensities of sound. In the USA Goldstein (1921) retried Urbantischitisch's ideas in a somewhat modified form. Sometime later Goldstein (1939) published a book on the acoustic method. Barczi (1934) introduced an acoustic training programme for profoundly deaf children, while Ewing and Ewing (1938) introduced what they called a hearing-lipreading method for deaf children.

The stage seemed set for continuous advances, but war intervened to delay the work for some years. A few workers were able to continue with their research during the war years particularly with deaf children (Johnson 1939; O'Connor 1940; Johnson 1943). Following the cessation of hostilities in the immediate post-war years the work continued (Fowler 1946; Harris 1946; Myklebust 1946; Ewing 1947; Carhart 1947; Whitehurst 1947, 1949; Hudgins 1948; Whitehurst and Monses 1952). It was now being advocated (Whetnall 1949) that auditory training should begin very early in life for deaf children and this was being provided for children of different ages and with differing degrees of deafness (Wedenberg 1951, 1954; Ewing and Ewing 1954; Hudgins 1954). It can be seen that interest in auditory training was still largely with deaf children.

However, alongside the developments in auditory training with deaf children there had been a move to help those adults who had become hard of hearing during the war years. A number of professional workers both in this country and America had become engaged in this process of aural rehabilitation and this helped the general public to get a better understanding of the problems which face hard-of-hearing people. It certainly caused many of the procedures suggested for auditory training to be systematically recorded. In some instances these and other training procedures have been published (Browd 1951, 1953; Oyer 1966). In the field of aural rehabilitation the work of Hutton and others was of considerable interest (Hutton et al 1959; Hutton 1959, 1960). Hutton considered that in speechreading no matter how effective the method or teacher, visual clues alone were not likely to provide enough information for efficient communication. He presented a rationale for combining auditory and visual stimuli in aural rehabilitation, a view which was supported by the more recent work of Siegenthaber and Gruber (1969). Ingeberg (1967) reviewed the rationale for auditory training and more recently Bode and Oyer (1970) have carried out further controlled studies of auditory training and speech discrimination.

In quite recent years more systematic work has been carried out in the field of auditory training. Significant contributions from the various workers would include that of Sanders (1971), Pollack (1975), Watts (1976), Watts and Pegg (1977), Davis and Silverman (1978) and Watts, Ballantyne and Pegg (1980). In particular it would include the extremely useful book on aural rehabilitation edited by Schow and Norbonne (1980).

The Basis of Auditory Training

Hearing rehabilitation or auditory training does not begin by clapping a pair of headphones on somebody's head and administering audiometric tests or even free-field speech discrimination tests. What is so extremely frustrating about hearing loss is that we cannot see what is going on; if someone has something wrong with an eye you can see it and it is easily accessible. Many hard of hearing people on the other hand find that on some days they hear quite well but on other days they find speech sounding like a distorted radio. This is puzzling, frightening and confusing and causes much impatience at home and at work. A frequent remark is 'He can hear well enough when he wants to ...' In point of fact he wants to hear well all the time but other people need a lot of convincing. It is difficult for a hearing person to imagine what it is like to have even a mild hearing loss. So it should be arranged for the domestic partner to attend and sit in on the tests, the findings and implications of which must be fully and clearly explained, and in this way a great deal of misunderstanding and tension can be cleared up.

When a person needs help for the first time, the first question must always be 'Now M... what seems to be wrong?' A person with a newly-acquired hearing loss may well be very disorientated due to his loss of the primitive or peripheral level of hearing of which most of us are unaware, and because of this he may feel very strange indeed. It is the primitive hearing level which keeps us in touch with our daily surroundings — the distant, 'unimportant' sounds that tell us we are not alone in a soundless empty world. Some people actually experience vertigo because of their degree of disorientation. The two most common descriptions for this state are 'It's like living in an empty world' and 'It's like living with my head in a bag'. The psychological problems of these newly hearing-impaired people can be immense, and many need very careful handling indeed, particularly if there is a lack of sympathy, or any resentment, at home or at work.

The person living alone, who may already suffer from loneliness, is likely to be as severely affected by acquired hearing loss, sometimes more so, than someone who has a companion to rely upon to be his 'ears' for the doorbell, the telephone, or to extend help and sympathy. 'Why should I bother with a hearing aid? I only talk to anybody when I go shopping, and it's useless then' is another defeatist attitude often met with by the hearing therapist. The feeling of being cut off from group chat with one's family, friends and workmates is an unpleasant experience; rather like a foreigner without knowledge of the local language, when an incident such as a group of people laughing about something and happening to glance at the sufferer may even give rise to suspicion of being mocked or derided. The reluctance of many new cases to admit that there is anything wrong with their hearing also makes them complain angrily that 'People mumble' or 'They mutter quietly to shut me out'. Often the hard of hearing person has been told by 'kind' relatives and friends or other professional people that he is 'deaf' (frequently in a derisory or impatient manner) or 'has a hearing loss' (frequently by a brisk professional person who then proceeds no further with comfort or advice). Once he accepts this situation it is difficult to persuade him that life may still have a great deal to offer him. Many moderately hard of hearing people have been told that they are 'deaf' and so they *become deaf*. Much valuable residual hearing is not used and they give up the struggle of trying to understand the imperfectly perceived speech they now hear.

Unlike someone who is born deaf, the hard of hearing person has been accustomed to the rapid, sophisticated code of running speech for exchanging communication without having any idea of the marvel of good hearing and the swift speech reception and decoding which goes on in the cortex of the brain. To have this all-important method of communication impaired is a bewildering and personality-diminishing experience. If the hearing loss is further exacerbated by tinnitus then the sufferer has additional problems which require careful explanation. Honest, realistic and positive assurances need to be given, together with suitable counselling and sympathetic discussion before any training is started. A frequently heard remark is 'You're the first person who has asked me about my problems and offered any help'. Already a hearing threshold may have been established and hearing loss referred to: a hearing aid may have been issued but with no one available to give the essential gradual training to make the maximum use of this device. The hearing therapist's concern should not be how much hearing loss there is, but how much residual hearing there is to use and train. The main concerns of the hearing therapist are as follows:

(1) To convince the sufferer that he is not alone and that the hearing therapist understands the problems and fears associated with hearing loss.

(2) To assure him that with suitable training and with amplification where appropriate, his inability to cope with the speech discrimination problems can be helped.

(3) To rebuild his shattered confidence and to make sure he realises that this is not 'weakness' on his part.

(4) To involve sympathetic personal and professional contacts.

(5) To ensure that he understands that he can, and has the right to, ask questions at all times; and that if he wants to talk out a set of problems, or a new difficulty, the rehabilitation programme must be set aside and the counselling take priority.

(6) To help the hearing-impaired person to become as socially acceptable as possible through improved use of his residual aided hearing, speechreading, and voice monitoring where appropriate.

(7) To keep extending the rehabilitation programme with more difficult work while constantly referring back to the much easier work which was necessary at the beginning, in order to demonstrate progress.

(8) To involve the hearing-impaired person as soon as possible in a speechreading class at a level suitable for his ability. In these early stages it is essential that he succeeds because success breeds success. If there is no suitable speechreading class or teacher available, the therapist must take on the speechreading and include it as part of the general rehabilitation programme.

The hearing therapist is very often the only person with knowledge of many of the problems which are only partly understood by the hearing-impaired person. One of the most frequent and resented misconceptions arises as a result of his having been 'told he has a nervous deafness' when the unfortunate term 'nerve deafness' has been used. A simple explanation of the anatomy of the ear and how it works as a conductor of sound to the 'decoding station' in the brain, where true hearing takes place, is essential in the early stages of rehabilitation. In situations where the hearing therapist administers the audiometric tests and the speech discrimination tests (the latter must be administered by the therapist), these must be explained and matched together in terms which the newly-handicapped person will understand, and the implications made absolutely clear. It is essential for the pure tone audiogram to be explained and for the client to understand where the gross speech sounds lie in relation to his hearing loss by tracing the speech envelope over the audiogram. The hearing therapist must demonstrate those sounds which may still be heard and explain why others are not heard or may be distorted in reception. To know is to understand. Seldom has a person not felt enlightened and better for having been shown the results of the tests, and for having the problems that have arisen explained as positively as possible. Often some of the fears experienced can be removed and puzzlement cleared up over such questions as 'Why can I hear this when I can't hear that?' The simple fact of having this test information explained and being encouraged to ask questions with the assurance of never being refused an answer is often one of the most important first steps on the road to rehabilitation.

For the hard of hearing person, it is immensely encouraging to be able to talk about his difficulties, fears and resentments not with someone who tells him he is 'imagining a lot of it', 'exaggerating it a bit', or is 'at the age when we've all got something, haven't we?' but with a hearing therapist who will listen carefully and accept the outpourings which have often been dammed up for a long time. It is often sufficient to send a person out of the room with head up and looking forward to the next visit with renewed hope for the future. This is why hearing therapists must be able to talk knowledgeably but non-technically about all aspects of the work, including audiology, speech sounds and their place in the frequency spectrum, relative sound levels, running speech, and the whys and wherefores of faulty speech discrimination. They must be thoroughly conversant with the various types of hearing aids and their suitability for the particular degree of hearing loss. It is necessary for the hearing therapist to build up a general rehabilitation programme as a basis for commencing training with the majority of cases, and to prepare material for specific needs to cover a large range of types of losses and ways in which the hearing-impaired cope with their problems.

Auditory Training and Rehabilitation — Basic Knowledge

The following breakdown shows an outline of the knowledge that the hearing therapist must possess in order to carry out this difficult work

The anatomy and physiology of the ear.
The anatomy and physiology of the voice.
Sound: The nature of sound.
  Speech discrimination and the interpretation of complex sound waves.
Hearing loss: Pure tone and speech audiograms: measurement, comparison, assessment and prescription of a suitable counselling/rehabilitation programme.
  Types of deafness and their effect on speech discrimination and speech production.
  Speech discrimination with impaired hearing with and without amplification.
  The ear-voice link.
The sounds of English speech:
  Articulation
  Running speech
  Co-articulation
  The speech chain
The psychology of spoken communication
Voice production:
  Tone quality
  Volume
  Pronunciation of unheard voice sounds
  Conservation of natural speech with severe or deteriorating hearing loss
Consultation and testing:
  Approach
  Testing for hearing threshold by pure tone method (air and bone conduction always).
  Testing speech discrimination:
    EP (on audiometer earphones)
    FF (in free-field, the therapist's voice monitored by sound level meter at 3ft, 6ft, and 9ft 60dBA voice level).
    Marking phonemically the responses given to the speech tests; deciding whether substitutions/omissions are acceptable according to the type of loss/established threshold or are bizarre.
  Ability to explain the implications of the tests and write up a full report.
  Tinnitus: a full report of any type of tinnitus present.
  Ability to take a concise history of past ear or hearing diffi-

culties and whether these have been manifest in other members of the family: childhood and adulthood illnesses, treatment/surgery/where known, any medication administered.

Auditory Training and Hearing Therapy – Basic Knowledge

Assessments of an individual's ability to cope with all aspects of acquired loss: regular re-assessment, comparison and regrading.

Use of hearing aid(s): ensuring that the individual has the most suitable aid for his hearing loss; training in the use of the aid (initial and ongoing); checking if a change of aid is necessary; listening training against background noise.

Training programmes covering the speech sounds in general texts and specific phonemic work: the compilation of suitable material for use in rehabilitation of the individual and for the various types of loss and severity of the handicap; follow-up procedures; re-weighting of compensatory training in cases of progressive or sudden deterioration in hearing acuity.

Counselling in all forms and at all times throughout the initial programme, the ongoing training and the follow-up blocks.

It must always be remembered that in every case of hearing impairment there are two aspects to be considered. These are the degree of *hearing loss* and the degree of *hearing handicap*. It will sometimes be found that cases with severe losses in hearing cope very well but that other cases with more residual hearing are unable to cope with their problems and may need much longer training and more support. The pure tone audiogram which establishes the threshold for hearing those tones is of use to medical and audiological specialists to indicate the degree of hearing loss: its value to the hearing therapist is to indicate how much residual hearing there remains to be trained and used.

The importance of the free-field speech discrimination test cannot be too heavily stressed. The omissions, errors and substitutions provided by such testing give a clear picture of how the individual is or is not using the residual hearing to discriminate speech, and whether the results show a reasonable measure of correlation with the shape of the threshold on the audiogram. This matching can also give some idea of the degree of distortion present in the discrimination of the victim of a sensorineural or mixed hearing loss. Often it is much better to apply the speech discrimination test in a free-field situation with live voice using a sound level meter set at 60 dBA weighting, placed always at the same distance from the therapist and always in the same position, than to try to use speech tapes through speakers attached to an audiometer. The same must be said for testing on the audiometer headphones, where the therapist's voice, monitored on the VU panel, should be used.

Many people, especially if they feel tense and stressed, or are elderly, need time to think of the monosyllabic word that has just been uttered. If speech tapes are used the reply very often comes back just as the voice on the tape speaks the next word. Using live voice, the words must always be pronounced as monosyllables; even on so-called professional test tapes, over-emphasis at word-endings makes a word like 'dog' sound like 'dogga', 'bed' as 'bedda', thus producing a two-syllable word. Heard also on such tapes have been unexpected rising inflexions on perfectly ordinary words such as bed, making the word sound like a question: bed? An unnatural rising or falling inflexion must be avoided: this gives the wrong 'tune' and therefore a spurious acoustic clue. The word-lists should be administered in a clear, forward-projected voice, with one eye always on the sound-level meter, using a monotone, crisply but not over-enunciated, and on a natural time-basis. Phonemic marking and scoring as well as whole-word scoring is essential: only by this method can the therapist decide whether the speech discrimination is mildly to grossly distorted, whether the result is what might be expected from the type of hearing loss and the pure tone audiogram and at what point in linguistic rehabilitation the training should begin. Many people who have had a hearing loss for some time with no help, training or amplification have literally forgotten the speech sounds and the stream of running speech. The longer they have been without help, the more difficult the problems are likely to be.

It is quite surprising how linguistic skills can slide down the scale and be lost to useful purpose: this is particularly true of people living alone and of older people, but it applies to many people who have acquired a hearing loss. There are many patients in hospitals in long-stay situations who have been pushed down the 'geriatric' scale simply because it has not been realised that they have a hearing problem and do not receive any linguistic stimulation, or not enough.

Auditory training programmes must be prepared so that all speech and communication difficulties caused by an acquired hearing loss can be worked upon. Unlike people who are born deaf, the hard of hearing have previously acquired their linguistic skills. The job in hand now must be to compensate for those sounds and groups of sounds in speech which are affected by the hearing loss and form the hearing handicap. While the material must cover all the groups of speech sounds (plosives, fricatives, sibilants, affricatives, approximates, long vowels and dipthongs, blends and clusters), it must in some parts be repetitive, and also include much work involving names, numbers, dates and questions. It must be presented as attractively as possible, based on interesting and suitable material, and made up so that it has a good visual appearance, especially if a sheet of card is held in front of and away from the therapist's lips to cut out lipreading. There are many advantages in making up the programmes in series: the client becomes familiar, and therefore at ease with, the format of the session and the work on each theme can become progressively more difficult. In this way people are encouraged to look forward as much to the continuation of a series of auditory training programmes as they do to the rehabilitation and counselling.

With seriously depressed cases, eye contact may at first be difficult. Even without deep depression, many people find eye contact embarrassing and a clearly visible picture or illustration of the subject on the client's side of the text card is not only pleasant to look at but is also a good talking point when introducing the study or encouraging conversation. Specific speech sounds should be contained in carefully constructed phonemically-weighted texts; then the words and phrases containing these sounds can be gone over again out of context and also included in question form at the end of the text. Here the technique is to train the client to repeat what the therapist says, have any substitutions or omissions explained, re-spoken twice, and then put back again into the text or the question. The questions should also be repeated. Question forms with their initial rush of words hurrying to reach the first important stress word are very difficult to discriminate, and the beginnings of why-where-when-which-what questions sound very much alike. Perception of speech is achieved in gestalts, or whole utterances, and single words should be used only as suggested because they are largely meaningless without contextual clues.

Making up material takes time, patience, and considerable knowledge of the gross phonemes, how they are affected by neighbouring phonemes in running of speech, and the rise and fall of the voice which can take place in uttering a single word. The ability to hear the speech sounds, the elisions and clusters, and to see them visually by writing them in phonetic script is essential for the therapist. It is not possible to read print and think of speech sounds. There are many permutations for use of the material to suit the very wide range of clients' needs. Some examples would include the needs of those who (1) require mostly training in improved use of residual aided/unaided hearing, with little lipreading, up to 4 ft, using normal conversational voice from 80-100 words a minute; (2) require more preparation with both voice and lipreading, more deliberate speech (never destroying the natural time-patterns or speech sounds) followed by work on the text and/or questions without lipreading; and (3) are unable to manage without deliberate very clear speech and lip pattern with both voice and lipreading, and visual clues.

In a half-hour session the material should be changed at least four times to cover all the parts of the programme required and to prevent fatigue and lapses of concentration. Very difficult cases should not be subjected to more than 15 minutes' work at first: immense concentration is required and most clients are over-anxious about not 'making a mistake' at the beginning of the session. They must be urged to give back whatever they think they heard the therapist say, even if it sounds odd. Then substitutions and omissions (never called errors or mistakes) can be pointed out and practised.

There are many in-betweens but these are the main groups into which clients tend to fall. The seriously handicapped client, whether through severe hearing handicap or psychological depression, needs attractive sets of picture card material. The picture subject can be voiced with the lead-in 'This is a . . . . . .' with the card held under the therapist's chin to be within lipreading range. Then the client is invited to discriminate between the objects by the therapist giving the lead-in every time: 'Show me the . . . . . .' Whether these are used with or without lipreading, the requests should be speeded up as the lesson progresses. Explanations of the stressed/unstressed syllables and relatively 'louder' or 'quieter' speech sounds should be given. More and more speech is substituted as the client's confidence grows, his attitude becomes more positive and the professional relationship develops. The series can have many uses for the therapist, containing in addition colours, shapes and numbers. Such basic series also help to improve attention span and auditory recall, two of the most important elements and continuants of therapy. It must be clearly understood that there is no such thing as 'simple' or 'easy' speech discrimination. 'The cat sat on the mat' is one of the most difficult utterances to discriminate and lipread in the English language.

Basic Training Programmes

The following programmes are suggested for basic training.

(1) A series of 10 cards containing short texts and questions on the weather: the time: today, tomorrow, and yesterday: five or six sentence texts with questions at the end, using only the words of the text: longer texts of three or four paragraphs with questions as before.

(2) Ten cards of longer texts with more difficult language and run-ons (about 100 words plus questions) with questions on the text using alternative words where possible.

(3) A set built around an interesting series (wild birds, flowers, motor vehicles, beauty spots and so on) covering the families of speech sounds in the following order: approximates, plosives, fricatives, sibilants, affricatives. The first half of this set should be in as uncomplicated a language as possible; then the phonemic families should be revised with longer texts, more difficult linguistically (about 20 cards). The speech families and how they are formed in the vocal tract must be explained: how some sound very similar and others are high-pitched and quiet while others are low-pitched and louder. Apart from being an essential part of the teaching, it helps to dispel the bewilderment 'Why I seem to hear some things quite well and others not at all'. It is also an essential for training people with gross distortion to re-learn the speech sounds; to re-train those who, without help over long periods, have literally forgotten the speech sounds; and, most difficult of all, to keep alive the memory of the speech sounds and prosody in cases with little or no usable hearing for speech.

(4) A set of 10 cards on a theme (old London, changing fashions, markets, methods of communication) to include as many names, numbers and dates as possible. (About 150-200 words each).

(5) A selection of very short jokes/puns/plays-on-words to end the session with a laugh and a shared joke. This is a more useful exercise than it appears to be on the surface; the hard of hearing are cut off from this form of group communication because of their mishearings and the fact that people drop their voices on a 'punch-line'.

When the client is ready, training against taped background noise should be included (10 minutes maximum) first with 'crowd' noises, then against a single voice. The therapist's voice should be raised only about 10dB above the background noise. The amplification of background noise creates many problems for a new user of a hearing aid, while those with sufficient hearing for it to be an added aggravation must be trained to concentrate through the central core of sound and follow the training material against background noise.

The hearing therapist's techniques in applying programmes must be carefully controlled and a well-projected 60 dB normal conversational voice must always be used. Clear enunciation is imperative. If a gestalt is split because it is too long to be recalled in its entirety, it must be split into phrases which make sense on their own. If a mouth-shield is being used it must only be in position when used for hiding the lips. At all other times it must be well lowered. Instructions such as 'Just repeat the question please' or other remarks such as 'That was very good' or 'I'm going back to the beginning of the sentence' must never be given with the mouth-shield up. Habits such as saying to oneself 'Where was I?', 'Right' must be eliminated, otherwise the client will think he has missed an utterance and will be confused instead of taught.

Conclusions

The field of linguistics is a complicated and wide-ranging one. This chapter has been able to give only a very bare outline of what is needed as a basis for auditory training and for helping one of the most unfortunate and uncared for handicapped groups. Very few cases fail to benefit from auditory training and the help of a hearing therapist. In numerous instances, busy workers with responsible jobs, who had previously thought despairingly of having to give up, have returned to successful work and in some cases promotion. Many older people have found pleasure again in coming out from a state of isolation and withdrawal and rejoining society. Many domestic difficulties, through knowledge, understanding and help, have been overcome.

Administratively, the hearing therapist must of course have a recall system. Some clients when re-assessed will report success which will show on their test results as well as in their outward behaviour. Others will perhaps show a slowed-down auditory response or a return to former difficulties, and they will need a few sessions of extra help. In the case of hearing deterioration, the person must be seen for much longer to build up the compensation in other communication directions. Hearing-impaired clients should always be invited to contact the therapist without awaiting recall if it is felt that the hearing is 'down' or the person is no longer coping. This is one of the most appreciated services we can offer — and there must always be time.

References

Barczi, G. (1934) Address to the International Congress of Logopedia and Phoneatrics in Budapest – see Wedenberg, E. (1951) *Acta Oto-Laryngol Suppl*, *94*, 25-27 and 'Hörerwecken und Hörerrzichen', Salzburg (1933)

Bode, D.L. and Oyer, H.J. (1970) 'Auditory Training and Speech Discrimination', *J Speech Hearing Research*, *13*, 839-855

Browd, V.L. (1951) *The New Way to Better Hearing*, Crown Publishers, New York

Browd, V.L. (1953) 'The New Way to Better Hearing: Through Hearing Reeducation', Faber and Faber, London

Carhart, R. (1947) 'Auditory Training' in Davis, H. (ed), *Hearing and Deafness: A Guide for Laymen*, Murray Hill Books

Davis, H. and Silverman, S.R. (1978) *Hearing and Deafness* (4th edn), Holt, Rinehart and Winston, New York

Ewing, A.W.G. (1947) 'Hearing Aids for the Deaf', *Practitioner*, *158*, 129-138

Ewing, I.R. and Ewing, A.W.G. (1938) *The Handicap of Deafness*, Longman Green, London

Ewing, I.R. and Ewing, A.W.G. (1954) *Speech and the Deaf Child*, Manchester University Press, Manchester

Ewing, A.W.G. and Littler, T.S. (1935) 'The Responses of Partially Deaf Patients to Amplified Speech at Controlled Intensities', Paper given at the annual meeting of the British Association, Norwich, 5 September

Fowler, E.P. (1946) 'Report of the Sub-committee on the evaluation of individual hearing aids in public schools', *Am Ann Deaf*, *91*, 397-402

Goldstein, M.A. (1921) An Acoustic Method. Report on the Proceedings of the Twenty-second meeting of the Joint Convention of American Instructors of the Deaf, US Government Printing Office, Washington DC, pp. 70-79

Goldstein, M.A. (1939) *The Acoustic Method*, Laryngoscope Press, St. Louis

Harris, G. (1946) 'An Acoustic Programme for Severely Deaf Children', *Volta Review*, *48*, 557-560

Hudgins, C.V. (1948) 'A Rationale for Acoustic Training', *Volta Review*, *50*, 484-490

Hudgins, C.V. (1954) 'Auditory Training: its Possibilities and limitations', *Volta Review*, *56*, 339-349

Hutton, B. (1959) 'Combining Auditory and Visual Stimuli in Aural Rehabilitation' *Volta Review*, *61*, 316-19

Hutton, C. (1960) 'A Diagnostic Approach to Combined Techniques in Aural Rehabilitation', *J Speech Hearing Disorders*, *25*, 267-272

Hutton, C., Curry, E.J. and Armstrong, M.B. (1959) 'Some diagnostic test materials for Aural Rehabilitation', *J Speech Hearing Disorders*, *24*, 319-329

Ingeberg, B.O. (1967) 'Rehabiliturrung Erwachsener mit Schwerhorigkeit', *J Laryngol Rhinol Otol*, *46*, 148-151

Johnson, C.W. (1943) 'A Survey of Acoustic Training Programmes and Accomplishments in the public residential schools for the Deaf', *Am Ann Deaf*, *88*, 279-295

Johnson, E.H. (1939) 'Testing Results of Acoustic Training', *Am Ann Deaf*, *84*, 223-233

Myklebust, H.R. (1946) 'The Use of Individual Hearing Aids in a Residential School for the deaf and Implications for Acoustic Training', *Am Ann Deaf*, *91*, 255-6

Oyer, H.J. (1966) *Auditory Communication for the Hard of Hearing*, Prentice Hall, Englewood Cliffs

O'Connor, C.D. (1940) 'The Use of Residual Hearing, *Volta Review*, *42*, 327-333

Pollack, M.C. (ed) (1975) *Amplification for the Hearing Impaired*, Grune and

Stratton, New York
Sanders, D.A. (1971) *Aural Rehabilitation*, Prentice Hall, Englewood Cliffs, New Jersey
Schow, R.L. and Nerbonne, M.A. (eds) (1980) *Introduction to Aural Rehabilitation*, University Park Press, Baltimore
Siegenthaler, B.M., and Gruber, V. (1969) 'Combining Vision and Audition for Speech Reception', *J Speech Hearing Disorders, 34*, 58-60
Watts, W.J. (1976) *Speechreading and Auditory Training in the Rehabilitation of Adults with Acquired Hearing Loss*, Phillips Research Unit, University of Sussex. Research Report made to the Department of Health and Social Security, London
Watts, W.J. and Pegg, K.S. (1977) 'The Rehabilitation of Adults with Acquired Hearing Loss', *Br J Audiol, 11*, 103-110
Watts, W.J., Ballantyne, J. and Pegg, K.S. (1980) Aural Rehabilitation. Further Investigation into the Rehabilitation of Adults with Acquired Hearing Loss. Phillips Research Unit, University of Sussex. Research Report made to the Department of Health and Social Security, London
Wedenberg, E. (1951) 'Auditory Training of Deaf and Hard of Hearing Children', *Acta Oto-Laryngologica, Suppl 94*
Wedenberg, E. (1954) 'Auditory Training of Severely Hard of Hearing Pre-School Children', *Acta Oto-Laryngologica, Suppl 110*
Whetnall, E. (1949) 'The Medresco in the Service of a Deafness Clinic', *J Largyngol Otol, 63*, 742-755
Whitehurst, M.W. (1947) 'Training the Hearing of a Young Deaf Child', *Volta Review, 49*, 215
Whitehurst, M.W. (1949) *Auditory Training for Children*, Hearing Rehabilitation Centre, New York
Whitehurst, M.W. and Monses, E.K. (1952) *Auditory Training for the Deaf*. Volta Bureau, Washington

14 SPEECH CONSERVATION

Ann Parker

The onset of hearing impairment in adult life is frequently associated with some degree of difficulty in communication. The initial and most obvious problem, which is described elsewhere in this book, concerns the individual's ability to understand the speech of others. For this reason, both rehabilitation practice and research literature have concentrated attention on the receptive part of the speech chain — the use of hearing aids, lipreading skills and other means to support comprehension of the spoken word. A further communication problem, but one which is much less well-documented, may result from an acquired hearing loss. This concerns the individual's own speech production. A change in the ability to monitor speech auditorily may cause a significant deterioration of speech in a previously normal speaker, and this may considerably worsen the overall communication problem if appropriate and early help is not given. This chapter discusses some of the difficulties of speech production which may develop, and it is suggested that the basis for improvement in a currently neglected area should be a different approach to monitoring and assessment of speech.

Previous Work

It is difficult to find original work on any aspect of the speech of deafened adults. By contrast, there is a great deal of published information about the speech of the congenitally deaf, and it is tempting to use such work as a basis for comparison with deteriorating speech patterns in the adventitiously hearing-impaired. However, as a substitute for direct information, such a comparison is inappropriate and deceptive, since in spite of their common basis in hearing impairment, the speech difficulties of the two groups are fundamentally different. The difference in extent of the problem is briefly noted by several writers on congenital impairment, and this is a predictably disappointing context in which to search for details about the speech of deafened adults. Rather than providing direct information about the latter, comments tend to have the effect of highlighting the very severe problems of the born deaf. Thus Ling (1976, p. 78) remarks that in deafened adults, control mechanisms being previously well established, 'auditory feedback is not essential'; similarly, Conrad (1979, p. 239) states that although deterioration may be rapid, 'speech rarely becomes unintelligible.'

Such brief comments tend to dismiss the problems of deafened adults. But the speech difficulties of the two groups are fundamentally different in nature, and not merely in extent. Children who are born with a profound hearing impairment, or who develop such a loss before learning to speak, have difficulty in acquiring every aspect of spoken language, with effects that can be observed from the very earliest stages of developing understanding to the severe educational and social difficulties that may result much later (Conrad, 1979). That the results of 'post-lingual' deafness are less severe than this is well-known; knowledge of a language, once acquired, is robust. Although an acquired hearing loss causes difficulties in perception and monitoring of speech it does not change the individual's ability, at a linguistic level, to understand the language once the message is conveyed, or to code and produce normal sentences. At the level of speech intelligibility, whereas both groups have problems, the deafened adult at least begins with a normal and complete set of sound contrasts, unlike the congenitally deaf child, whose abnormal phonetic output has been described as being 'coupled to a nonstandard, aberrant ... phonology' (Binnie et al 1982, p. 181; see also Fisher et al 1983).

The important distinction between phonetic and phonological levels is ignored in most of the rehabilitation literature on speech conservation, with the result that too much emphasis is placed on the speech problems of congenitally deaf children as a basis for assessment of deafened adults' speech production. For example Jackson (1982) notes that the task for the clinician is 'conservation of existing skills rather than the development of new ones' but the description of speech problems which follows uses almost exclusively data from work on children born with hearing impairment, basing suggestions about assessment on information from such studies as those of Hudgins and Numbers (1942) and Nickerson (1975). A short note in McCarthy and Alpiner (1982) offers some data for both pre- and post-lingual deafness, but again the distinction between phonetic and phonological levels is absent. A serious result of this type of description is that the initially more subtle phonetic changes in the speech of deafened adults are not accounted for, and speech may not be recognised as abnormal until deterioration approaches very marked and obvious levels. If speech conservation is to replace crisis-level remediation, this is an unsatisfactory state of affairs. Assessment of the speech of adults with acquired hearing impairment should therefore be based primarily on comparison with normal speech.

Patterns of Speech Change Following Hearing Loss

In the case of a hearing impairment which is acquired well after the normal development of speech, and in the absence of any other reason for a language or communication disorder, the primary areas of concern are the naturalness and the intelligibility of speech production, and not the way in which words are used and combined to form sentences (the lexicon and syntax of the speaker, which should not change as a result of acquired hearing impairment). There are three broad areas of consideration when discussing normal speech production as a basis for assessment of the results of hearing loss. Firstly, the nature of speech is conditioned by the nature of the apparatus — auditory and vocal — which is concerned. The study of the speech sounds which are produced by the human vocal tract and perceived by the ear is known as phonetics. Secondly, the language which is used by the speaker-listener concerned utilises a limited range of the possible sounds in a systematic set of contrasts and sequences. The study of the speech sounds used in particular languages is known as phonology, and it should be noted that particular examples from the phonology of one language are not generally applicable to other languages, with their different ranges of sounds and rules. Thirdly, the amount of normal individual variation which is possible between different speakers of the same language is an important consideration.

Analysis of the pronunciation of English is traditionally divided into two areas. These are the segmental features (speech sounds) of the language, and the suprasegmental (non-segmental, or prosodic) features which provide the overall qualities of the language — its timing, rhythm, voice quality and intonation patterns. Problems associated with acquired hearing impairment may also be considered in these broad categories, but of course there is considerable overlap and interaction between different types of feature. In addition, other factors such as overall tension, eye contact and facial expression may influence the effectiveness of spoken communication. It should also be remembered that other problems of language and communication are found in adults, and are especially relevant when assessing the geriatric population.

With the exception of Penn's early (1955) but valuable study, quantitative information concerning frequency and types of speech problem is not available. Penn studied speech production patterns in 200 cases of acquired (100 conductive and 100 perceptive) loss, concluding that there were 'significant relationships between the types of hearing loss and specific voice and speech deviations, clusters of voice and speech deviations, and numbers of voice and speech deviations' (Penn 1955).

Several writers have opinions about influential factors. Bergman (1952) claims a close relationship between types of loss and types of speech problem, quoting examples of 'typical' problems for patients in four categories (conductive, high-frequency, nerve and total deafness respectively) but adds that other physical and environmental factors also have influence. Cowie *et al* (1982) found deterioration of speech in all the twelve totally deaf individuals studied, but reported considerable variability between subjects, which appeared to be related to age of onset of loss. McCarthy and Alpiner (1982) cite rate of onset, claiming that relatively few speech problems are seen because of the slow onset of loss in the majority of cases. Jackson (1982) lists influential factors as being the degree and configuration of the loss, age of onset, hearing aid history, accompanying problems and the need to use speech. The particular problems which are mentioned later are taken from the literature; in particular, a certain amount of information can be gained from reports by Kinney (1948), Penn (1955), Bergman (1952), Carhart (1947, 1960), Griffith (1969), Markides (1977), Douglas-Cowie *et al* (1979, 1983), Cowie *et al* (1982, 1983) and Binnie *et al* (1982)) or have been recorded in clinical practice by the writer. For reasons which have been discussed earlier, data on congenital deafness are excluded. For convenience, the 'normal' examples in this section are taken from the particular variety of South-Eastern British English which is known as 'Received Pronounciation' (Gimson 1962) but it should be noted that the standard used for assessment of an individual speaker will be the particular accent or dialect which is used.

Suprasegmental Features

The untrained listener may find it difficult to assess the non-segmental features of speech, partly because of the emphasis traditionally placed on the segmental aspects of speech production — vowels and consonants — and partly because this area is the least documented in the rehabilitation literature. Unfortunately, it is also an area where misguided efforts, however informal, by an untrained observer to 'correct' speech may prove particularly counterproductive, and in time actually contribute to the problem.

Breathing Patterns

A variety of disturbances are found in normal breathing patterns for speech. Breathing problems may involve overall tension when attempting to understand and be understood, and may be the basis of several other speech production problems. The speaker may be unaware of the auditory result of speaking with an inadequate amount of air (see next section on voice) and in consequence may speak for too long after one intake of breath. Intake may become inadequate, or be normal but wasted during expiration, with the result that frequent, disruptive pauses for breath, or general voice production problems become evident. Intake of air may actually become distractingly audible because of inappropriate constriction at some point in the vocal tract (see also Penn 1955). Some speakers with particularly abnormal patterns (such as a deliberate intake of air through the nose, accompanied by raised shoulders) have reported they are making such efforts as a result of exhortations to 'take deeper breaths' by well-meaning associates. Remedial work on breathing should be based on a thorough understanding and explanation of the normal mechanism of breathing for speech.

Voice

Normal speech depends on the normal production of voice by means of appropriate control of airflow and vocal fold vibration. A number of aspects of production may be disturbed as a result of hearing impairment, but before discussing such effects in more detail a vitally important point must be emphasised. There is a particular danger for hearing-impaired adults that the onset of an additional voice problem may be overlooked altogether. A number of laryngeal difficulties are actually caused by abnormal use of the vocal folds and there is a further important reason to ensure the involvement of the ENT consultant in the assessment of voice. Greene (1972) states the position unequivocally:

> No case of hoarseness should ever be accepted for treatment ... without first having obtained a report from the laryngologist. It is imperative that malignancy should be excluded besides other illness, and there is grave danger to the patient in treating even the

mildest case of hoarseness without obtaining a laryngological inspection and diagnosis first.

The speech therapist who deals with voice disorders normally has good and ready access to advice from ENT colleagues and is well aware of the necessity for swift referral after voice change, but because hearing-impaired individuals may be dealt with initially by other staff, this point cannot be overstressed.

In relationship to acquired hearing impairment, Bergman (1952) is in no doubt as to the importance of voice assessment, stating that the 'first detectable change usually occurs in voice quality, regardless of the type of deafness.' In Kinney's study (1948) voice change was detectable appreciably earlier than other 'loss of speech' in 27 out of 29 postmeningitic cases. While it is to be hoped that, in the years since these reports appeared, developments in amplification provision have modified the position for many individuals, voice change continues to be reported in more recent studies (Binnie *et al* 1982; Cowie *et al* 1983).

Early voice change may involve simple difficulty with monitoring of loudness, and many individuals report that under changing acoustic conditions considerable embarrassment and sometimes unintelligibility may result. In many cases the development of a simple cueing system with a hearing spouse or friend may help, as may the use of special electronic aids (Summers *et al* 1981). The long-term effect of loudness problems may be more complex for certain individuals, and necessitate professional guidance from the speech therapist. This is because in the absence of adequate auditory information, which would immediately cue a different strategy, the person may attempt to change speech production in abnormal ways. For example, excessive tension of the laryngeal area may cause various types of production that may be perceived as 'harsh', 'hoarse', or 'high-pitched', and a more detailed assessment of speech production will then be necessary. If the speaker has developed habitual use of an abnormal (such as creaky or breathy) voice quality, no amount of direct work on simple increase or decrease of loudness will be effective, but may very well compound the problem and in addition cause an increase of tension and anxiety. Similarly, if abnormal phonation type is used, simple attempts to change pitch range are likely to be inappropriate, and therefore ineffective, until normal voice has been re-established. Even where normal voice production is concerned, any impression of inappropriate pitch or 'monotone' needs further investigation prior to remediation. Pitch may simply be high-pitched overall, but such an impression may also be caused by a

240 *Speech Conservation*

Figure 14.1: Examples of Different Patterns of Production Underlying Reported 'High Pitch' (Female (2) and Male (2)) and 'Loudness' (Female (3)) Problems, as Shown on a Visual Display of Fundamental Frequency (see Wright, 1982)

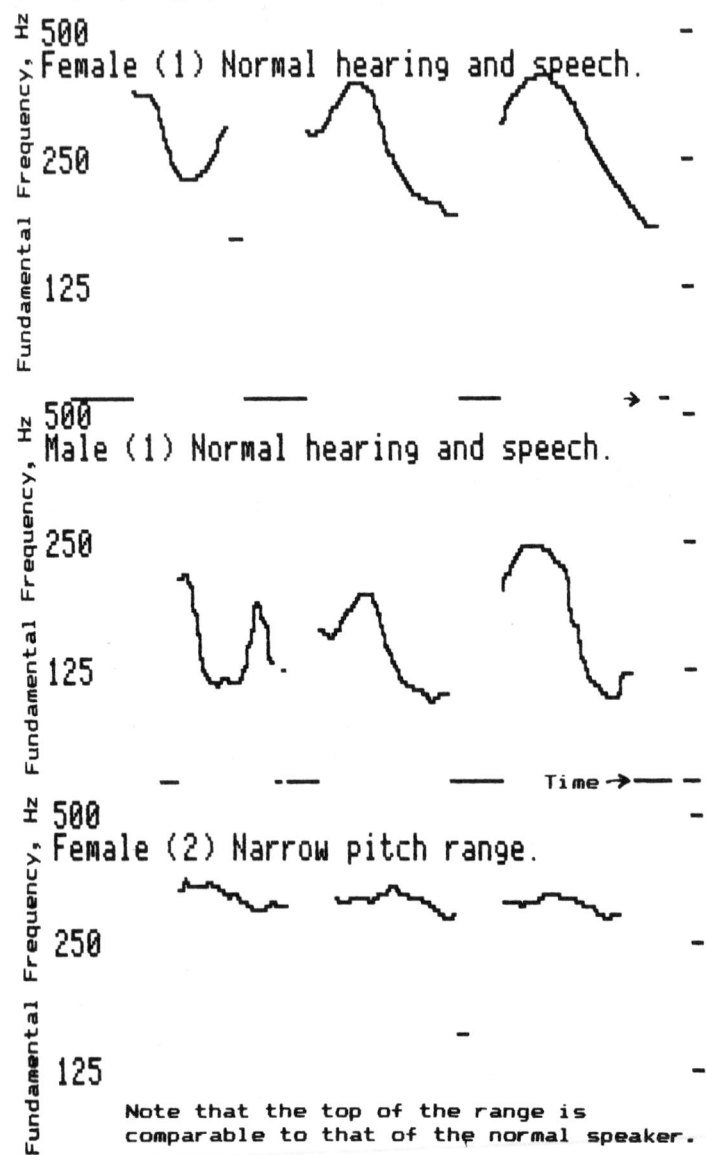

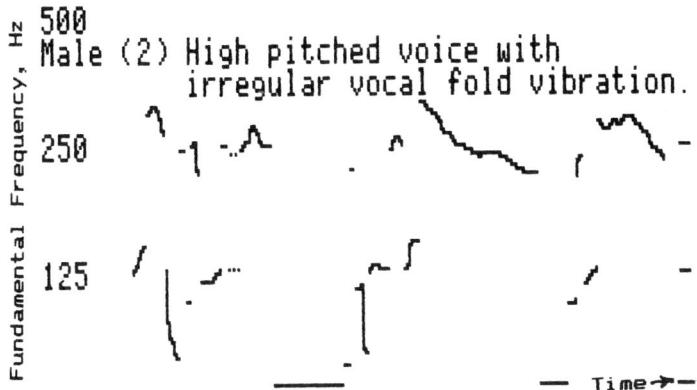

Note that this inadequate excitation of the vocal tract completely precludes normal intonation contrasts.

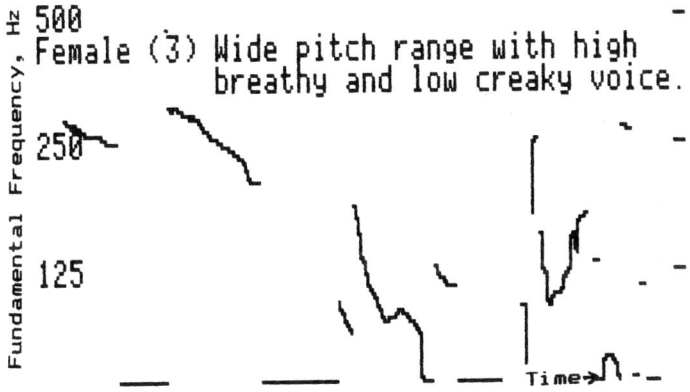

Note that this patient was referred as having a "loudness" problem.

narrowing in pitch range which involves a normal upper limit with deletion of the lower range. Simple attempts to lower overall pitch in such cases will merely amount to replacing the former 'high monotone' with a new 'low monotone'. Figure 14.1 shows examples of different voice problems in individuals referred to speech therapy for 'high-pitched voice'.

Assessment of voice, then, involves attention not only to reported and observed overall loudness and its modification under different acoustic conditions, but also careful evaluation of voice quality, pitch and pitch range, supported where possible by instrumental measurement. Problems may involve several factors which underlie a simple reported problem, as exemplified by a 35-year-old woman who, several months after the sudden onset of a profound bilateral loss, was referred to speech therapy with a 'loudness problem' (see Figure 14.1). Her speech patterns already involved fluctuating pitch, with use of a high-pitched, breathy voice range at the beginning of a breath group and a sudden switch into a much lower, creaky range as airflow diminished. Both types of production were too quiet for efficient communication. Work on relaxation, breathing and intonation using a visual display enabled considerable improvement, obviating any need for work on the 'loudness' problem (which might well have caused further deterioration in this case).

Intonation

The characteristic intonation patterns of English are primarily produced by changing rates of vocal fold vibration (giving a corresponding change in fundamental frequency, which is heard as the pitch of the voice). The patterns used are not random, or dependent on the whim of the individual speaker, but form a highly systematic way of communicating meaning at different linguistic levels (Crystal 1969 and 1977; O'Connor and Arnold 1961; Halliday 1967) which is learnt early by the child acquiring English as a native language. Of particular importance in the system is the use of the nuclear tone (a rising, falling or complex pitch change) to stress the most important word in a phrase.

The use of intonation is well-established in the normally hearing adult's linguistic competence. Although the underlying system is unlikely to be lost quickly or completely by the deafened adult, a number of early phonetic changes may take place which affect the realisation of the linguistic contrast. Firstly, any abnormality of voice quality may restrict the ability to make smooth pitch changes, and marked abnormality will make normal intonation impossible (see Figure 14.1). Either an abnormally restricted or an extended pitch range may be responsible for uncomfortable misunderstandings of the speaker's attitude, the former tending to give an impression of lack of interest or depression while the latter, involving as it may the use of 'high fall' in place of the less emphatic 'low fall' as a nuclear tone, often sounds much more aggressive than the speaker intends, especially if combined with overall excessive loudness.

Overall loudness change is primarily used to adapt speech levels to different acoustic conditions, pitch change and contrasting syllable length being primarily responsible for emphasis on particular syllables and words in speech (see also next section on rhythm). The popular view of stress, however, involves the idea that syllables which are perceived as more prominent than others must be louder. This is an erroneous view (Ladefoged 1979) with possible unfortunate consequences for the deafened adult, who without skilled guidance may attempt to improve intonation (and/or rhythm) by a marked increase in loudness on the relevant syllable. This will certainly contribute to the problem and may even completely change the intonation pattern because of the relationship between laryngeal tension and pitch. Any attempt to modify intonation must be based on a thorough understanding of both the intonation system of English and its phonetic correlates. For this purpose, detailed phonetic description is a more useful basis for assessment than much of the rehabilitation literature, since comments in the latter are frequently based on impressionistic and over-generalised statements. For example, the assertion that 'in English speech, the voice tends to drop in pitch at the end of a sentence' (Bergman 1952) may have some statistical truth but if applied as a rule for the basis of speech assessment and therapy without reference to linguistic meaning, would produce a great number of stereotyped and extremely bizarre utterances. Similarly, the popular notion that all statements fall and questions rise is quite inadequate. Again, the use of a visual display of fundamental frequency (Wright 1982) is relevant both for assessment and therapy.

Timing and Rhythm

Timing changes in speech are responsible for many difficulties at both suprasegmental and segmental levels. Although speakers of English 'talk at a fairly constant rate, about 210-220 syllables a minute' (Lenneberg 1967) the overall rate of utterance may vary considerably without sounding abnormal. However, the relative length of different syllables in an utterance is more constrained, being the basis of rhythm in English (Ladefoged 1975; Allen 1975). As with intonation, English rhythm is language-specific and systematic, and again early changes are usually concerned with the phonetic realisation rather than with the application of the rules of placement of stress (though in time the severity of phonetic deterioration may disrupt the system). In normal speech, certain syllables are made, and perceived as, more prominent than others, and the spacing between these more prominent, 'stressed' syllables gives the impression of regularity which is known as rhythm. English is said to be a 'stress-timed language' (unlike, for example, French, which is 'syllable-timed') because of the perceived regularity of occurrence of stressed syllables. (However, see Roach 1982 for a critical view.) The phonetic source of this perceived 'isochrony' is two-fold. Firstly, stressed syllables tend to have greater duration than unstressed ones. Secondly, the vowels of the briefer, unstressed syllables tend to change in quality to a more centralised form.

Thus the sentence

"He ˈsaid he was ˈtired of ˈexploiˋtation."
    *   * *   *   * *

can be said to have two types of syllable (stressed and unstressed), each with two levels of prominence.

ˋ precedes the nuclear syllable, which in this case is given primary stress by a falling pitch. Note that the place of the nucleus can be moved to another word.

ˈ precedes syllables which are stressed by a difference in length but ar not 'pitch-prominent'.

* marks unstressed syllables, which are comparatively brief, and in all but the diphthong the vowels have reduced forms, either /ɪ/ or /ə/.

Changes may involve exaggeration, abnormal realisation or reduction of these contrasts in speech, or a combination of the three. Simple exaggeration of the normal length contrast, for example, would involve over-extended length for stressed syllables, and possibly such rapidity for unstressed ones, particularly in polysyllabic words, that whole segments are omitted or distorted. Clearly this may involve a drastic loss of intelligibility.

Reduction of contrast, on the other hand, may actually be fostered by attempts to produce speech more carefully, in that word-by-word pronunciation tends to keep the full (unreduced) form of the vowels, producing the 'citation' form of each word (for example /hi/ instead of /hɪ/ for 'he', and even /eɪ/ instead of /ə/ for 'a'). The impression which results is of rather stilted, syllable-timed speech, and if overall tempo is fast, may be responsible for the 'staccato' effects reported by some investigators. A further complication may be the substitution (instead of increased duration) of a marked loudness increase on stressed syllables. Despite the widely held view to the contrary, loudness is not a primary correlate of stress in English (Ladefoged 1975) and this type of production causes an impression of over-assertive speech. Such an abnormal realisation of stress may underlie an impression that speech is generally too loud, and if it is accompanied by a corresponding reduction of loudness for unstressed syllables (especially if the timing difficulties described above co-exist) intelligibility may be quite drastically reduced, in addition to the embarrassing effects of the abnormal speech production which are referred to by Cowie *et al* (1982).

Other Overall Changes

Hypernasality of speech has been reported as a problem for some deafened adults (Penn 1955), though Binnie *et al* (1982) point out that in the case of perceived nasality of words which have nasal consonants, this is an exaggeration of a normal co-articulation effect rather than a complete abnormality. In addition, some profoundly deaf speakers may begin, in addition to audible breathing during pauses, to insert additional syllables between sounds and even between words (Bergman 1952; Penn 1955). Again, attempts to improve articulation without adequate guidance may be responsible for some of these effects (Binnie *et al* 1982; further comments below).

Segmental Features

Segmental phonology is concerned with description of the way in which speech sounds are contrasted with one another (examples are the single phoneme change involved in such minimal pairs as 'pin/bin' and 'heart/hard') and combined in certain sequences (compare 'pin/spin' and 'hard/harder', for example) to convey meaning in language. An adequate speech assessment is concerned not only with this level of phonological contrast, but also with the phonetic detail on which perception of such contrasts is based. Without an adequate account of both levels, the assessment may lead to inappropriate intervention. For example, one writer ascribes the loss of the voiced-voiceless contrast in word-final position to a tendency 'for all final-voiced consonants ... to become unvoiced' (Bergman 1955). But phonetically, the lost phonological contrast depends in syllable-final position on contrasting length of the preceding vowel, and not on the voicing of the consonant itself, which is normally 'devoiced'. Loss of the contrast is therefore another example of a timing change, and speech therapy will be concerned with re-establishing additional length for the

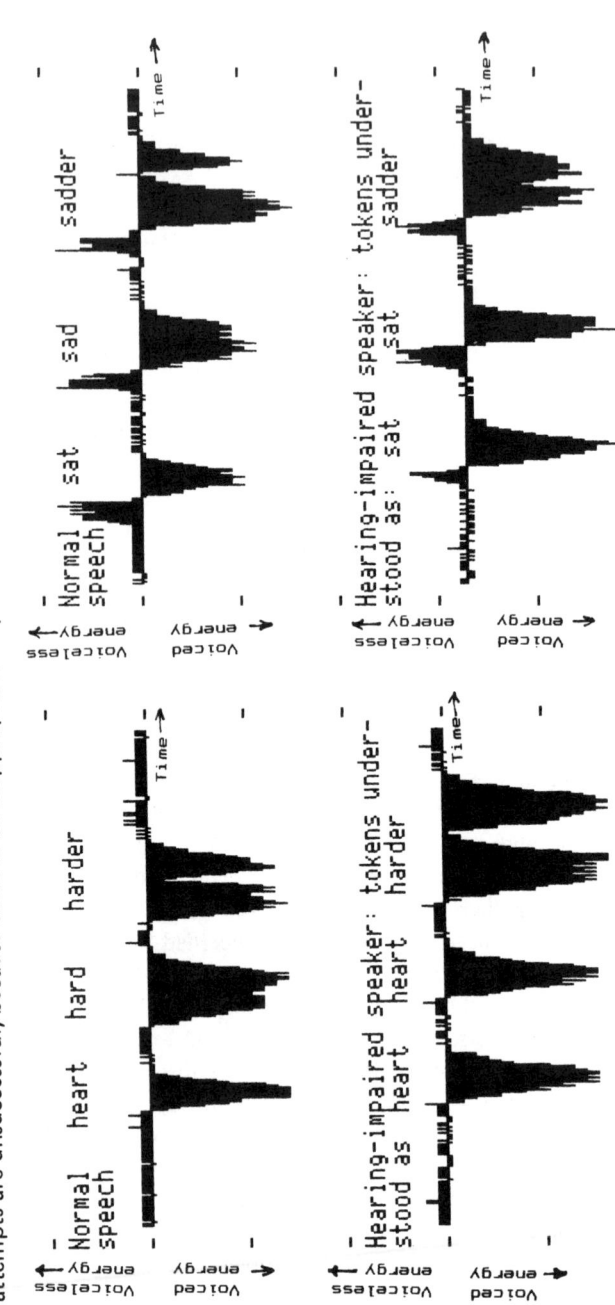

Figure 14.2: Top — Timing Contrasts as the Phonetic Basis for the 'Voiced/Voiceless Distinction' and for Syllable Number in Normal English, as Shown on a Time-base Display of Voiced (Low Frequency) vs Voiceless (High Frequency) Energy. Below — The Hearing-impaired Speaker is Misunderstood. The intended words were 'heart' and 'hard', and 'sat' and 'sad', but the length contrast is lost for the first pair in each set. The attempts to clarify 'hard' and 'sad' in the third attempts are unsuccessful, because there is an inappropriate emphasis on the final 'voiced' consonant.

vowel which precedes the 'voiced' consonant (see Figure 14.2). Any attempt to induce full word-final voicing in such consonants as /b,d,g,v,z/ would risk causing a new error. For example, previous production of 'heart' instead of 'hard' might be changed to 'harder'; Binnie *et al* (1982) ascribe such 'syllabification of syllable-final consonants' to development of exaggerated consonant articulation.

There is some conflicting evidence in the literature about the amount of segmental change which is found, which illustrates the range of results of hearing impairment and the need for detailed individual assessment. In their single case-study of a child with an acquired profound loss, Binnie *et al* (1982) found abnormal phonetic quality and reduced intelligibility, but commented that 'most intended sounds were present and representative of their phonemic class', whereas in 'the case of R.K. — high-frequency deafness', Bergman (1952) quotes examples of phonological reduction in the case of /s/:

> For example, you will hear him say 'Today's date' as 'Today-date'. 'Eighty-second street' sounds like 'eighty-secon treet'. He finds it particularly difficult to include both sounds when it occurs in combination with other consonants. 'Six' is pronounced as 'si-s'.

In spite of the fact that there are more details in the literature concerning segmental features than for prosodics, the exact problem may be different in each case, and careful assessment is indicated in any case of noticeable deterioration. Some brief comments about possible difficulties may be made.

Vowels

Centralisation of vowels may occur, in which case contrasts may become progressively obscured. Another tendency was found in the study by Binnie *et al* (1982) who report diphthongisation of single vowels, possibly resulting from an attempt to compensate for loss of auditory feedback by increasing orosensory feedback. The same writers report that vowels are less often altered than consonants in the case studied.

Consonants

Place of articulation for consonants may remain comparatively stable (partly because lipreading ability tends to strengthen awareness of this aspect). Other problems, particularly of place and manner, which are most apparent may be related to the nature of the English system of phonological contrasts, and the relationship between visible and audible contrasts. For example, English has a number of alveolar and near-alveolar pairs, which are distinguished only by the manner of their articulation (such as stop/fricative /t/ vs /s/; stop/nasal /d/ vs /n/; stop/approximant /d/ vs /l/) such that only a small amount of phonetic change may cause a phonological confusion. On the other hand, the incidence of only two phonemes at labiodental place (fricatives, voiced/voiceless /v/ vs /f/) allows rather more room for slight changes, and even the use of a homorganic stop may not cause misunderstanding, especially if the listener also lipreads the place of contact. A particularly common source of intelligibility reduction is the deletion of one or more consonants in a cluster, as in the example cited from Bergman (1952). Again, where the sequence is of several consonants at the same place of articulation (homorganic consonants) disruption of the normal sequence may be more likely. Conversely, careful over-articulation may lead to the addition of syllables, and this should be a consideration in speech therapy.

Discussion: Speech Conservation

The term 'speech conservation' suggests the prevention of speech deterioration. There are, however, practical difficulties with the establishment of a successful programme to maintain normal speech. Firstly, in the absence of adequate research concerning the prevalence of speech deterioration, any individual who loses a significant amount of hearing may be considered to be at risk. This implies a need for routine speech evaluation as part of the total communication assessment by the audiology team, and if such information were properly documented the much-needed research data would become available. However, the provision of appropriate amplification is an important factor in the prevention of speech deterioration, and clearly many individuals who are able to benefit from hearing aid use will not develop speech production difficulties. Detailed speech assessment for this group is neither necessary nor possible.

Among speakers whose speech does deteriorate, two types of problem have been described. Subtle, phonetic deterioration may affect speech acceptability at an early stage, and furthermore may anticipate the more extensive phonological changes which threaten speech intelligibility more seriously. Both types of problem need early detection, but it is claimed that neither is susceptible to adequate analysis or remediation by observers with only a superficial knowledge of normal speech. In most English-speaking countries, the only clinically-based training which involves sufficiently detailed study of phonology and phonetics is that of speech therapists (known as speech/language pathologists in the USA), but it is only in the last ten years that British speech therapy services have developed sufficiently to enable specialist appointments for work with the hearing-impaired (Quirk 1969; Byers-Brown 1981).

At the Royal National Institute for the Deaf in London, where many more adults are seen for hearing advice than need or could receive detailed assessment by one speech therapist, a two-level approach for detection and assessment of problems has been adopted. A standard screening procedure, involving high-quality tape-recording of a brief structured interview, is available for routine use by all the advisory staff. Training in the use of the procedure is given by the speech therapist, who reviews and discusses the results on a regular basis. The availability of a permanent record of speech, taken at regular intervals for an individual, enables monitoring of any subsequent deterioration. Detailed assessment and advice on speech conservation and speech therapy can be arranged as soon as it is needed. In addition, the data collected will provide a source of further information about the speech of adults with acquired hearing loss and of training material for speech therapists and their colleagues in the rehabilitation team. Finally, it is hoped that experience and evaluation of the procedure itself will provide a model for use in other centres.

References

Allen, G.D. (1975) 'Speech Rhythm: its Relation to Performance Universals and Articulatory Timing, *J Phonetics*, *3*, 87-98
Bergman, M. (1952) 'Special Methods of Audiological Training of Adults', *Acta Otolaryngol*, *40*, 336-45
Binnie, C.A., Danilof, R.G. and Buckingham, H.W. (1982) 'Phonetic Disintegration in a five-year-old following Sudden Hearing Loss.' *JSHD*, *47*, 181-9
Byers-Brown, B. (1981) *Speech Therapy: Principles and Practice*, Churchill Livingstone, Edinburgh
Carhart, R. (1947) 'Conservation of Speech', in Davis, H. (ed), *Hearing and Deafness*, Staples Press, New York
Carhart, R. (1960) 'Auditory Training', in Davis and Silverman (eds) *Hearing and Deafness*, Holt, Rinehart, and Winston, New York
Conrad, R. (1979) *The Deaf Schoolchild*, Harper & Row, London
Cowie, R., Douglas-Cowie, E. and Kerr, A.G. (1982) 'A Study of Speech Deterioration in Post-lingually Deafened Adults, *J Laryngol Otol*, *96*, 101-12
Cowie, R.I.D. and Douglas-Cowie, E. (1983) 'Speech Production in Profound Postlingual Deafness', in M.E. Lutman and M.P. Haggard (eds) *Hearing*

Science and Hearing Disorders, Academic Press. London
Crystal, D. (1969) *Prosodic Systems and Intonation in English*, Cambridge University Press, Cambridge
Crystal, D. (1975) *The English Tone of Voice*, Arnold, London
Douglas-Cowie, E. and Cowie, R. (1979) 'Speaking without Hearing', *J N Ireland Speech Lang Forum*, 5, 54-70
Fisher, J., King, A.B., Parker, A. and Wright, R.D. (1983) 'Assessment of Speech Production and Speech Perception as a basis for Speech Therapy,' in Hochberg, I., Levitt, H., and Osberger, M.J., *Proceedings of the 1979 CUNY Conference on Speech of the Hearing Impaired*, University Park Press, Baltimore
Gimson, A.C. (1962) *An Introduction to the Pronunciation of English*, Arnold, London
Greene, M. (1972) *The Voice and its Disorders*, 3rd edn, Pitman, London
Griffith, J. (1969), 'Assessment and Evaluation: Diagnosis of Speech and Language disorders', in Griffith, J. (ed) *Persons with Hearing Loss*, Thomas, Springfield, Illinois
Halliday, M.A.K. (1967) *Intonation and Grammar in British English*, Mouton, The Hague
Hudgins, C.V. and Numbers, F.C. (1942). 'An Investigation of the Intelligibility of the Speech of the Deaf', *Genetic Psych Mono*, 25, 289-392
Jackson, P.L. (1982) 'Techniques for Speech Conservation', in Hull, R.H. (ed) *Rehabilitation Audiology*, Grune and Stratton, New York
Kinney, C.E. (1948) 'Loss of Speech due to Meningitic Deafness', *Archives Otol*, 47, 303-9
Ladefoged, P. (1975) *A Course in Phonetics*, Harcourt Brace, New York
Lenneberg, E.H. (1967) *Biological Foundations of Language*, Wiley, New York
Ling, D. (1976) *Speech and the Hearing-Impaired Child: Theory and Practice*, Bell, Washington DC
Markides, A. (1977 'Rehabilitation of People with Acquired Deafness in Adulthood', *BJA, Suppl 1*
McCarth, P.A. and Alpiner, J.G. (1982) 'The Remediation Process', in Alpiner, J.G. (ed), *Handbook of Adult Rehabilitative Audiology*, 2nd edn, Williams & Wilkins, Baltimore
Nickerson, R.S. (1975) Characteristics of the Speech of Deaf Persons *Volta Review*, 77, 342-62
O'Connor, J.D. and Arnold, G.F. (1961) *Intonation of Colloquial English*, Longmans, London
Penn, J.P. (1955) Voice and speech patterns of the hard of hearing. *Acta Otolaryngol. Suppl 124*, p. 69
Quirk, R. (chairman) (1972) *Speech Therapy Services (Report of the Committee)*, HMSO, London
Roach, P. (1982) 'On the Distinction between "Stress-timed" and "Syllable-timed" languages', in Crystal, D. (ed) *Linguistic Controversies*, Arnold, London
Summers, I.R., Peake, M.A. and Martin, M.C. (1981) 'Field Trials of a Tactile Acoustic Monitor for the Profoundly Deaf', *BJA*, 15, 195-9
Wright, R.D. (1982) 'Visual Indicators and Displays', *Talk*, 103, 13-14

15 HEARING THERAPY

Christine Richardson

During the last few decades, an increasingly enlightened social attitude towards the disabled has emerged. There is a growing recognition of the problems of the physically handicapped and a collective feeling that something practical should be done to help solve these problems. Outward signs of this awareness can be seen in small changes in our environment which help to minimise the effects of physical handicap; ramps and wider doorways for wheelchair access in public places are just two examples. However, society is much less well-informed about the effects of hearing loss, apart from the obvious difficulties in communication. The social and educational needs of those who are born deaf or prelingually deafened have been met for some years, but very little has been done for the adult with acquired deafness. Indeed, the problems confronted by such a person are barely appreciated by the rest of society.

The desire for communication with other people is one of our most basic needs. It is hardly surprising, therefore, that a person who becomes deaf in adult life may become discouraged, depressed and frustrated as communication becomes increasingly difficult.

There are a variety of causes of hearing loss in adults, but very often the impairment develops gradually. At first, the hearing-impaired person may not even be aware that there is a problem. Often he blames other people for not speaking sufficiently loudly or complains that they mumble. As a result, tensions may emerge between the person with the hearing loss and his family and friends. He may even become suspicious of half-heard remarks and withdraw from stressful social situations. Problems may be even worse at work. If the hearing-impaired person is finding it difficult to cope at home, at work his troubles may be intensified by the attitudes of people around him. Most people are ignorant of the effects of an acquired hearing loss and may treat the deafened adult with embarrassment and impatience. Others may ignore him completely or treat him as if he was almost mentally deficient.

'People just talk to you as though you are daft — or else talk to my husband as if I wasn't there'!

'I avoid telling people I cannot hear as they don't understand. If I say I lipread they start speaking unnaturally — that doesn't help at all! Many people just lose patience and say "it doesn't matter".'

'You learn which people to avoid. Very few understand my problem; most get annoyed and blame me for being deaf!'

In time, the hearing-impaired adult may be forced to accept that there is a problem with his hearing. Often under family pressure, he visits the local hospital and may well be told the impairment cannot be cured by drugs or surgery. However, he is to be fitted with a hearing aid. The deafened adult may now feel happier as this small device will restore his hearing. Sadly, he is soon disappointed. Sounds are much louder, but conversation is not necessarily much clearer and this comes as a shock. Communication is still a strain and family and friends cannot understand why he cannot hear with his aid. They may accuse him of not trying to listen or may simply ignore him. The deafened adult may well be further depressed by being cut off from those familiar reassuring sounds of daily living, sounds that he was scarcely aware of when he was a hearing person.

Hearing Therapy Services

Not all deafened adults find it difficult to accept and to adjust to their hearing difficulties. However, for those who do, advice and support are urgently needed as soon as possible after medical and audiological assessment of the impairment. Hearing therapy is vital for such individuals before the hearing loss has a damaging effect on their whole personality.

Hearing therapy services for adults with an acquired hearing loss are somewhat sparse throughout the world. Emphasis for habilitation and rehabilitation has always focused on children, but there is a growing awareness of the rehabilitation needs of the adult hearing-impaired person. However, in many countries, aural rehabilitation is still not offered routinely to the deafened adult. For those fortunate enough to be referred for hearing therapy, the settings in which this is provided vary tremendously, as other contributions to this book have pointed out. In the USA, the hearing-impaired person may go to a university speech and hearing centre, a community centre, a hearing aid dealer or a veterans hospital. In Britain he is most likely to be offered limited help in the local NHS hospital. In Scandinavia he may well be seen in a state hearing centre. Aural rehabilitation practices in these various settings may differ slightly, but all appear to have similar basic aims: to integrate the hearing-impaired person back into the hearing community by helping him to come to terms with his hearing loss and by training him to maximise his communication skills.

Acceptance of Hearing Loss

Such acceptance is a major step in the process of aural rehabilitation. Unless the individual fully understands the problem, he may well shy away from wearing a hearing aid and from further rehabilitative procedures. After initial assessment of the hearing impairment, it seems that the majority of deafened adults should be provided with basic information on deafness and its effects, particularly in relation to their own hearing loss. The provision of such information to the deafened adult and his family helps to relieve the anxiety so often caused by incorrect or misinformed appraisal of the basic facts.

Benefits and Limitations of a Hearing Aid

Before a person is fitted with a hearing aid, its benefits and limitations should be discussed, because many hearing-impaired adults have unrealistic expectations of the hearing aid and are severely disappointed when it does not restore their hearing. If the limitations of the aid have been discussed by the patient, his family and the hearing therapist, the hearing-impaired adults may be more inclined to accept the aid. Once it is fitted, the wearer will naturally need to be instructed about the controls, the batteries, the insertion of the earmould and the general care of the hearing aid. He will also need to be made aware of the local arrangements for repairs and the replacement of batteries.

The new hearing aid wearer should also be helped to adjust to sound again. As a general principle, he is advised to begin wearing the new aid in quiet surroundings with a gradual transition to more difficult listening conditions. At first he may wear the hearing aid for a short while, lengthening the periods of use as he becomes more familiar with regulating the aid and his tolerance to amplified sound increases. During the initial months of orientation to the hearing aid, the new wearer will require much support and advice from his local audiology centre. Many people do not find the hearing aid an immediate success, but one hopes they would not become sufficiently discouraged to stop using it if they received adequate instruction and encouragement. In time, the new hearing aid wearer should satisfactorily adjust to the aid and use it to its maximum benefit.

Environmental Aids

While the deafened adult is getting used to his hearing aid, he also needs to be acquainted with the range of environmental aids available, such as amplified handsets on telephones, the loop system, flashing light doorbells and television amplifiers. For some people, a particular environmental aid may be of more benefit than a hearing aid — the elderly person who only has problems in knowing when somebody is at the door may be very happy to have an extra loud doorbell fitted. The installation of environmental aids may also ease family tension; for example, a television amplifier would allow a deafened adult to listen to the television at a suitable volume for him without disturbing the rest of the family.

Communication Tactics

The deafened adult may also be helped by a discussion of communication tactics. There are many ploys the hearing-impaired individual may use to help him in difficult communication situations. Such simple tactics as looking at the speaker's face, expressions and gestures, and the provision of good lighting, may well ease a potentially stressful situation.

For the majority of adult hearing-impaired people, a basic hearing therapy course on deafness, hearing aids, environmental aids and communication tactics is sufficient for them to develop the necessary attitudes to cope and live with their impairment. Others may require more extensive and specialised help. Such patients may be offered training in speechreading and auditory training, speech correction and conservation, and additional counselling.

Total Communication Therapy

After full adjustment and orientation to the hearing aid, some individuals may require more intensive communication rehabilitation. In the past, much emphasis has been placed on the importance of speech-reading as the primary means of improving communication. However, in recent years, there has been a trend towards total communication therapy, involving training both the auditory and visual channels. The aims of auditory training courses are to help the hearing-impaired individual to make full use of his residual hearing and to learn to recognise sound again through his hearing aid. Certainly, the act of listening is more of a conscious act for the person with a hearing loss and he needs to become more alert and attentive. Practice is given in the therapy session with and without background noise, thus simulating more closely the real-life situations. It is also essential to use vocabulary appropriate to the person's communication needs. Whatever the philosophy regarding a unisensory or bisensory approach to aural rehabilitation, speechreading may still be seen as an essential part of the therapy programme. It may well be helpful to the hearing-impaired adult to recognise the sounds of speech and it is certainly beneficial to make him more aware of visual clues; facial expressions, gestures and body movements that accompany everyday conversation. Such communication training may be carried out with individuals or on a group therapy basis. It is often found that the group approach is particularly valuable, as it gives each individual practice in speechreading and auditory training in conversation with other group members. Even more important is the counselling role of the group. The hearing-impaired individual now knows that he is not the only one with hearing difficulties and may be more willing to share his problems with other group members rather than the therapist. Similarly, family and friends can be invited to group therapy sessions to improve their understanding of the problems and to discuss ways to ease the effects of the hearing impairment. Hopefully, such an intensive communication and counselling programme will give the deafened adult renewed confidence in himself and make it easier for him to be part of the hearing world again.

From this brief discussion of the place of hearing therapy in the aural rehabilitation of adults with acquired deafness it is clear that much more help and support could be provided for such people. The first handicap of deafness is communication but it often seems that a very close second is the attitude of hearing people towards those with this handicap. The average hearing person takes the sense of hearing very much for granted and knows little about the problems that hearing impairment may provoke. Deafened people are often met with embarrassment and even fear by some hearing people, whose emotions are usually due to ignorance. Deafness may affect many of us at some time in our lives, yet there appears to be little positive information available about the handicap and much widespread misinformation and misunderstanding. One of the essential aims of those involved in hearing therapy in its broadest sense is to educate the hearing world about the problems of the hearing-impaired. Such education is vital if there is to be a substantial change in the attitude of society which will help to alleviate many of the needs of those who suffer from acquired deafness.

CONTRIBUTORS

John C. Ballantyne, FRCS Hon FRCS (I) DLO Emeritus Consultant Ear, Nose and Throat Surgeon, The Royal Free Hospital, London

Winifred S. Brinson, NFF NCTB CTD Senior Lecturer City Lit Centre for the Deaf, London

Peggy Chalmers, SRN Technical Co-ordinator (Audiology), The Royal National Throat, Nose and Ear Hospital, London

Gaynor M. Freestone, AGSM CTD Lecturer in Hearing Therapy, City Lit Centre for the Deaf, London

Larry Fisch, MD DLO Consultant Audiological Physician, Hospital for Sick Children, Great Ormond Street, London

John Groves, MB BS FRCS, Consultant Ear, Nose and Throat Surgeon, The Royal Free Hospital, London

John J. Knight, PhD F INST P FIOA Physicist to the Institute, Institute of Laryngology and Otology, University of London. Honary Consulting Physicist, Royal National Throat, Nose and Ear Hospital, London

Andreas Markides, PhD MEd Dp Audiol. Senior Lecturer in the Education of the Deaf, Department of Audiology and Education of the Deaf, University of Manchester

Michael C. Martin, OBE BSc Head of Scientific and Technical Department, Royal National Institute for the Deaf, London

Ann Parker, MCST Scientific and Technical Department, Royal National Institute for the Deaf, London

Kenneth S. Pegg, OBE MA MPhil Former Head of Centre, City Lit Centre for the Deaf, London

John D. Pym, BEd CTD Lecturer in Hearing Therapy, City Lit Centre for the Deaf, London

Christine Richardson, Cert Ed CHT CTL Hearing Therapist, Area Hearing Therapy Service, Croydon, Surrey

William J. Watts, DPhil Senior Research Fellow and Director Phillips Research Unit, University of Sussex. On loan to City Lit Centre for the Deaf, London

Roger Wills, MSHAA Senior Chief PMT (Audiology), Audiology Department, Royal Berkshire Hospital, Reading

INDEX

Acquired hearing loss, adult with
    ability to speechread 53
    adjustment to life 13
    amplification 13
    auditory rehabilitation 54
    auditory training 12
    Beethoven 26
    experiences of 50-4
    housewife 27
    overcoming handicap 51
    problem, the 52
    problem of communication 12
    speechreading 12
Adolescence
    as a process 40
    ego identity 41
    idea of crisis 41
    identity formation 41-2
    self discovery 42
Adult
    adult personality 42
    compromise 43
    creative activity 43
    creative energy 44
    ideas of mortality 44
    integrity 43
    mid-life 43-4
    work identity 43
Ageing
    aspects of death 46-7
    bereavement 47
    depressive feelings 46
    gerontology 46
    human life path 47
    life potential 45
    social competence 45
    success in ageing 45
    work role 45
Audiological physician
    audiological medicine 134-5
    developments in audiology 134
    job description 135-8
    see also Clinical work of 139-43
    see also Audiology team and clinic 143-5
Audiology team and clinic
    confidentiality 144
    examination environment 144-5
    general philosophy 144
    patient communication 145
    starting rehabilitation 145
    stigma of deafness 144
    team work 143-4
Auditory Training
    alternative approaches 15
    auditory rehabilitation 54
    availability 15
    basic training programmes 230-1
    basis of 221-4
    development 219-21
    hearing therapy basic knowledge 226-31; assessments 226; counselling 226-7; making up material 228; training programmes 226
    pioneer work 14
    rehabilitation basic knowledge 224-5; communication 225; consultation and testing 225; hearing loss 225; psychology of 225; sound 225; sounds of English 225; voice production 225
Aural rehabilitation
    Denmark as a model 55-85
    defined 11
    North America 23-4
    psychological framework 26
    psychologically 11
    rehabilitation techniques 11
    Western Europe 23-4

Birth
    communication 30
    eyes 30
    odour discrimination 30
    psychological organisation 30
    relaxed harmony 30
    response to sound 30
    spatial discrimination 30

Classification of hearing aids
    automatic gain control 166
    magnetic and electrical inputs 164
    peak clipping 166
    see also Design and use of 146-53

Index 259

see also Hearing aid characteristics 154-63
see also Subjective aspects of
   hearing aid measurement 167-72
Clinical Work of the Audiological
   Physician
   disorders of balance 140-1
   neuro-otology 141
   noise damage 141-2
   otological examination 141
   research and epidemiology 142-3
   sudden deafness 139-40
Communication rehabilitation
   difficulties in acceptance 13-14
   in recent years 13
   in the past 13

Design and use of hearing aids
   basic design 147-50; amplifier 148;
      earphone 148; microphone
      147-8; power 149
   in the past 146
   hearing aid performance 151-3;
      acoustic couplers 153; artificial
      ears 153; audiometric zero 153;
      equipment for measuring 152;
      hearing aid characteristics 153;
      on site measurements 153;
      initial evaluation 173; suggested
      test battery 173; technological
      steps 146; see also Basic hearing
      aid characteristics 154-63; see
      also Classification of hearing
      aids 164-6; see also Subjective
      aspects of hearing aid measure-
      ment 167-72
Differential diagnosis
   acoustical chain 108
   acoustic impedance 112-14
   calibrated instruments 108-9
   electrophysiological tests 114-17
   identifying location 108
   nature of disturbance 108
   present clinical situation 117
   pure tone audiometry 109
   self-recording audiometry 112
   sound treated rooms 108
   speech audiometry 112

Ear impressions and earmoulds
   clinical considerations 174-5
   conclusion 188
   earmould fitting 185-6
   earmould processing 180-4
   impression techniques 175-9;
      acoustic feedback 187; dis-
      comfort 186; materials 175-6;
      preparation 176-9; problems
      with earmoulds 186-8; skin
      reactions 187-8
   problems with impressions 184-5
Environmental acoustics and listening
   areas
   amplification in public places 202-3
   floors, ceilings, walls, windows &
      furniture 190-1
   suppression of sound from out-
      side 191-2
   see also Environmental aids 189-
      204
Environmental aids
   co-operation of others 189
   sympathetic hearing scheme 189-90
   see also Environmental acoustics
      and listening areas 190-2
   see also Household environmental
      aids 192-6, 201-2
   see also Vibrating and amplified
      environmental aids 198-200

Hearing aid characteristics
   basic characteristics 154
   distortion 156
   harmonic distortion 157
   harmony versus intermodulation
      160
   intermodulation distortion 158
   phase distortion 163
   signal to noise ratio 163
Hearing Therapy
   acceptance of hearing loss 253
   communication tactics 254
   environmental aids 254
   hearing aids 253-4
   hearing therapy services 252
   social attitude 251
   total communication therapy
      255
Household environmental aids
   audible door bells and chimes 192-3
   clocks 194
   specific television aids 201-2;
      headphones 201; inductive
      loop system 201-2; micro-
      phone aids 201
   telephone attachments 194-6;
      amplified headset 195; exten-
      sion bells 194-5; inductive
      coupler 195; loudspeaker
      telephones 196; portable

telephones 194; visual telephones 196; visual doorbells and alarm lights 193-4; *see also* Environmental aids 189-204

Human development and communication
a psychological framework 26
adolescence 40
conception, birth and first months 28-30
developing intellect 34-6
empathetic understanding 27
maturity 42-4
passing years and ageing 44-7
speech and the early years 31-4
thinking and language 36-40

Intellectual development
model building 34
Piaget's contemporary theory 34-6
schema 34
sensori-motor activity 34

Model of aural rehabilitation
Denmark as a model 55; audiometric section 61; earmould construction section 66; hearing aid section 62-6; legislative basis 55-6; local human care service 58; medical section 60-1; medical-audiological service 59; organisation of services 56-7; state hearing centres 59-75; social service 58; technical section 62-4; technical-audiological services 57
aural rehabilitation section 66-7, 71-8; administration 68; audiological diagnosis 71; aural rehabilitation 71-8; in-patient section 67-8; pedagogical service 71-8; physical accommodation 71; referrals 68-9; research 68; staffing 69-70; workload 71
state hearing institute Frederica, 78-84
summary 84-5

Otologist
at work 89-92
change in specialisation 88-9
further investigations 90-92; blood tests 91; electrocochleography 91; evoked response 91; patient co-operation 91-2; reality of situation 92; tests of vestibular function 91; thermal reactions 91; x-ray examination 91
hearing assessment 90
otological examination 89-90
otological expertise 87
role of 87-92

Pregnancy
later stages 29
refining imaginative activity 29
Prevention of deafness
aminoglycoside antibiotics 106
deafness due to noise 105
drug damage 106
firearms and weapons 106
hearing protectors 106
summary 107

Speech
babbling 31
early prelinguistic 31
emotional relationships 31
first word 31-3
framework of development 33-4
impulse to communicate 31
maturational factors 31
real linguistic significance 31
Speechreading
ability to speechread 53
alternative approaches 15
availability 15
pioneer work 14
Speechreading in practice
consequences of acquired deafness 206-9
development of speechreading 205-6
postscript 217-18
principles of speechreading 215-17; drill 215-16; practical 216; involvement 216; intellectual aspect 216; listening 217
Speech conservation
previous work 234-6
speech change 236-7
suprasegmental features 237-45; breathing patterns 238; intonation 242; other overall changes 245; timing and rhythm 243; voice 238
segmental features 245-8; consonants 247; segmental phonology 245; vowels 247

speech conservation 248-9; detection and assessment 249; phonetic deterioration 248; phonological changes 248; speech therapy services 249
Subjective hearing and measurement
benefit from using 167
processing time 172
pure tone measurements 168
qualitative tests 170
quantitative tests 171
speech testing 170
threshold improvements 168

Thinking and language
definition of language 37
definition of thinking 36
developing logical actions 39
Furth 39-40
operative thinking 40
Piaget 38-9
relationship between 37-8
symbolic function 38-40
Treatment and prevention of deafness
causes of conductive deafness 93-4
causes of sensorineural deafness 94
treatment of conductive deafness 94-101; myringoplasty 97; ossiculoplasty 99-101; stapedectomy 95-6; tympanoplasty 97
treatment of sensorineural deafness 101-4; cochlear implants 102-4; hearing aids 101; hearing therapy 101; sudden onset 102; syphilitic deafness 102; total deafness 102

Validation of speechreading and auditory training
background to investigation 16-18
conditions 22-3
hypothesis 18
instruction 18
results 19-22
tests used 19
conclusions 22-3
Vibrating amplified environmental aids
amplified stethoscopes 200
domestic high-fidelity equipment 199
extra loudspeakers 200
headset radio 200
portable cassettes and radios 200
portable communicator 198-9
reflectors 200
radio microphones 200
separate earpiece 200
speech trainers 199
tone controls 200
see also Environmental aids 189-204
Visual environmental aids
badges 197
electronic devices 197; Palantype 198; Prestel 198; subtitles 197-8; Teletext 197
fingerspelling and gesture 197
flashing lights 197
pen, pencil and paper 197
queueing systems 197
visual indicators 197
see also Environmental aids 189-204